Written

Questions In

Data Structures

Written Test Questions In Data Structures

By

Yashavant Kanetkar
Asang Dani

BPB PUBLICATIONS
B-14, CONNAUGHT PLACE, NEW DELHI-1

FIRST EDITION 2010

ISBN –978-81-8333-331-3

LIMITS OF LIABILITY AND DISCLAIMER OF WARRANTY

Distributors:

COMPUTER BOOK CENTRE
12, Shrungar Shopping Centre, M.G. Road,
BANGALORE-560001 Ph: 25587923, 25584641

MICRO BOOKS
Shanti Niketan Building, 8, Camac Street
KOLKATTA-700017 Ph: 22826518/9

BUSINESS PROMOTION BUREAU
8/1, Ritchie Street, Mount Road,
CHENNAI-600002 Ph: 28410796, 28550491

BPB PUBLICATIONS
B-14, Connaught Place, NEW DELHI-110001
Ph : 23325760, 23723393, 23737742

BPB BOOK CENTRE
376, Old Lajpat Rai Market, DELHI-110006
Ph: 23861747

MICRO MEDIA
Shop No.5, Mahendra Chambers, 150 D.N. Rd,
Next to Capital Cinema V.T. (C.S.T.) Station,
MUMBAI-400001 Ph: 22078296, 22078297

DECCAN AGENCIES
4-3-329, Bank Street,
HYDERABAD-500195 Ph: 24756400, 24756967

INFO TECH
G-2, Sidhartha Building , 96, Nehru Place,
NEW DELHI-110019
Ph: 26438245, 26415092, 26234208

INFO TECH
Shop No. 2, F-38, South Extention Part-I
NEW DELHI-110049
Ph: 24691288

Published by **Manish Jain** for BPB Publications, B-14, Connaught Place, New Delhi-110001 and Printed by him at Akash Press, New Delhi.

Dedicated to

Nalinee and Prabhakar Kanetkar

- Yashavant Kanetkar

Dedicated to

Neelima and Kamalakar Dani

- Asang Dani

About the Authors

Yashavant Kanetkar

Through his original works in the form of books and Quest Video Courseware CDs Yashavant has created, moulded and groomed lacs of IT careers in the last decade and half. In recognition of his contribution he has been awarded the "Best .NET Technical Contributor" and "Most Valuable Professional" awards by Microsoft. Yashavant holds a BE from VJTI Mumbai and M.Tech. from IIT Kanpur. Yashavant's current affiliations include being a Director of KICIT and KSET, companies engaged in training and Embedded Systems development.

Asang Dani

Asang holds a BE in Electronics Engineering from VRCE, Nagpur and ME in Computer Science from IISc, Bangalore. Asang has a rich Real-time Embedded Systems and Storage Networking experience that he obtained while working for companies like Veritas, Microsoft and Dow Jones. Asang's current areas of interest include .NET Technologies, Window CE, Device Drivers and Embedded Linux. Asang is currently Director of KICIT and KSET.

Yashavant's and Asang's current activities can be tracked at
http://quest.ksetindia.com/

Contents

Preface

As most of you are aware, the road to a successful career in Software starts with a series of Written Technical Tests conducted by most IT companies in India. These companies test your fundamental skills in programming and design in three major areas—C Programming, Data Structures and C++ Programming. Most of you may have prepared for that "dream test" without knowing the exact pattern, the level and the difficulty of questions that appear in such tests. As a result, you are not able to give your best performance in these tests.

This "Written Test Questions" series addresses these concerns and is aimed at giving you the necessary practice and confidence to help you crack these tests. This series presents a whole gamut on questions on different topics in each of these three subjects—C, DS and C++. The volume that you are holding in your hands right now deals with questions in Data Structures.

The questions have been separated topic-wise so that you can learn and prepare a topic and then test your strength and confidence in it by attempting questions on that topic, before you switch to another topic. At the end of each chapter you will find correct answers to the questions in that chapter. We have tried to avoid the questions whose answers are most obvious because the idea was not to increase the number of questions, but to present questions that would force the readers to think twice before answering.

We are sure that if you practice the questions in this book enough, you would not face any problem in clearing the written test in Data Structures. We hope you will find this book useful.

Once you are through with this book and want to now test your strength in Data Structures, you can take practice test in Data Structures by visiting http://www.smartcertindia.com/

Needless to say we are willing to hear all that you have to say about this edition and more. We are available at *kanetkar@ksetindia.com* and *asang@ksetindia.com*. So roll your sleeves and get on with the real questions. All the best!!

Yashavant Kanetkar *Asang Dani*

1

Analysis Of Algorithm

Question 1

Which of the following statement is correct?

I. Algorithm is a step-by-step procedure to solve any problem in finite number of steps.

II. Algorithm is a step-by-step procedure to solve only mathematical problem in finite number of steps.

(a) Only I is correct.

(b) Only II is correct.

(c) Both I and II are correct.

(d) Both I and II are not correct.

Question 2

Which of the following are the measures of complexity?

(a) Time

(b) Space

(c) Data

(d) Both A and B

Question 3

Which of the following are the basic categories of algorithms?

(a) Iterative algorithms

(b) Recursive algorithms

(c) Structured algorithms

(d) Both A and B

Question 4

Which of the following statement is correct?

I. Iterative algorithms typically use loops and conditional statements.

II. Recursive algorithm uses a 'divide and conquer' strategy.

(a) Only I is correct.

(b) Only II is correct.

(c) Both I and II are correct.

(d) Both I and II are not correct.

Question 5

Which of the following statement is correct about the analysis of algorithms?

I. The analysis of algorithms takes care of any mathematical problems and provides efficient way for solving the problems.

II. The analysis of an algorithm provides information that gives us an idea of how long an algorithm will take for solving a problem.

(a) Only I is correct.

(b) Only II is correct.

(c) Both I and II are correct.

(d) Both I and II are not correct.

Question 6

Which of the followings are the properties of an algorithm?

I. Input

II. Output

III. Finiteness

IV. Definiteness

V. Effectiveness

(a) Only I, II and III.

(b) Only III, IV and V.

(c) Only I and II.

(d) All I, II, III, IV and V.

Question 7

____________ algorithms break down a larger problem into small pieces and then applies algorithm on each pieces.

(a) Iterative algorithms

(b) Repetitive algorithm

(c) Recursive algorithm

(d) Structured algorithm

Question 8

Under which of the following categories does a "procedure which goes on performing a series of steps infinitely" falls?

(a) Recursive algorithm

(b) Iterative algorithm

(c) Repetitive algorithm

(d) This procedure is not an algorithm as it performs the steps infinite number of times

Question 9

Which of the following factors are not involved while selecting a good algorithm?

(a) Type of computer.

(b) Instruction set used by the Microprocessor.

(c) Amount of memory available.

(d) Optimizations that the computer performs in the executable code.

Question 10

Which of the following statement is correct?

I. The analysis of algorithms should be done regardless of the computer on which the program that implements the algorithm is going to get executed.

II. By moving a program to a faster computer, the algorithm would become better.

(a) Only I is correct.

(b) Only II is correct.

(c) Both I and II are correct.

(d) Both I and II are incorrect.

Question 11

Which of the following are the classes of operations that are typically chosen for the significant operation while analyzing an algorithm?

(a) arithmetic

(b) comparison

(c) number of additions

(d) Both A and B

Question 12

Which of the following statement is correct about Sequential Search Algorithm?

I. The Sequential Search Algorithm is the simplest searching algorithm.

II. The Sequential Search Algorithm search looks at elements, one at a time, from the first in the list until a match is found.

(a) Only I is correct.

(b) Only II is correct.

(c) Both I and II are correct.

(d) Both I and II are incorrect.

Question 13

Which of the following are essential statement types for describing algorithms?

(a) Sequence

(b) Selection

(c) Repetition

(d) A, B and C

Question 14

Which of the following will mainly impact the efficiency of the algorithm in most sorting algorithms?

(a) Absence of recursive technique.

(b) Number of elements in list.

(c) Number of comparisons that are made.

(d) Which element is chosen as a pivot element.

Question 15

Which of the following are the cases to consider during analysis of algorithms?

(a) best case

(b) bad case

(c) good case

(d) better case

Question 16

Which of the following input makes an algorithm to take shortest time to execute?

(a) Best case input

(b) Worst case input

(c) Average case input

(d) Standard input

Question 17

Which of the following input gives an idea of the most time an algorithm will ever take to execute?

(a) Best case input

(b) Worst case input

(c) Average case input

(d) Standard input

Question 18

Which of the following is the worst case scenario for sequential search algorithm?

I. The value being searched matches the last element in the list.

II. The value being searched is not present in the list.

(a) Only I

(b) Only II

(c) Both I and II

(d) Neither I nor II

Question 19

While using Sequential Search Algorithm for searching an element '5' in the given set of data containing 5 elements, which of the following will be the worst case?

(a) 5 lying in the first position.

(b) 5 lying in the fifth position.

(c) 5 lying in the second position.

(d) 5 lying in the fourth position.

Question 20

Which of the following set of data represents best case for a sorting algorithm?

(a) { 2, 4, 1, 3, 0 }

(b) { 1, 3, 9, 4, 2 }

(c) { 3, 6, 9, 12, 15 }

(d) { 4, 6, 2, 1, 0 }

Question 21

Which of the following is correct number of comparisons required to search an element using linear search algorithm?

(a) O (n)

(b) O (n2)

(c) O (log n)

(d) O (2 log n)

Question 22

Which of the following two algorithms will require more space?

Algorithm 1

```
big  = a
if ( b > big )
      big = b
if ( c > big )
      big = c
```

Algorithm 2

```
if ( a > b )
      if ( a > c )
            return a
      else
            return c
else if ( b > c)
      return b
else
      return c
```

(a) Algorithm 1 will occupy more space.

(b) Algorithm 2 will occupy more space.

(c) Both algorithms will occupy same amount of space.

(d) Both algorithms will not occupy any space.

Question 23

Which of the following function is correct to search an element n in an array A of N elements using sequential search?

(a)
```
function ( int *p, int N )
{
        int i = 0 ;
        while ( i < N )
        {
              if ( * ( p + i ) == n )
                    return i + 1 ;
              i ++ ;
        }
        return -1 ;
}
```

(b)
```
function ( int *p, int N )
{
        int i = 0 ;
        while ( i < N )
        {
              if ( * ( p + i ) == n )
                    return i – 1 ;
              i ++ ;
        }
        return -1 ;
}
```

(c)
```
function ( int *p, int N )
{
        int i = 0 ;
        while ( i < N – 1 )
        {
              if ( * ( p + i ) == n )
                    return i ;
              i ++ ;
        }
        return -1 ;
}
```

(d)
```
function ( int *p, int N )
{
    int i = 0 ;
    while ( i < N )
    {
        if ( * ( p + i++ ) == n )
            return i – 1 ;
        i ++ ;
    }
    return -1 ;
}
```

Question 24

Which of the following alternative form is correct about the given conditional flow of selection logic algorithms?

If condition Then :
    [Module A]
Else :
    [Module B]
[End of If Structure]

(a) Above program is single alternative form of conditional flow.

(b) Above program is double alternative form of conditional flow.

(c) Above program is multiple alternative form of conditional flow.

(d) Above program is structured alternative form of conditional flow.

Question 25

Which one of the option represents the worst case complexity of the code given below?

```
for ( i = 1 ; i < N ; i++ )
{
      for ( j = 1 ; j < N – 1 ; j++ )
      {
            [ body of loop ]
      }
}
for ( k = 0 ; k < N ; k++ )
{
      [ body of loop ]
}
```

(a) O (N)

(b) O (N2)

(c) O (log N)

(d) O (2 log N)

Question 26

What will be the complexity of the following loop?

```
for ( int i = 1 ; i < n - 2 ; i++ )
      /* body of loop */
```

(a) O (n)

(b) O (n – 2)

(c) O (n2)

(d) O (log n)

Question 27

What will be the complexity of the following loops?

```
while ( i < N )
{
    while ( j < M )
    {
        for ( k = 1 ; k < P ; k ++ )
        {
            /* Some Code Here */
        }
    }
}
```

(a) O (N)

(b) O (N * M)

(c) O (N * M * P)

(d) O (N M * P)

Question 28

How many number of comparisons are there in average case of sequential search algorithm for N elements?

(a) N

(b) N / 2

(c) N2

(d) N – 4

Question 29

Which of the following represents the best case for Binary Search Algorithm?

(a) The element to be searched lies at the beginning of the set.

(b) The element to be searched lies at the end of the set.

(c) The element to be searched lies at the middle of the set.

(d) Both A and B.

Question 30

Which of the following statement is correct?

I. Average case complexity of Quick sort algorithm is same as that of Heap sort algorithm.

II. Worst case complexity of Quick sort algorithm is same as that of Heap sort algorithm.

(a) Only I is correct.

(b) Only II is correct.

(c) Both I and II are correct.

(d) Both I and II are incorrect.

Question 31

What is the worst case complexity of Bubble sort algorithm?

(a) O (n)

(b) O (log n)

(c) O (n2)

(d) O (n log n)

Question 32

What is the worst case complexity of Quick sort algorithm?

(a) O (n)

(b) O (log n)

(c) O (n2)

(d) O (n log n)

Question 33

Which of the following is not a sorting algorithm?

(a) Insertion sort.

(b) Heap sort.

(c) Merge sort.

(d) Calculation sort.

Question 34

What is Average case complexity of Bubble sort algorithm?

(a) O (n)

(b) O (n2)

(c) O (log n2)

(d) O (n2 log n2)

Question 35

Which of the following represents the worst case for Binary Search algorithm?

(a) The element to be searched lies at the beginning of the set.

(b) The element to be searched lies at the end of the set.

(c) The element to be searched is not present in the set.

(d) All of the above.

Question 36

Which of the following are the two techniques of sorting algorithms?

(a) procedural sort, objective sort

(b) internal sort, external sort

(c) procedural sort, external sort

(d) combine sort, internal sort

Question 37

What is Average case complexity of Heap sort algorithm?

(a) O (log n)

(b) O (n log n)

(c) O (log n2)

(d) O (n2 log n2)

Question 38

Which of the following statement is correct?

I. Average case complexity of Merge Sort algorithm is same as that of its Worst case.

II. Best case complexity of Merge Sort algorithm is same as that of its Worst case.

(a) Only I is correct.

(b) Only II is correct.

(c) Both I and II are correct.

(d) Both I and II are incorrect.

Question 39

Which of the following function will search a string 'str' in an array S[5][20] using Linear

Search?

(a) int Search (char S[ ][10], char *str)
```
{
    int i ;
    for ( i = 0 ; i < 5 ; i ++ )
    {
        if ( strcmp ( S[ i ], str ) == 0 )
            return i + 1 ;
    }
    return -1 ;
}
```

(b) int Search (char S[ ][10], char *str)
```
{
    int i ;
    for ( i = 0 ; i < 5 ; i ++ )
    {
        if ( strcmp ( S[ i ], str ) == 0 )
            return i - 1 ;
    }
    return -1 ;
}
```

(c) int Search (char S[ ][10], char *str)
```
{
    int i ;
    for ( i = 1 ; i < 5 ; i ++ )
    {
        if ( strcmp ( S[ i ], str ) == 0 )
            return i + 1 ;
    }
    return -1 ;
}
```

(d) int Search (char S[ ][10], char *str)

```
{
        int i ;
        for ( i = 1 ; i <= 5 ; i ++ )
        {
            if ( strcmp ( S[ i ], str ) == 0 )
                return i + 1 ;
        }
        return -1 ;
}
```

Question 40

What will be the complexity of the following loop?

```
for ( i = 0 ; i < n ; i ++ )
{
    for ( j = 0 ; j <= i ; j ++ )
    {
        /* body of loop */
    }
}
```

(a) O (n2)

(b) O (n)

(c) O (n * i)

(d) O (log n)

Question 41

Which of the following statement is correct?

I. Internal sorting methods are used if all the data that is to be sorted can be accommodated at a time in memory.

II. External sorting methods are used if all the data that is to be sorted cannot be accommodated at a time in memory.

(a) Only I is correct.

(b) Only II is correct.

(c) Both I and II are correct.

(d) Both I and II are incorrect.

Question 42

Which of the following function will sort the array 'arr' in ascending order using Bubble Sort method?

(a)
```
void Function ( int *arr )
{
    int i, j, t ;
    for ( i = 0 ; i < 5 ; i ++ )
    {
        for ( j = 0 ; j < 5 - i ; j ++ )
        {
            if ( *( arr + j ) > *( arr + j + 1 ) )
            {
                t = *( arr + j ) ;
                *( arr + j ) = *( arr + j + 1 ) ;
                *( arr + j + 1 ) = t ;
            }
        }
    }
}
```

(b)
```
void Function ( int *arr )
{
    int i, j, t ;
    for ( i = 0 ; i < 5 ; i ++ )
    {
```

```
            for ( j = 0 ; j < 5 - i ; j ++ )
            {
                if ( *( arr + j ) < *( arr + j + 1 ) )
                {
                    t = *( arr + j ) ;
                    *( arr + j ) = *( arr + j + 1 ) ;
                    *( arr + j + 1 ) = t ;
                }
            }
        }
    }
```

(c) void Function (int *arr)

```
    {
        int i, j, t ;
        for ( i = 0 ; i < 5 ; i ++ )
        {
            for ( j = 0 ; j < 5 - i ; j ++ )
            {
                if ( *( arr + j ) > *( arr + j + 1 ) )
                {
                    t = *( arr + j ) ;
                    *( arr + j ) = *( arr + j + 1 ) ;
                    *( arr + j  ) = t ;
                }
            }
        }
    }
```

(d) void Function (int *arr)

```
    {
        int i, j, t ;
        for ( i = 0 ; i < 5 ; i ++ )
        {
            for ( j = 0 ; j < 5 - i ; j ++ )
```

```
        {
            if ( *( arr + j ) > *( arr + j + 1 ) )
            {
                t = *( arr + j ) ;
                *( arr + j ) = *( arr + i ) ;
                *( arr + i ) = t ;
            }
        }
    }
}
```

Question 43

Which of the following statement is correct?

I. Average case complexity of the binary tree sort algorithm is same as that of its Best case.

II. Average case complexity of the binary tree sort algorithm is same as that of its Worst case.

(a) Only I is correct.

(b) Only II is correct.

(c) Both I and II are correct.

(d) Both I and II are incorrect.

Question 44

What is the worst case complexity of Heap sort algorithm?

(a) O (n)

(b) O (log n)

(c) O (n2)

(d) O (n log n)

Question 45

Which of the following data structure's element cannot be sorted using any sorting algorithm?

(a) Arrays

(b) Linked List

(c) Tree

(d) Stack

Question 46

Which of the following function will sort the array 'arr' in ascending order using Selection Sort method?

(a)
```
void Function ( int *arr )
{
    int i, j, t ;
    for ( i = 0 ; i < 5 ; i ++ )
    {
        for ( j = 0 ; j < 5 - i ; j ++ )
        {
            if ( *( arr + j ) > *( arr + j + 1 ) )
            {
                t = *( arr + j ) ;
                *( arr + j ) = *( arr + j + 1 ) ;
                *( arr + j + 1 ) = t ;
            }
        }
    }
}
```

(b)
```
void Function ( int *arr )
{
    int i, j, t ;
```

```
        for ( i = 0 ; i < 5 ; i ++ )
        {
            for ( j = 0 ; j < 5 - i ; j ++ )
            {
                if ( *( arr + j ) < *( arr + j + 1 ) )
                {
                    t = *( arr + j ) ;
                    *( arr + j ) = *( arr + j + 1 ) ;
                    *( arr + j + 1 ) = t ;
                }
            }
        }
    }
```

(c) void Function (int *arr)

```
    {
        int i, j, t ;
        for ( i = 0 ; i < 4 ; i ++ )
        {
            for ( j = i + 1 ; j < 5  ; j ++ )
            {
                if ( *( arr + i ) > *( arr + j ) )
                {
                    t = *( arr + j ) ;
                    *( arr + j ) = *( arr + i ) ;
                    *( arr + i ) = t ;
                }
            }
        }
    }
```

(d) void Function (int *arr)

```
    {
        int i, j, t ;
        for ( i = 0 ; i < 4 ; i ++ )
```

```
    {
        for ( j = i + 1 ; j < 5  ; j ++ )
        {
            if ( *( arr + i ) < *( arr + j ) )
            {
                t = *( arr + j ) ;
                *( arr + j ) = *( arr + i ) ;
                *( arr + i ) = t ;
            }
        }
    }
}
```

Question 47

Which of the following is the worst case complexity of the binary tree sort algorithm?

(a) O (n log n)

(b) O (n)

(c) O (n2)

(d) O (log n)

Question 48

Which of the following function is the correct implementation of algorithm of push operation on stack implemented using array having maximum capacity of MAX elements?

(a)
```
void push ( struct stack *s, int item )
{
    if ( s -> top == MAX - 1 )
    {
        printf ( "Stack is full" ) ;
        return ;
    }
    s -> arr[ s -> top ] = item ;
```

```
}
```

(b)
```
void push ( struct stack *s, int item )
{
    if ( s -> top == MAX - 1 )
    {
        printf ( "Stack is full" ) ;
        return ;
    }
    s -> top ++ ;
    s -> arr[ s -> top ] = item ;
}
```

(c)
```
void push ( struct stack *s, int item )
{
    s -> top ++ ;
    s -> arr[ s -> top ] = item ;
}
```

(d)
```
void push ( struct stack *s, int item )
{
    if ( s -> top == MAX - 1 )
    {
        printf ( "Stack is full" ) ;
    }
    s -> top ++ ;
    s -> arr[ s -> top ] = item ;
}
```

Question 49

Which of the following function will correctly return the location of element 'n' in array 'A' of N elements, or -1 if 'n' is not found using binary search method? Assume that 'A' is sorted in ascending order?

(a)
```
int Search ( int *a, int e )
```

```
{
    int s = 0, m, n = 2 ;
    while ( s <= e )
    {
        m = ( s + e ) / 2 ;
        if ( *( a + m ) == n )
            return *( a + m ) ;
        else if ( *( a + m ) > n )
            e = m - 1 ;
        else
            s = m + 1 ;
    }
    return -1 ;
}
```

(b)
```
int Search ( int *a, int e )
{
    int s = 0, m, n = 2 ;
    while ( s <= e )
    {
        m = ( s + e ) / 2 ;
        if ( *( a + m ) == n )
            return m + 1 ;
        else if ( *( a + m ) > n )
            e = m - 1 ;
        else
            s = m + 1 ;
    }
    return -1 ;
}
```

(c)
```
int Search ( int *a, int e )
{
    int s = 0, m, n = 2 ;
    while ( s <= e )
```

```
    {
        m = ( s + e ) / 2 ;
        if ( *( a + m ) == n )
            return m + 1 ;
        else if ( *( a + m ) < n )
            e = m - 1 ;
        else
            s = m + 1 ;
    }
    return -1 ;
}
```

(d)
```
int Search ( int *a, int e )
{
    int s = 0, m, n = 2 ;
    while ( s <= e )
    {
        m = ( s + e ) / 2 ;
        if ( *( a + m ) > n )
            e = m - 1 ;
        else
            s = m + 1 ;
    }
    return -1 ;
}
```

Question 50

Which of the following function is the correct implementation of algorithm of adding an item to the queue represented using Linked list? Assume suitable structure for Queue.

(a)
```
void add ( struct queue *q, int n )
{
    struct node *temp ;
    temp = ( struct node* ) malloc ( sizeof ( struct node ) ) ;
    if ( temp == NULL )
```

```
            printf ( "Queue is full" ) ;
        temp -> data = n ;
        temp -> link = NULL ;
        if ( q -> front == NULL )
        {
            q -> rear = q -> front = temp ;
            return ;
        }
        q -> rear -> link = temp ;
        q -> rear = q -> rear -> link ;
    }
```

(b)
```
    void add ( struct queue *q )
    {
        struct node *temp ;
        temp = ( struct node* ) malloc ( sizeof ( struct node ) ) ;
        if ( temp == NULL )
            printf ( "Queue is full" ) ;
        temp -> data = n ;
        temp -> link = NULL ;
        if ( q -> front == NULL )
        {
            q -> rear = q -> front = temp ;
            return ;
        }
        q -> rear -> link = temp ;
        q -> rear = q -> rear -> link ;
    }
```

(c)
```
    void add ( struct queue *q, int n )
    {
        struct node *temp ;
        temp = ( struct node* ) malloc ( sizeof ( struct node ) ) ;
        if ( temp == NULL )
            printf ( "Queue is full" ) ;
```

```
        temp -> data = n ;
        temp -> link = NULL ;
        if ( q -> front == NULL )
        {
            q = q -> front = temp ;
            return ;
        }
        q -> rear -> link = temp ;
        q -> rear = q -> rear -> link ;
    }
```

(d)
```
    void add ( struct queue *q, int n )
    {
        struct node *temp ;
        temp = ( struct node* ) malloc ( sizeof ( struct node ) ) ;
        if ( temp == NULL )
            printf ( "Queue is full" ) ;
        temp -> data = n ;
        temp -> link = NULL ;
        if ( q -> front == NULL )
        {
            q -> rear = q -> front = temp ;
            return ;
        }
        q -> link = temp ;
        q -> rear = q -> link ;
    }
```

Question 51

Which of the following is the correct implementation of algorithm of adding a node in the linked list whose starting address is stored in variable p?

(a)
```
    void add ( int n )
    {
        struct MyList *q, *q1 ;
        q = ( struct MyList * ) malloc ( sizeof ( struct MyList ) ) ;
```

```
        q -> data = n ;
        q -> Link = NULL ;
        q1 = p ;
        while ( q1 -> Link != NULL )
            q1 = q1 -> Link ;
        q1 -> Link = q ;
    }
```

(b)
```
    void add ( int n )
    {
        struct MyList *q, *q1 ;
        q = ( struct MyList * ) malloc ( sizeof ( struct MyList ) ) ;
        q -> data = n ;
        q -> Link = NULL ;
        if ( p == NULL )
            p = q ;
        else
        {
            q1 = p ;
            while ( q1 != NULL )
                q1 = q1 -> Link ;
            q1 -> Link = q ;
        }
    }
```

(c)
```
    void add ( int n )
    {
        struct MyList *q, *q1 ;
        q = ( struct MyList * ) malloc ( sizeof ( struct MyList ) ) ;
        q -> data = n ;
        q -> Link = NULL ;
        if ( p == NULL )
            p = q ;
        else
        {
```

```
            q1 = p ;
            while ( q1 -> Link != NULL )
                  q1 = q1 -> Link ;
            q1 = q ;
      }
}
```

(d)
```
void add ( int n )
{
      struct MyList *q, *q1 ;
      q = ( struct MyList * ) malloc ( sizeof ( struct MyList ) ) ;
      q -> data = n ;
      q -> Link = NULL ;
      if ( p == NULL )
            p = q ;
      else
      {
            q1 = p ;
            while ( q1 -> Link != NULL )
                  q1 = q1 -> Link ;
            q1 -> Link = q ;
      }
}
```

Question 52

What is Average case complexity of Quick sort algorithm?

(a) O (log n)

(b) O (n log n)

(c) O (log n2)

(d) O (n2 log n2)

Question 53

What will be the output of the following program?

```
# include <stdio.h>
void Sorting ( int * ) ;
int main( )
{
      int EmployeeID[ ] = { 720, 545, 123, 458, 120 } ;
      int i ;
      Sorting ( EmployeeID ) ;
      for ( i = 0 ; i < 5 ; i++ )
            printf ( "%d ", EmployeeID[ i ] ) ;
      return 0 ;
}
void Sorting ( int *EmpID )
{
      int a ;
      int i, j ;
      for ( i = 1 ; i < 4 ; i++ )
      {
            for ( j = i + 1 ; j < 4 ; j++ )
            {
                  if ( *( EmpID + i ) > *( EmpID + j ) )
                  {
                        a = *( EmpID + i ) ;
                        *( EmpID + i ) = *( EmpID + j ) ;
                        *( EmpID + j ) = a ;
                  }
            }
      }
}
```

(a) 120 123 458 545 720

(b) 720 545 458 123 120

(c) 720 123 458 545 120

(d) 720 120 123 458 545

Question 54

Which of the following function is the correct implementation of algorithm of inorder traversal of a tree? Assume suitable structure for tree.

(a)
```
void inorder ( struct node *root )
{
        if ( root != NULL )
        {
                inorder ( root -> left ) ;
                printf ( "%c ", root -> data ) ;
                inorder ( root -> right ) ;
        }
}
```

(b)
```
void inorder ( struct node *root )
{
        if ( root != NULL )
        {
                inorder ( root -> right ) ;
                printf ( "%c ", root -> data ) ;
                inorder ( root -> left ) ;
        }
}
```

(c)
```
void inorder ( struct node *root )
{
        if ( root != NULL )
        {
                inorder ( root -> right ) ;
                inorder ( root -> left ) ;
```

```
            printf ( "%c ", root -> data ) ;
        }
}
```

(d)
```
void inorder ( struct node *root )
{
    if ( root != NULL )
    {
        inorder ( root -> left ) ;
        inorder ( root -> right ) ;
        printf ( "%c ", root -> data ) ;
    }
}
```

Question 55

Which of the following function will return the location of element 'n' in array 'A' of N elements or -1 if 'n' not found using linear search method assuming that 'A' is sorted in ascending order?

(a)
```
int Search ( int *a, int N )
{
    int i = 0, n = 3 ;
    for ( i = 0 ; i < N ; i ++ )
    {
        if ( * ( a + i ) == n )
            return i + 1 ;
        else if ( * ( a + i ) >= n )
            return -1 ;
    }
    return -1 ;
}
```

(b)
```
int Search ( int *a, int N )
{
    int i = 0, n = 3 ;
```

```
        for ( i = 0 ; i < N ; i ++ )
        {
            if ( * ( a + i ) == n )
                return i + 1 ;
            else if ( * ( a + i ) > n )
                return -1 ;
        }
        return -1 ;
    }
```

(c)
```
    int Search ( int *a, int N )
    {
        int i = 0, n = 3 ;
        for ( i = 0 ; i < N ; i ++ )
        {
            if ( * ( a + i ) == n )
                return i + 1 ;
            else if ( * ( a + i ) < n )
                return -1 ;
        }
        return -1 ;
    }
```

(d) Both A and B are correct.

Question 56

Which of the following function is the correct implementation of algorithm for pop operation on stack implemented using array having maximum capacity of MAX elements?

(a)
```
    int pop ( struct stack *s )
    {
        int data ;
        if ( s -> top = -1 )
        {
            printf ( "Stack is empty" ) ;
```

```
            return NULL ;
        }
        data = s -> arr[ s -> top ] ;
        s -> top -- ;
        return data ;
    }
```

(b) int pop (struct stack *s)

```
    {
        int data  ;
        data = s -> arr[ s -> top ] ;
        s -> top -- ;
        return data ;
    }
```

(c) int pop (struct stack *s)

```
    {
        int data ;
        if ( s -> top = -1 )
        {
            printf ( "Stack is empty" ) ;
            return NULL ;
        }
        data = s -> arr[ s -> top ] ;
        return data ;
    }
```

(d) int pop (struct stack *s)

```
    {
        int data ;
        if ( s -> top = -1 )
        {
            printf ( "Stack is empty" ) ;
            return NULL ;
        }
```

```
        data = s -> arr[ s -> top ] ;
        s -> top ++ ;
        return data ;
    }
```

Question 57

Which of the following statement is correct about the program given below?

```
# include <stdio.h>
# include <string.h>
int Search ( char S[][10], char * ) ;
char strarray[ ][10] = { "Shashi", "Shashi", "Raj", "Brijesh", "Abhay" } ;
int main( )
{
    int A ;
    A = Search ( strarray, "Shashi" ) ;
    if ( A == -1 )
        printf ( "Searched String not found" ) ;
    else
        printf ( "String %s found at position %d", strarray[ A – 1 ], A ) ;
    return 0 ;
}
int Search ( char S[ ][10], char *str )
{
    int s = 0, e = 5, m ;
    while ( s <= e )
    {
        m = ( s + e ) / 2 ;
        if ( strcmp ( S[ m ], str ) == 0 )
            return m + 1 ;
        else if ( strcmp ( S[ m ], str ) > 0 )
            e = m - 1 ;
        else
            s = m + 1 ;
```

```
    }
    return -1 ;
}
```

(a) Above program will display the message "String Shashi found at position 0".

(b) Above program will display the message "String Shashi found at position 1".

(c) Above program will display the message "Searched String not found".

(d) Above program will go into an infinite loop.

Question 58

Which of the following sort function will sort the link list in ascending order whose starting address is stored in pointer p?

(a)
```
void sort ( void )
{
    struct MyList *t,*t1, *t2 ;
    t = t1 = p ;
    t2 = ( struct MyList* ) malloc ( sizeof ( struct MyList ) ) ;
    while ( t != NULL )
    {
        t1 = t ;
        while ( t1 != NULL )
        {
            if ( t -> data < t1 -> data)
            {
                t2 -> data = t -> data ;
                t -> data = t1 -> data ;
                t1 -> data = t2 -> data ;
            }
            t1 = t1 -> Link ;
        }
        t = t -> Link ;
    }
```

```
}
```

(b)
```
void sort ( void )
{
    struct MyList *t,*t1, *t2 ;
    t = t1 = p ;
    t2 = ( struct MyList* ) malloc ( sizeof ( struct MyList ) ) ;
    while ( t != NULL )
    {
        t1 = t ;
        while ( t1 != NULL )
        {
            if ( t -> data > t1 -> data)
            {
                t2 -> data = t -> data ;
                t -> data = t1 -> data ;
                t1 -> data = t2 -> data ;
            }
            t1 = t1 -> Link ;
        }
        t = t -> Link ;
    }
}
```

(c)
```
void sort ( void )
{
    struct MyList *t,*t1, *t2 ;
    t = t1 = p ;
    t2 = ( struct MyList* ) malloc ( sizeof ( struct MyList ) ) ;
    while ( t -> Link != NULL )
    {
        t1 = t ;
        while ( t1 -> Link != NULL )
        {
            if ( t -> data > t1 -> data)
```

```
                {
                        t2 -> data = t-> data ;
                        t -> data = t1 -> data ;
                        t1 -> data = t2 -> data ;
                }
                t1 = t1 -> Link ;
            }
            t = t -> Link ;
        }
    }
```

(d) void sort (void)

```
    {
        struct MyList *t,*t1, *t2 ;
        t = t1 = p ;
        t2 = ( struct MyList* ) malloc ( sizeof ( struct MyList ) ) ;
        while ( t != NULL )
        {
            while ( t1 != NULL )
            {
                if ( t -> data > t1 -> data)
                {
                    t2 -> data = t -> data ;
                    t -> data = t1 -> data ;
                    t1 -> data = t2 -> data ;
                }
                t1 = t1 -> Link ;
            }
            t = t -> Link ;
        }
    }
```

Question 59

What will be the output of the following program?

```
# include <stdio.h>
# include <string.h>
# include <malloc.h>
int display ( struct MyList *ptr, int ) ;
void add ( int n ) ;

struct MyList
{
      int data ;
      struct MyList *Link ;
} *p ;

int main( )
{
      p = NULL ;
      add ( 0 ) ;
      add ( 10 ) ;
      add ( 20 ) ;
      add ( 30 ) ;
      display ( p , 20 ) ;
      return 0 ;
}
void add ( int n )
{
      struct MyList *q, *q1 ;
      q = ( struct MyList * ) malloc ( sizeof ( struct MyList ) ) ;
      q -> data = n ;
      q -> Link = NULL ;
      if ( p == NULL )
            p = q ;
      else
      {
            q1 = p ;
            while ( q1 -> Link != NULL )
```

```
            q1 = q1 -> Link ;
        q1 -> Link = q ;
    }
}
int display ( struct MyList *ptr, int n )
{
    static int i, j ;
    while ( ptr != NULL )
    {
        if ( ptr -> data == n )
            return printf ( "%d", ptr -> data ) ;
        printf ( "%d ", ptr -> data ) ;
        ptr = ptr -> Link ;
    }
    return -1 ;
}
```

(a) 0 10 20 30

(b) 0 10 20 2

(c) 0 10 20

(d) 0 10

Question 60

Which of the following function will search a string 'str' in an array S[5][20] using Binary Search?

(a)
```
int Search ( char S[ ][10], char *str )
{
    int s = 0, e = 5, m ;
    while ( s <= e )
    {
        m = ( s + e ) / 2 ;
        if ( strcmp ( S[m], str ) == 0 )
```

```
                return m + 1 ;
            else if ( strcmp ( S[m] , str ) > 0 )
                s = m + 1 ;
            else
                e = m - 1 ;
        }
        return -1 ;
    }
```

(b)
```
    int Search ( char S[ ][10], char *str )
    {
        int s = 0, e = 5, m ;
        while ( s <= e )
        {
            m = ( s + e ) / 2 ;
            if ( strcmp ( S[m], str ) == 0 )
                return m + 1 ;
            else if ( strcmp ( S[m], str ) > 0 )
                s = m + 1 ;
        }
        return -1 ;
    }
```

(c)
```
    int Search ( char S[ ][10], char *str )
    {
        int s = 0, e = 5, m ;
        while ( s <= e )
        {
            m = ( s + e ) / 2 ;
            if ( strcmp ( S[m], str ) == 0 )
                return m + 1 ;
            else if ( strcmp ( S[m], str ) < 0 )
                s = m + 1 ;
            else
                e = m - 1 ;
```

```
        }
        return -1 ;
    }
```

(d)
```
    int Search ( char S[ ][10], char *str )
    {
        int s = 0, e = 5, m ;
        while ( s <= e )
        {
            m = ( s + e ) / 2 ;
            if ( strcmp ( S[m], str ) == 0 )
                return m + 1 ;
            else if ( strcmp ( S[m], str ) > 0 )
                e = m + 1 ;
        }
        return -1 ;
    }
```

Answers

Q. 1 – A	Q. 2 – D	Q. 3 – D
Q. 4 – C	Q. 5 – B	Q. 6 – D
Q. 7 – C	Q. 8 – D	Q. 9 – C
Q. 10 – C	Q. 11 – D	Q. 12 – C
Q. 13 – D	Q. 14 – D	Q. 15 – A
Q. 16 – A	Q. 17 – B	Q. 18 – C
Q. 19 – B	Q. 20 – C	Q. 21 – A
Q. 22 – A	Q. 23 – A	Q. 24 – B
Q. 25 – B	Q. 26 – A	Q. 27 – C
Q. 28 – B	Q. 29 – C	Q. 30 – A
Q. 31 – C	Q. 32 – C	Q. 33 – D
Q. 34 – B	Q. 35 – D	Q. 36 – B
Q. 37 – B	Q. 38 – C	Q. 39 – A
Q. 40 – A	Q. 41 – C	Q. 42 – A
Q. 43 – A	Q. 44 – D	Q. 45 – D
Q. 46 – C	Q. 47 – C	Q. 48 – B

Q. 49 – B	Q. 50 – A	Q. 51 – D
Q. 52 – B	Q. 53 – C	Q. 54 – A
Q. 55 – D	Q. 56 – A	Q. 57 – C
Q. 58 – B	Q. 59 – C	Q. 60 – A

2

Arrays, Strings and Pattern Matching

Question 1

In which of the following type of data structure its elements form a sequence?

(a) Arrays

(b) Trees

(c) Graphs

(d) Binary Trees

Question 2

Which of the following code snippet is correct that will create and initialize a matrix mat[3][3]?

(a)
```
void create ( int mat[3][3] )
{
        int i, j ;
        for ( i = 0 ; i < 3 ; i++ )
        {
                for ( j = 0 ; j < 3 - i ; j++ )
                {
                        printf ( "Enter the element: " ) ;
                        scanf ( "%d", &mat[i][j] ) ;
                }
        }
}
```

(b)
```
void create ( int mat[3][3] )
{
        int i, j ;
        for ( i = 0 ; i < 2 ; i++ )
        {
                for ( j = 0 ; j < 2 ; j++ )
                {
```

```
            printf ( "Enter the element: " ) ;
            scanf ( "%d", &mat[i][j] ) ;
        }
    }
}
```

(c)
```
void create ( int mat[3][3] )
{
    int i, j ;
    for ( i = 0 ; i < 3 ; i++ )
    {
        for ( j = 0 ; j < 2 ; j++ )
        {
            printf ( "Enter the element: " ) ;
            scanf ( "%d", &mat[i][j] ) ;
        }
    }
}
```

(d)
```
void create ( int mat[3][3] )
{
    int i, j ;
    for ( I = 0 ; i < 3 ; i++ )
    {
        for ( j = 0 ; j < 3 ; j++ )
        {
            printf ( "Enter the element: " ) ;
            scanf ( "%d", &mat[i][j] ) ;
        }
    }
}
```

Question 3

Which of the following statements regarding array are correct?

I. Arrays are useful when the number of elements to be stored will vary.

II. Unsorted arrays will be allowed while merging them.

(a) I is correct II is not correct.

(b) Both I and II are correct.

(c) II is correct I is not correct.

(d) Both I and II are not correct.

Question 4

Which of the following statements is correct about the given code snippet?

```
int fun ( int mat[3][3] )
{
    int sum, i, j, k, p ;
    sum = 0 ; j = 1 ; k = 2 ;
    for ( i = 0 ; i < 3 ; i++ )
    {
        p = pow ( -1, i ) ;

        if ( i == 3 - 1 )
            k = 1 ;
        sum = sum + ( mat[0][i] * ( mat[1][j] * mat[2][k] - mat[2][j] * mat[1][k] ) ) * p ;
        j = 0 ;
    }
    return sum ;
}
```

(a) The code initializes a 3 X 3 matrix.

(b) The code adds a 3 X 3 matrix elements.

(c) The code finds determinant value of a 3 X 3 matrix.

(d) The code obtains transpose of a 3 X 3 matrix.

Question 5

Which of the following statements regarding array are correct?

I. The addresses present in an array of pointers can be addresses of isolated variables or even the addresses of other array elements.

II. A matrix is called orthogonal if the determinant value of a matrix is 0.

(a) I is correct II is not correct.

(b) Both I and II are correct.

(c) II is correct I is not correct.

(d) Both I and II are not correct.

Question 6

Which of the following code snippet is correct that will multiply two 3 X 3 matrices?

(a)
```
void matmul ( int m1[3][3], int m2[3][3], int m3[3][3] )
{
    int i, j, k ;
    for ( k = 0 ; k < 3 ; k++ )
    {
        for ( i = 0 ; i < 3 ; i++ )
        {
            for ( j = 0 ; j < 3 ; j++ )
                m3[k][i] += m1[k][j] * m2[j][i] ;
        }
    }
}
```

(b)
```
void matmul ( int m1[3][3], int m2[3][3], int m3[3][3] )
{
    int i, j, k ;
    for ( k = 0 ; k < 3 ; k++ )
    {
```

```
            for ( i = 0 ; i < 3 - k ; i++ )
            {
                m3[k][i] = 0 ;
                for ( j = 0 ; j < 2 ; j++ )
                    m3[k][i] += m1[k][j] * m2[j][i] ;
            }
        }
    }
```

(c) void matmul (int m1[3][3], int m2[3][3], int m3[3][3])

```
    {
        int i, j, k ;
        for ( k = 0 ; k < 3 ; k++ )
        {
            for ( i = 0 ; i < 3 ; i++ )
            {
                m3[k][i] = 0 ;
                for ( j = 0 ; j < 3 ; j++ )
                    m3[k][i] += m1[k][j] * m2[j][i] ;
            }
        }
    }
```

(d) void matmul (int m1[3][3], int m2[3][3], int m3[3][3])

```
    {
        int i, j, k ;
        for ( k = 0 ; k < 3 ; k++ )
        {
            for ( i = 0 ; i < 3 - k ; i++ )
            {
                for ( j = 0 ; j < 3 - k ; j++ )
                    m3[k][i] += m1[k][j] * m2[j][i] ;
            }
        }
    }
```

Question 7

How will you represent a 3D array "arr" with two 2D arrays each of which is having 5 rows and 3 columns?

(a) arr[1][4][2]

(b) arr[5][3][2]

(c) arr[2][5][3]

(d) arr[3][6][4]

Question 8

Which of the following statement is correct about the function fun( ) given below? (Array elements are initialized using the constructor.)

```
class sample
{
    int arr[5], x, y ;
    public :
        void fun( )
        {
            x = arr[0] ;
            y = arr[4] ;
            for ( int i = 1 ; i <= 4 ; i++ )
            {
                if ( x < arr[i] )
                {
                    y = x ;
                    x = arr[i] ;
                }
                else if ( y < arr[i] && arr[i] < x )
                    y = arr[i] ;
            }
        }
```

```
};
```

(a) The function fun( ) finds the biggest and second biggest element of the array "arr".

(b) The function fun( ) interchanges the elements of the array "arr".

(c) The function fun( ) sorts the elements of the array "arr".

(d) The function fun( ) finds the biggest and smallest element of the array "arr".

Question 9

Which of the following is the correct for the given array?

```
int arr[ ][ ][ ] = {
            {
                {2, 8 },
                {0, 6 },
                {4, 7 },
                {1, 5 }
            },
            {
                {3, 2 },
                {8, 6 },
                {1, 6 },
                {4, 5 }
            },
            {
                {3, 9 },
                {1, 8 },
                {6, 5 },
                {4, 0 }
            }
    };
```

(a) int arr[2][3][1]

(b) int arr[3][4][2]

(c) int arr[4][5][3]

(d) int arr[4][2][3]

Question 10

Which of the following statement is correct about the function fun( ) given below? (Array elements are initialized using the constructor.)

```
class sample
{
    private :
        int mat[3][3] ;
    public :
        int fun( )
        {
            sample m1 = // Find the transpose of given matrix.
            sample m2 = // Perform the multiplication of elements of m1.
            for ( int i = 0 ; i < 3 ; i++ )
            {
                if ( m2.mat[i][i] == 1 )
                    continue ;
                else
                    break ;
            }
            if ( i == 3 )
                return 1 ;
            else
                return 0 ;
        }
};
```

(a) It finds whether the given matrix is singular.

(b) It finds the determinant of the given matrix.

(c) It finds whether the matrix is orthogonal.

(d) It determines whether the matrix is upper triangular.

Question 11

Which of the following statements regarding Polynomials are correct?

I. Polynomials can be maintained using an array.

II. While maintaining the polynomial it is assumed that the exponent of each successive term is less than that of the previous term.

(a) I is correct II is not correct.

(b) Both I and II are correct.

(c) II is correct I is not correct.

(d) Both I and II are not correct.

Question 12

Which of the following statement is correct about the given code snippet?

```
struct term
{
    int coeff ;
    int exp ;
} ;

struct poly
{
    struct term t [10] ;
    int noofterms ;
} ;
void polynomial ( struct poly *p )
```

```
{
    int i ;
    p -> noofterms = 0 ;
    for ( i = 0 ; i < 10 ; i++ )
    {
        p -> t[i].coeff = 0 ;
        p -> t[i].exp = 0 ;
    }
}
```

(a) The code adds polynomial terms to an array.

(b) The code builds an array to represent polynomial.

(c) The code creates a space for an array in memory to represent a polynomial.

(d) The code initializes the elements of structure poly.

Question 13

Which of the following statements regarding Polynomials are correct?

I. To represent a polynomial of degree "n" as an array is to store the coefficient of (n + 1) terms of a polynomial in an array.

II. Each element of the array representing a polynomial should consist of two values, namely coefficient and exponent.

(a) I is correct II is not correct.

(b) Both I and II are correct.

(c) II is correct I is not correct.

(d) Both I and II are not correct.

Question 14

Which of the following is the simplest way to represent a polynomial of degree n?

(a) To store the coefficient of n terms of a polynomial in an array.

(b) To store the coefficient of (n – 1) terms of a polynomial in an array.

(c) To store the coefficient of (n + 1) terms of a polynomial in an array.

(d) To store the coefficient of (n * n) terms of a polynomial in an array.

Question 15

How many values should each element of array consist to represent a polynomial as an array?

(a) 1

(b) 2

(c) 3

(d) 4

Question 16

Which of the following statements regarding Strings are correct?

I. A string cannot be represented using a linked list.

II. A string not terminated by a '\0' cannot be considered as a string.

(a) I is correct II is not correct.

(b) Both I and II are correct.

(c) II is correct I is not correct.

(d) Both I and II are not correct.

Question 17

Which of the following code snippet is correct that will search for the first occurrence of a character in the string?

(a) int search (char *str, char ch)

```
{
    int i = 0 ;
    while ( *str )
    {
        if ( *str == ch )
            return i ;
        str++ ;
        i++ ;
    }
    return -1 ;
}
```

(b)
```
int search ( char *str, char ch )
{
    int i = 0 ;
    while ( str )
    {
        if ( str == ch )
            return i ;
        str++ ;
        i++ ;
    }
    return -1 ;
}
```

(c)
```
int search ( char *str, char ch )
{
    int i = 0 ;
    while ( *str )
    {
        if ( *str == ch )
            return i ;
        *str++ ;
    }
    return -1 ;
```

```
    }
```

(d)
```
int search ( char *str, char ch )
{
    int i = 0 ;
    while ( *str )
    {
        if ( str = ch )
            return i ;
        *str++ ;
        i++ ;
    }
    return -1 ;
}
```

Question 18

Which of the following statements regarding Strings are correct?

I. While using array of pointers to strings, we cannot initialize it by receiving the string from the keyboard.

II. It is not possible to manipulate a string if we use an array of pointers to store it.

(a) I is correct II is not correct.

(b) Both I and II are correct.

(c) II is correct I is not correct.

(d) Both I and II are not correct.

Question 19

Which of the following statement is correct about the given code snippet?

```
void funstr ( char *t, char *s )
{
```

```
    while ( *t )
        t++ ;
    while ( *s )
        *t++ = *s++ ;
    *t = '\0' ;
}
```

(a) The above code copies one string to another.

(b) The above code finds the first occurrence of one string into another.

(c) The above code concatenates the two strings.

(d) The above code compares two strings.

Question 20

Which of the following algorithm is used for pattern matching?

(a) Kruskal's Algorithm

(b) Shortest Path Algorithm

(c) Dijkstra's Algorithm

(d) Brute Force Algorithm

Question 21

Which of the following statement is correct about the given code snippet?

```
char *names[6] ;
void funstr ( int i, int j )
{
    char *temp ;
    temp = names[i] ;
    names[i] = names[j] ;
    names[j] = temp ;
```

}

(a) The above code swaps the names at given two positions.

(b) The above code adds the names at given two positions.

(c) The above code compares the names at given two positions.

(d) The above code concatenates the names at given two positions.

Question 22

Which of the following statements regarding string are correct?

I. A pointer to the linked list identifies a string represented by a linked list.

II. Each node in the list contains a character and a pointer to the next character in the string.

(a) Only I is correct.

(b) Only II is correct.

(c) Both I and II are correct.

(d) Both I and II are incorrect.

Question 23

Which of the following is the correct sequence of steps for replacing "pattern1" string in the given text with "pattern2" string?

I. Add "pattern2" string to a temporary variable.

II. Delete "pattern1" string.

III. Index the text for "pattern1" string and record the position.

IV. Copy contents of text from beginning to the position into the temporary string variable.

V. Copy contents of text from position + 1 into the temporary variable.

(a) I, II, III, IV and V

(b) I, III, V, IV and II

(c) III, II, IV, I and V

(d) III, IV, I, V and II

Question 24

Which of the following is a string with zero length?

(a) Zero string

(b) End string

(c) Blank string

(d) Empty string

Question 25

Which of the following statement is correct about the code snippet given below?

```
class string
{
    private :
        char *str ;
    public :
        void operator < ( string s )
        {
            int l1 = strlen ( str ) ;
            int l2 = strlen ( s.str ) ;
            int l = l1 + l2 + 1 ;
            char *t = new char[l + 1] ;
            strcpy ( t, str ) ;
            strcat ( t, s.str ) ;
            delete str ;
            str = new char[l + 1] ;
            strcpy ( str, t ) ;
```

```
        }
};
```

(a) The overloaded operator < initializes the string "str".

(b) The overloaded operator < copies the string "s" to "str".

(c) The overloaded operator < concatenates strings "str" and "s".

(d) The overloaded operator < compares string "str" with "s".

Answers

Q. 1 – A	Q. 2 – D	Q. 3 – D
Q. 4 – C	Q. 5 – A	Q. 6 – C
Q. 7 – C	Q. 8 – A	Q. 9 – B
Q. 10 – B	Q. 11 – B	Q. 12 – D
Q. 13 – B	Q. 14 – C	Q. 15 – B
Q. 16 – C	Q. 17 – A	Q. 18 – A
Q. 19 – C	Q. 20 – D	Q. 21 – A
Q. 22 – C	Q. 23 – C	Q. 24 – D
Q. 25 – C		

Kanetkar's
New Arrival
Interview Questions In C Programming
Interview Questions In C++ Programming
Rs. 399/-
Rs. 399/-
• Data types
• Operators
• Pointers Advanced
• Storage Classes
• Arrays
• Structures
• Control Instructions
• Functions
• Pointer Concepts
• Preprocessor Directives
• Strings
• Unions
• OOPS Concepts
• Enhancement To Functions
• References
• Objects and Classes
• Constructors and Destructors
• Free Memory Store
• Function Overloading
• Operator Overloading
• Friends Functions
• Inheritance
• Files and Streams
• Exception Handling
• Templates
Available at all leading booksellers

3

Linked List

Question 1

Linked list is used to store ________________.

(a) Similar type of data

(b) Character type of data

(c) Integer type of data

(d) Floating type of data

Question 2

Linked list is a collection of ______________.

(a) structures

(b) Nodes

(c) functions

(d) arrays

Question 3

In linked List each node contains ___________ parts.

(a) one

(b) three

(c) two

(d) four

Question 4

Which of the following statement is correct?

(a) First part of the node contains address of the next node and second part contains element.

(b) First part of the node contain element of the next node and second part contains address.

(c) First part of the node contains NULL value and second part contains element.

(d) First part of the node contains element and second part contains address of the next node.

Question 5

A link is a ____________ that indicates explicitly the location of the node containing the successor of the list element.

(a) pointer

(b) element

(c) node

(d) structure

Question 6

Which of the following is used to indicate the last node in the linked list?

(a) Pointer

(b) Null

(c) End

(d) Garbage value

Question 7

Which of the following is used to allocate space for the node in memory?

(a) calloc( )

(b) malloc( )

(c) reserved( )

(d) Both A and B

Question 8

Which of the following statement is correct?

(a) The size of the doubly linked list is less than the size of the two way linked lists.

(b) The size of the singly linked list is less than the circular linked list.

(c) The size of the singly linked list is greater than the size of the doubly linked list.

(d) The size of the singly linked list is smaller than the size of the doubly linked list.

Question 9

Which of the following linked list does not have a first or last node?

(a) Singly linked list

(b) Doubly linked list

(c) Circular linked list

(d) Trees

Question 10

Which of the following two linked list structure declaration is similar?

(a) Singly linked list and doubly linked list

(b) Doubly linked list and circular linked list

(c) Circular linked list and singly linked list

(d) Both A and C

Question 11

All nodes in the linked list are usually in ___________.

(a) contiguous

(b) non contiguous

(c) adjacent

(d) Both A and C

Question 12

It is necessary that the _________ in a linked list must contain NULL.

(a) node part of the first node

(b) node part of the last node

(c) link part of the first node

(d) link part of the last node

Question 13

Which of the following represent the structure of a node of a doubly linked list?

(a)
```
struct node
{
    struct node *pre ;
    int data ;
    struct node *next ;
};
```

(b)
```
struct node
{
    int data ;
    struct node *middle ;
};
```

(c)
```
struct node
{
      struct node *pre ;
      struct node *next ;
};
```

(d)
```
struct node
{
      struct node *pre ;
      int data ;
      int next_data ;
};
```

Question 14

In which of the following linked list pointer of the last node points back to the first node?

(a) Singly linked list

(b) Doubly linked list

(c) Circular linked list

(d) Trees

Question 15

Which part/s of doubly linked list contains NULL value?

(a) Previous of first node

(b) Next of last node

(c) Both A and B

(d) Previous of last node

Question 16

Linked list is a series of ________________.

(a) Structures

(b) Pointers

(c) Arrays

(d) Unions

Question 17

Which of the following operator / function is used to free memory allocated by a node of linked list?

(a) delete

(b) new

(c) calloc( )

(d) free( )

Question 18

What does the previous part of first node of a doubly linked list contain?

(a) NULL

(b) Garbage

(c) Address of first node

(d) Address of last node

Question 19

Doubly linked list node contains________________.

(a) A pointer to last node

(b) A pointer to last node, data and pointer to previous node

(c) A pointer to previous node, data and pointer to last node

(d) A pointer to previous node, pointer to last node and data

Question 20

What will be the output of the following program?

```
# include <stdio.h>
# include <malloc.h>
void add ( int ) ;
struct node
{
    int data ;
    struct node *link ;
} ;
struct node *p ;
int main( )
{
    int n = 100 ;
    p = NULL ;
    add ( n ) ;
    return 0 ;
}
void add ( int n )
{
    struct node *r ;
    r = ( struct node * ) malloc ( sizeof ( struct node ) ) ;
    r -> data = n ;
    r -> link = p ;
    printf ( "%d %d", r -> data, r -> link ) ;
}
```

(a) 100 NULL

(b) 100 \0

(c) 100 0

(d) 100 Garbage value

Question 21

Which of the following statement is correct about the code snippet given below?

```
# include <stdio.h>
# include <malloc.h>
void add ( struct node **, int ) ;
void dis ( struct node * ) ;
struct node
{
    int data ;
    struct node *link ;
} ;
struct node p ;
int main( )
{
    p = NULL ;
    add ( &p, 10 ) ;
    dis ( p ) ;
    return 0 ;
}
void add ( struct node **s, int n )
{
    struct node *r ;
    r = ( struct node * ) malloc ( sizeof ( struct node ) ) ;
    r -> data = n ;
    r -> link = NULL ;
    *s = r ;
}
void dis ( struct node *q )
```

```
{
    while ( q != NULL )
    {
        printf ( "%d", q -> data ) ;
        q = q -> link ;
    }
}
```

(a) The program will print the output 10.

(b) The program will report an error.

(c) The program will print the output as garbage value.

(d) The program will cause an exception.

Question 22

Which of the following statement is correct about the program given below?

```
# include <stdio.h>
# include <malloc.h>
# define reserved ( struct node * ) malloc ( sizeof ( struct node ) )
# define structure struct node
void fun ( structure **, int ) ;
struct node
{
    int data ;
    struct node *link ;
} ;
structure *p ;
int main( )
{
    int i = 0 ;
    p = NULL ;
    fun ( &p , 40 ) ;
```

```
    fun ( &p , 30 ) ;
    fun ( &p , 20 ) ;
    fun ( &p , 10 ) ;
    printf ( "%d ", *p ) ;
    return 0 ;
}
void fun ( structure **q, int num )
{
    static int flag = 0 ;
    structure *r ;
    r = reserved ;
    if ( flag == 0 )
    {
        r -> data = num ;
        r -> link = NULL ;
        *q = r ;
        flag = 1 ;
    }
    else
    {
        r -> data = ( *q ) -> data - num ;
        *q = r ;
    }
}
```

(a) The program will report an error.

(b) The program will print the output as garbage value.

(c) The program will print the output as 20.

(d) The program will print the output as -20.

Question 23

What will be the output of the program given below?

```
# include <stdio.h>
# include <malloc.h>
struct node
{
      int data ;
      struct node *link ;
} ;
struct node *p ;
void add ( int n ) ;
void display ( struct node *q ) ;
int main( )
{
      p = NULL ;
      add ( 10 ) ;
      add ( 5 ) ;
      add ( 8 ) ;
      add ( 14 ) ;
      display ( p ) ;
      return 0 ;
}
void add ( int n )
{
      struct node *t, *t1 ;
      t = malloc ( sizeof ( struct node ) ) ;
      t -> data = n ;
      t -> link = NULL ;
      if ( p == NULL )
            p = t ;
      else
      {
            t -> link = p -> link ;
            p = t ;
      }
}
void display ( struct node *q )
```

```
{
    while ( q != NULL )
    {
        printf ( " %d", q -> data ) ;
        q = q -> link ;
    }
}
```

(a) 10 5 8 14

(b) 14 8 5 10

(c) 14

(d) 14 10 5 8

Question 24

Which of the following statement is correct about the program given below?

```
# include <stdio.h>
# include <malloc.h>
int main( )
{
    struct node
    {
        char str[ 20 ] ;
        struct node *link ;
    } *p, p1 ;
    struct node *t ;
    p = NULL ;
    strcpy ( p1.str, "BOMBAY" ) ;
    t = ( struct node * ) malloc ( sizeof ( struct node ) ) ;
    strcpy ( t -> str, p1.str ) ;
    t -> link = p ;
    printf ( "%s", t -> str ) ;
```

```
    return 0 ;
}
```

(a) The program will print the output BOMBAY.

(b) The program will report an error.

(c) The program will print the output as garbage value.

(d) The program will cause an exception.

Question 25

Which of the following statement is correct about the program given below?

```
# include <stdio.h>
# include <malloc.h>
void add ( struct node **, int ) ;
void dis ( struct node * ) ;
struct node
{
    int data ;
    struct node *link ;
} ;
struct node *p ;
int main( )
{
    p = NULL ;
    add ( &p, 100 ) ;
    add ( &p, 200 ) ;
    add ( &p, 300 ) ;
    dis ( p ) ;
    return 0 ;
}
void add ( struct node **q, int num )
{
```

```
    struct node *t ;
    t = ( struct node * ) malloc ( sizeof (struct node ) ) ;
    t -> data = num ;
    t -> link = *q ;
    *q = t ;
}
void dis ( struct node *q )
{
    while ( q!= NULL )
    {
        printf ( "%d", *q ) ;
        q = q -> link ;
    }
}
```

(a) The program will report an error.

(b) The program will cause an exception.

(c) The program will print the output as 100 200 300.

(d) The program will print the output as 300 200 100.

Question 26

Which of the following statement is correct about the program given below?

```
# include <stdio.h>
# include <malloc.h>
struct node
{
    int data ;
    struct node *link ;
} ;
void add ( struct node **, struct node **, int ) ;
void display ( struct node * ) ;
```

```
int main( )
{
      struct node *f, *r ;
      f = r = NULL ;
      add ( &f, &r, 10 ) ;
      add ( &f, &r, 17 ) ;
      add ( &f, &r, 5 ) ;
      display( ) ;
      return 0 ;
}
void add ( struct node **f, struct node **r, int item )
{
      struct  node *q ;
      q = malloc ( sizeof ( struct node ) ) ;
      q -> data = item ;
      if ( *f == NULL )
            *f = q ;
      else
            ( *r ) -> link = q ;
      *r = q ;
      ( *r ) -> link = *f ;
}
void display ( struct node *f )
{
      struct node *q = f , *p = NULL ;
      while ( q != p )
      {
            printf ( "%d", q -> data ) ;
            q = q -> link ;
            p = f ;
      }
}
```

(a) The program will cause an exception.

(b) The program will print the output as 10 17 5.

(c) The program will print garbage values.

(d) The program will report an error.

Question 27

Which of the following statement is correct about the program given below?

```
# include <stdio.h>
# include <malloc.h>
void add ( int ) ;
int main( )
{
    struct node
    {
        int data ;
        struct node *link ;
    } ;
    struct node *p ;
    int n = 1000 ;
    p = NULL ;
    add ( n ) ;
    return 0 ;
}
void add ( int n )
{
    struct node *r ;
    r = ( struct node * ) malloc ( sizeof ( struct node ) ) ;
    r -> data = n ;
    r -> link = p ;
    printf ( "%d %d", r -> data, r -> link ) ;
}
```

(a) The program will print the output as 1000 0.

(b) The program will report an error.

(c) The program will print the output as 1000 \0.

(d) The program will cause an exception.

Question 28

What will be the output of the following program?

```
# include <stdio.h>
# include <malloc.h>
void fun ( struct node **, int ) ;
void dis ( struct node *, int * ) ;
struct node
{
      int data ;
      struct node *pre ;
      struct node *next ;
} ;
struct node *p ;
int main( )
{
      int d = 0 ;
      p = NULL ;
      fun ( &p, 10 ) ;
      fun ( &p, 20 ) ;
      fun ( &p, 30 ) ;
      fun ( &p, 40 ) ;
      dis ( p, &d ) ;
      printf ( "%d", d ) ;
      return 0 ;
}
void fun ( struct node **s, int num )
```

```
{
    struct  node *t, *r ;
    if ( *s == NULL )
    {
        *s = ( struct node* ) malloc ( sizeof ( struct node ) ) ;
        ( *s ) -> data = num ;
        ( *s ) -> pre = NULL ;
        ( *s ) -> next = NULL ;
    }
    else
    {
        t = *s ;
        while ( t -> next != NULL )
            t = t -> next ;
        r = ( struct node * ) malloc ( sizeof ( struct node ) ) ;
        r -> data = num ;
        r -> pre = t ;
        r -> next = NULL ;
        t -> next = r ;
    }
}
void dis ( struct node *q, int *count )
{
    while ( q -> next != NULL )
    {
        count++ ;
        q = q -> next ;
    }
}
```

(a) 0

(b) 2

(c) 3

(d) 4

Question 29

Which of the following statement is correct about the program given below?

```
# include <stdio.h>
# include <malloc.h>
void dis ( struct node * ) ;
void add ( struct node **, int ) ;
struct node
{
    int data ;
    struct node *link ;
} ;
struct node *p ;
int main( )
{
    p = NULL ;
    add ( &p, 200 ) ;
    add ( &p, 300 ) ;
    dis ( p ) ;
    return 0 ;
}
void add ( struct node **q, int num )
{
    static int flag = 0, flag1 = 0 ;
    static int nos = 0 ;
    struct node *t ;
    t = ( struct node * ) malloc ( sizeof ( struct node ) ) ;
    if ( flag == 0 )
    {
        t -> data = num ;
        t -> link = NULL ;
        *q = t ;
```

```
        flag = 1 ;
    }
    if ( flag1 == 0 )
    {
        nos = t -> data ;
        flag1 = 1 ;
    }
    else
    {
        printf ( "%d", nos ) ;
        t -> data = ( num + nos ) ;
        t -> link = NULL ;
        *q = t ;
    }
}
void dis ( struct node *q )
{
    while ( q != NULL )
    {
        printf ( "%d", *q ) ;
        q = q -> link ;
    }
}
```

(a) The program will report an error.

(b) The program will print the output as 300 200.

(c) The program will print the output as 200 300.

(d) The program will print the output as 200 500.

Question 30

Which of the following statement is correct about the program given below?

```
# include <stdio.h>
# include <malloc.h>
void add ( struct node **, struct node **, int ) ;
void dis ( struct node * ) ;
struct node
{
    int data ;
    struct node *link ;
} ;
int main( )
{
    struct node *f, *r ;
    f = r = NULL ;
    add ( &f, &r, 10 ) ;
    add ( &f, &r, 20 ) ;
    add ( &f, &r, 30 ) ;
    dis ( f ) ;
    return 0 ;
}
void add ( struct node **f, struct node **r, int item )
{
    struct node *q ;
    q = malloc ( sizeof ( struct node ) ) ;
    q -> data = item ;
    if ( *f == NULL )
        *f = q ;
    else
        ( *r ) -> link = q ;
    *r = q ;
    ( *r ) -> link = *f ;
}
void dis ( struct node *f )
{
    struct node *q = f, *p = NULL ;
    while ( q != p )
```

```
    {
        printf ( "%d ", q -> data ) ;

        q = q -> link ;
        p = f ;
    }
}
```

(a) The program will print the output as 10 20 30.

(b) The program will print three garbage values.

(c) The program will report an error.

(d) The program will cause an exception.

Question 31

What will be the output of the following program?

```
# include <stdio.h>
# include <malloc.h>
# include <stdarg.h>
void add ( int ) ;
int dis ( struct node * ) ;
fun ( int,... ) ;
struct node
{
    int data ;
    struct node *link ;
} ;
struct node *s, *p ;
int main( )
{
    int nos = 0 ;
    p = NULL ;
```

```
    s = p ;
    fun ( 5, 11, 22, 33, 44, 55 ) ;
    nos = dis ( s -> link ) ;
    printf ( "%d", nos ) ;
    return 0 ;
}
fun ( int n,... )
{
    int i = 0 ;
    va_list s ;
    va_start ( s, n ) ;
    for ( i = 0 ; i <= 4 ; i++ )
    {
        add ( va_arg ( s ,int ) ) ;
    }
}
void add ( int n )
{
    struct node *r , *t ;
    if ( s == NULL)
    {
        r = ( struct node * ) malloc ( sizeof ( struct node * ) ) ;
        r -> data = n ;
        r -> link = NULL ;
        s = r ;
    }
    else
    {
        t = s ;
        r = ( struct node * ) malloc ( sizeof ( struct node * ) ) ;
        r -> data = n ;
        r -> link = NULL ;
        while ( t -> link != NULL )
        {
            t = t -> link ;
```

```
        }
        t -> link = r ;
    }
}
int dis ( struct node *q )
{
    int c = 0 ;
    while ( q -> link != NULL )
    {
        c ++ ;
        q = q -> link ;
    }
    return ( c ) ;
}
```

(a) 1

(b) 3

(c) 4

(d) 5

Question 32

What will be the output of the following program?

```
# include <stdio.h>
# include <malloc.h>
void add ( struct node **, int ) ;
void dis ( struct node * ) ;
struct node
{
    int data ;
    struct node *link ;
} ;
```

```
struct node *p ;
int main( )
{
    p = NULL ;
    add ( &p, 65 ) ;
    add ( &p, 66 ) ;
    add ( &p, 119 ) ;
    dis ( p ) ;
    return 0 ;
}
void add (struct node **q, int num)
{
    struct node *t ;
    t = ( struct node * ) malloc ( sizeof ( struct node ) ) ;
    t -> data = num ;
    t -> link = NULL ;
    *q = t ;
}
void dis ( struct node *q )
{
    while ( q != NULL )
    {
        printf ( "%c ", *q ) ;
        q = q -> link ;
    }
}
```

(a) 65 66 119

(b) A B W

(c) w

(d) a

Question 33

Which of the following statement is correct about the program given below?

```
# include <stdio.h>
# include <stdarg.h>
# include <malloc.h>
void fun ( int ) ;
void dis ( struct node * ) ;
struct node
{
    int data ;
    struct node *link ;
} ;
struct node *p ;
int main( )
{
    p = NULL ;
    fun ( 10 ) ;
    fun ( 20 ) ;
    fun ( 30 ) ;
    dis ( p ) ;
    return 0 ;
}
void fun ( int num )
{
    struct node *r ;
    if ( p == NULL )
    {
        r = ( struct node * ) malloc ( sizeof ( struct node ) ) ;
        r -> data = num ;
        r -> link = NULL ;
        p = r ;
    }
    else
```

```
    {
        r = ( struct node * ) malloc ( sizeof ( struct node ) ) ;
        r -> data = num ;
        r -> link = NULL ;
        while ( p -> link != NULL )
            p = p -> link ;
        p -> link = r ;
    }
}
void dis ( struct node *q )
{
    while ( q != NULL )
    {
        printf ( "%d", q -> data ) ;
        q = q -> link ;
    }
}
```

(a) The program will print the output as 10 20 30.

(b) The program will print the output as 20 30.

(c) The program will cause an exception.

(d) The program will report an error.

Question 34

Which of the following statement is correct about the program given below?

```
# include <stdio.h>
# include <malloc.h>
void fun ( int ) ;
void insert ( struct node **, int ) ;
void dis ( struct node * ) ;
struct node
```

```
{
    int data ;
    struct node *link ;
} ;
struct node *p ;
int main( )
{
    p = NULL ;
    fun ( 100 ) ;
    fun ( 200 ) ;
    fun ( 300 ) ;
    fun ( 400 ) ;
    fun ( 500 ) ;
    insert ( &p, 200 ) ;
    dis ( p ) ;
    return 0 ;
}
void fun ( int num )
{
    struct node *r, *t ;
    if ( p == NULL )
    {
        r = ( struct node * ) malloc ( sizeof ( struct node ) ) ;
        r -> data = num ;
        r -> link = NULL ;
        p = r ;
    }
    else
    {
        t = p ;
        r = ( struct node * ) malloc ( sizeof ( struct node ) ) ;
        r -> data = num ;
        r -> link = NULL ;
        while ( t -> link != NULL)
            t = t -> link ;
```

```
        t -> link = r ;
    }
}
void dis ( struct node *q )
{
    while ( q != NULL)
    {
        printf ( "%d", q -> data ) ;
        q = q -> link ;
    }
}
void insert ( struct node **q, int num )
{
    struct node *t ;
    int i = 0 ;
    while ( ( *q ) != NULL )
    {
        if ( ( *q ) -> data == num )
        {
            t = ( *q ) -> link ;
            ( *q ) = ( *q ) -> link -> link ;
            break ;
        }
        ( *q ) = ( *q ) -> link ;
    }
    t -> link = ( *q ) ->link ;
}
```

(a) The program will report an error.

(b) The program will print the output as 100 300 400 500.

(c) The program will print the output as 300 400.

(d) The program will print the output as 400 500.

Question 35

Which of the following statement is correct about the program given below?

```
# include <stdio.h>
# include <malloc.h>
void add ( struct node **, int ) ;
void dis ( struct node * ) ;
void insert (struct node *, int, int ) ;
struct node
{
    int data ;
    struct node *link ;
} ;
struct node *p ;
int main( )
{
    static int i ;
    static int s = 1 ;
    p = NULL ;
    for ( i = 0 ; i < 3 ; i++ )
    {
        add ( &p, ( s += i ) ) ;
    }
    insert ( p, 3, 3 ) ;
    dis ( p ) ;
    return 0 ;
}
void add ( struct node **q, int num )
{
    struct node *r, *t ;
    r = ( struct node * ) malloc ( sizeof ( struct node ) ) ;
    r -> data = num ;
    r -> link = NULL ;
    if ( p == NULL )
```

```
        p = r ;
    else
    {
        t = p ;
        while ( t -> link != NULL )
        {
            t = t -> link ;
        }
        t -> link = r ;
    }
}
void dis ( struct node *p )
{
    while ( p != NULL )
    {
        printf ( "%d", *p ) ;
        p = p -> link ;
    }
}
void insert (struct node *q, int z, int num )
{
    struct node *t ;
    int i ;
    for ( i = 0 ; i < z - 2 ; i++ )
    q = q -> link ;
    t = ( struct node * ) malloc ( sizeof ( struct node ) ) ;
    t -> data = num ;
    t -> link = q -> link ;
    q -> link = t ;
}
```

(a) The program will cause an exception.

(b) The program will report an error.

(c) The program will print the output as 1 2 3 3.

(d) The program will print the output as 1 2 3 4.

Question 36

What will be the output of the following program?

```
# include <stdio.h>
# include <malloc.h>
# include <stdarg.h>
fun ( int,... ) ;
void add ( int ) ;
void check ( struct node ** ) ;
void dis ( struct node * ) ;
struct node
{
    int data ;
    struct node *link ;
} ;
struct node *p, *start ;
int main( )
{
    p = NULL ;
    start = p ;
    fun ( 4, 'a', 'b' , 'c' , 'd' ) ;
    check ( &start ) ;
    dis ( start ) ;
    return 0 ;
}
fun ( int n,...)
{
    int i = 0 ;
    va_list s ;
    va_start ( s, n ) ;
    for ( i = 0 ; i <= 3 ; i++ )
    {
```

```
            add ( va_arg ( s, int ) ) ;
      }
}
void add ( int n )
{
      struct node *r, *t ;
      if ( start == NULL )
      {
            r = ( struct node * ) malloc ( sizeof ( struct node * ) ) ;
            r -> data = n ;
            r -> link = NULL ;
            start = r ;
      }
      else
      {
            t = start ;
            r = ( struct node * ) malloc ( sizeof ( struct node * ) ) ;
            r -> data = n ;
            r -> link = NULL ;
            while ( t -> link != NULL )
            {
                  t = t -> link ;
            }
            t -> link = r ;
      }
}
void dis ( struct node *q )
{
      while ( q != NULL )
      {
            printf ( "%c ", q -> data ) ;
            q = q -> link ;
      }
}
void check ( struct node **x )
```

```
{
    struct node *q, *r, *s ;
    q = *x ;
    r = NULL ;
    while ( q != NULL )
    {
        s = r ;
        r = q ;
        q = q -> link ;
        r -> link = s ;
    }
    *x = r ;
}
```

(a) a b c d

(b) b a d c

(c) d c a b

(d) d c b a

Question 37

What will be the output of the following program?

```
# include <stdio.h>
# include <malloc.h>
struct node
{
    int data ;
    struct node *link ;
} ;
struct node *p ;
void add ( int n ) ;
int search ( int n, struct node *q ) ;
```

```
int main( )
{
    p = NULL ;
    add ( 10 ) ;
    add ( 5 ) ;
    add ( 8 ) ;
    add ( 14 ) ;
    printf ( "%d", search ( 5, p ) ) ;
    return 0 ;
}
void add ( int n )
{
    struct node *t, *t1 ;
    t = malloc ( sizeof ( struct node ) ) ;
    t -> data = n ;
    t -> link = NULL ;
    if ( p == NULL )
        p = t ;
    else
    {
        t1 = p ;
        while ( t1 -> link != NULL )
            t1 = t1 -> link ;
        t1 -> link = t ;
    }
}
int search ( int n, struct node *q )
{
    while ( q != NULL )
    {
        if ( q -> data == n )
            return ( q -> link -> link -> data ) ;
        q = q -> link ;
    }
    return -1 ;
```

```
}
```

(a) 5

(b) 8

(c) 14

(d) -1

Question 38

What will be the output of the following program?

```
# include <stdio.h>
# include <malloc.h>
void check ( struct node **, int ) ;
void addafter ( struct node *, int, int ) ;
void show ( struct node * ) ;
struct node
{
    struct node *prev ;
    int data ;
    struct node * next ;
} ;
int main( )
{
    struct node *p ;

    p = NULL ;
    check ( &p , 11 ) ;
    check ( &p , 22 ) ;
    check ( &p , 33 ) ;
    check ( &p , 44 ) ;
    check ( &p , 55 ) ;
    addafter ( p , 2, 100 ) ;
```

```
    show ( p ) ;
    return 0 ;
}
void check ( struct node **s, int num )
{
    struct node *r, *q = *s ;
    if ( *s == NULL )
    {
        *s = malloc ( sizeof ( struct node ) ) ;
        ( *s ) -> prev = NULL ;
        ( *s ) -> data = num ;
        ( *s ) -> next = NULL ;
    }
    else
    {
        while ( q -> next != NULL )
            q = q -> next ;
        r = malloc ( sizeof ( struct node ) ) ;
        r -> data = num ;
        r -> next = NULL ;
        r -> prev = q ;
        q -> next = r ;
    }
}
void addafter ( struct node *q, int loc, int num )
{
    struct node *temp ;
    int i ;
    for ( i = 0 ; i <= loc ; i++ )
    {
        q = q -> next ;
        if ( q == NULL )
        {
            printf ( "\nThere are less than %d elements", loc ) ;
            return ;
```

```
            }
        }
        q = q -> prev ;
        temp = malloc ( sizeof ( struct node ) ) ;
        temp -> data = num ;
        temp -> prev = q ;
        temp -> next = q -> next ;
        temp -> next -> prev = temp ;
        q -> next = temp ;
}
void show ( struct node *q )
{
        printf ( "\n" ) ;
        while ( q != NULL )
        {
                printf ( "%d", q -> data ) ;
                q = q -> next ;
        }
}
```

(a) 11 22 33 44 55 100

(b) 11 22 33 100 55

(c) 11 22 33 100 44 55

(d) 11 22 100 33 44 55

Question 39

Which of the following statement is correct about the program given below?

```
# include <malloc.h>
# include <stdio.h>
void fun ( struct node **, int ) ;
typedef struct node
```

```
{
    int data ;
    struct node *link ;
} structure ;
structure s ;
structure *p ;
int main( )
{
    p = NULL ;
    fun ( &p, 75 ) ;
    fun ( &p, 125 ) ;
    fun ( &p, 100 ) ;
    printf ( "%d", s.data ) ;
    return 0 ;
}
void fun ( structure **q, int n )
{
    structure *r ;
    r = ( structure * ) malloc ( sizeof ( structure ) ) ;
    s.data += n ;
    s.link = NULL ;
    *q = r ;
}
```

(a) The program will print output as garbage value.

(b) The program will print the output as 100.

(c) The program will report an error.

(d) The program will print the output as 300.

Question 40

What will be the output of the following program?

```
# include <stdio.h>
# include <malloc.h>
void arr ( struct node **, int ) ;
struct node
{
    int data ;
    struct node *link ;
} ;
struct node *p ;
static int a[ 5 ] ;
int main( )
{
    int j ;
    p = NULL ;
    arr ( &p, 10 ) ;
    arr ( &p, 20 ) ;
    arr ( &p, 30 ) ;
    arr ( &p, 40 ) ;
    for ( j = 0 ; j <= 4 ; j++ )
    printf ( "%d", a [ j ] ) ;
    return 0 ;
}
void arr ( struct node **q, int n )
{
    struct node *r, *t ;
    static int flag = 0, i = 0 ;
    r = ( struct node * ) malloc ( sizeof ( struct node ) ) ;
    r -> data = n ;
    r -> link = NULL ;
    if ( p == NULL )
    {
        p = r ;
        flag = 1 ;
        i = flag ;
        flag++ ;
```

```
    }
    else
    {
        t = p ;
        while ( t -> link != NULL )
        t = t -> link ;
        t -> link = r ;
        if ( flag == 2 )
        {
            a[ i ] = r -> data ;
            i++ ;
        }
    }
}
```

(a) 10 20 30 40 50

(b) 0 0 0 0 0

(c) 0 20 30 40 0

(d) 0 0 20 30 40

Question 41

Which of the following statement is correct about the program given below?

```
# include <stdio.h>
# include <malloc.h>
void add ( struct count **, int ) ;
struct count
{
    int data ;
    struct count *link ;
} ;
struct count *n ;
```

```
int main( )
{
    n = NULL ;
    add ( &n, printf ( "GOOD" ) ) ;
    printf ( " %d ", *n ) ;
    return 0 ;
}
void add ( struct count **q, int n )
{
    struct count *r ;
    r = ( struct count * ) malloc ( sizeof ( struct count ) ) ;
    r -> data = n ;
    r -> link = NULL ;
    *q = r ;
}
```

(a) The program will report an error.

(b) The program will print the output as garbage value.

(c) The program will print the output as GOOD.

(d) The program will print the output as GOOD 4.

Question 42

Which of the following statement is correct about the program given below?

```
# include <stdio.h>
# include <stdarg.h>
# include <malloc.h>
fun ( int, ...) ;
void dis ( struct node * ) ;
struct node
{
    int data ;
```

```
    struct node *link ;
} ;
struct node *p ;
int main( )
{
    p = NULL ;
    fun ( 3, 75 , 150 , 225 ) ;
    dis ( p ) ;
    return 0 ;
}
fun ( int num,... )
{
    struct node *r, *t ;
    va_list z ;
    int i = 0 ;
    va_start ( z, num ) ;
    for ( i = 0 ; i < num ; i++ )
    {
        t = p ;
        if ( p == NULL )
        {
            r = ( struct node * ) malloc ( sizeof ( struct node ) ) ;
            r -> data = va_arg ( z , int ) ;
            r -> link = NULL ;
            p = r ;
        }
        else
        {
            r = ( struct node * ) malloc ( sizeof ( struct node ) ) ;
            r -> data = va_arg ( z, int ) ;
            r -> link = NULL ;
            while ( t -> link != NULL )
            t = t -> link ;
            t -> link = r ;
        }
```

```
    }
}
void dis ( struct node *q )
{
    while ( q != NULL )
    {
        printf ( "%d", q -> data ) ;
        q = q -> link ;
    }
}
```

(a) The program will print the output as 75 150 225.

(b) The program will print the output as three garbage values.

(c) The program will report an error.

(d) The program will print the output as garbage value.

Question 43

Which of the following statement is correct about the program given below?

```
# include <malloc.h>
# include <stdio.h>
void fun ( struct node **, int ) ;
void dis ( struct node * ) ;
struct node
{
    int data ;
    struct node *link ;
} ;
struct node *p, *s ;
int main( )
{
    int i = 1 ;
    p = NULL ;
```

```
    fun ( &p, ( i * 10 ) ) ;
    i++ ;
    fun ( &p, ( i * 10 ) ) ;
    i++ ;
    fun ( &p, ( i * 10 ) ) ;
    i++ ;
    fun ( &p, ( i * 10 ) ) ;
    i++ ;
    fun ( &p, ( i * 10 ) ) ;
    dis ( p ) ;
    return 0 ;
}
void fun ( struct node **q , int n )
{
    struct node *r, *t ;
    t = p ;
    if ( p == NULL )
    {
        r = ( struct node * ) malloc ( sizeof ( struct node ) ) ;
        r -> data = n ;
        r -> link = NULL ;
        p = r ;
    }
    else
    {
        r = ( struct node * ) malloc (sizeof ( struct node ) ) ;
        r -> data = n ;
        r -> link = NULL ;
        while ( t -> link != NULL )
            t = t -> link ;
        t -> link = r ;
    }
}
void dis ( struct node *p )
{
```

```
    if ( p != NULL )
    {
        dis ( p -> link ) ;
        printf ( "%d", p -> data ) ;
    }
}
```

(a) The program will report an error.

(b) The program will print the output as 10 20 30 40 50.

(c) The program will cause an exception.

(d) The program will print the output as 50 40 30 20 10.

Question 44

Which of the following statement is correct about the program given below?

```
# include <stdio.h>
# include <malloc.h>
void test ( int ) ;
void order ( struct node * ) ;
void dis ( struct node * ) ;
struct node
{
    int data ;
    struct node *link ;
} ;
struct node *p, *z ;
int main( )
{
    p = NULL ;
    p = z ;
    test ( 5 ) ;
    test ( 4 ) ;
```

```
    test ( 3 ) ;
    test ( 2 ) ;
    test ( 1 ) ;
    order ( &z ) ;
    dis ( p ) ;
    return 0 ;
}
void test ( int num )
{
    struct node *r , *t ;
    if ( p == NULL )
    {
        r = ( struct node * ) malloc ( sizeof ( struct node ) ) ;
        r -> data = num ;
        r -> link = NULL ;
        p = r ;
    }
    else
    {
        t = p ;
        r = ( struct node * ) malloc ( sizeof ( struct node ) ) ;
        r -> data = num ;
        r -> link = NULL ;
        while ( t -> link != NULL )
            t = t -> link ;
        t -> link = r ;
    }
}
void order( struct node  *q )
{
    struct node *s ;
    int i, j, t ;
    s = ( struct node * ) malloc ( sizeof ( struct node ) ) ;
    s = q -> link ;
    s = q -> data ;
```

```
    while ( s != NULL)
    {
        while ( q -> link != NULL )
        {
            if ( s -> data > q -> data )
            {
                t = s -> data ;
                s -> data = q -> data ;
                q -> data = t ;
            }
                q = q ->link ;
        }
        s = s -> link ;
    }
}
void dis ( struct node *q )
{
    while ( q != NULL )
    {
        printf ( "%d ", q -> data ) ;
        q = q -> link ;
    }
}
```

(a) The program will report an error.

(b) The program will print the output as 5 4 3 2 1.

(c) The program will cause an exception.

(d) The program will print the output as 1 2 3 4 5.

Question 45

What will be the output of the following program?

```
# include <stdio.h>
# include <malloc.h>
# include <string.h>
void name ( char * ) ;
void dis ( struct node * ) ;
struct node
{
        char str[ 20 ] ;
        struct node *link ;
} ;
struct node *p ;
int main( )
{
        p = NULL ;
        name ( "bombay" ) ;
        name ( "nagpur" ) ;
        name ( "chennai" ) ;
        name ( "pune" ) ;
        name ( "delhi" ) ;
        dis ( p ) ;
        return 0 ;
}
void name ( char *s )
{
        struct node *r, *t ;
        if ( p == NULL )
        {
                r = ( struct node * ) malloc ( sizeof ( struct node ) ) ;
                strcpy ( r -> str, s ) ;
                r -> link = NULL ;
                p = r ;
        }
        else
        {
                t = p ;
```

```
        r = ( struct node * ) malloc ( sizeof ( struct node ) ) ;
        strcpy ( r -> str, s ) ;
        r -> link = NULL ;
        while ( t -> link != NULL )
            t = t -> link ;
        t -> link = r ;
    }
}
void dis ( struct node *q )
{
    static int i = 0 ;
    while ( q != NULL )
    {
        if ( i < 5 )
        {
            i++ ;
            dis ( q -> link ) ;
            printf ( "%s ",  q -> str ) ;
        }
        else
            break ;
    }
}
```

(a) bombay nagpur chennai pune delhi

(b) bombay chennai delhi nagpur pune

(c) delhi pune chennai nagpur Bombay

(d) Garbage value garbage value garbage value garbage value garbage value

Question 46

What will be the output of the following program?

```
# include <stdio.h>
# include <malloc.h>
# include <stdarg.h>
fun ( int, ... ) ;
void add ( int ) ;
void dis ( struct node  * ) ;
struct node
{
      int data ;
      struct node *link ;
} ;
struct node *p , *start ;
int main( )
{
      p = NULL ;
      start = p ;
      fun ( 5, 10, 20, 30, 40, 50 ) ;
      dis ( start ) ;
      return 0 ;
}
fun ( int n,...)
{
      int i = 0 ;
      va_list s ;
      va_start ( s, n ) ;
      for ( i = 0 ; i <= 4 ; i++ )
      {
            add ( va_arg ( s, int ) ) ;
      }
}
void add ( int n )
{
      struct node *r , *t ;
      if ( start == NULL )
      {
```

```
        r = ( struct node * ) malloc ( sizeof ( struct node * ) ) ;
        r -> data = n ;
        r -> link = NULL ;
        start = r ;
    }
    else
    {
        t = start ;
        r = ( struct node * ) malloc ( sizeof ( struct node * ) ) ;
        r -> data = n ;
        r -> link = NULL ;
        while ( t -> link != NULL )
        {
            t = t -> link ;
        }
        t -> link = r ;
    }
}
void dis ( struct node *q )
{
    while ( q -> link != NULL )
    {
        printf ( "%d ", q -> link -> data ) ;
        q = q -> link -> link ;
    }
}
```

(a) 10 40

(b) 10 30

(c) 20 40

(d) 30 50

Question 47

Which of the following statement is correct about the following program?

```
# include <stdio.h>
# include <malloc.h>
struct node
{
      int data ;
      struct node *link ;
};
struct node *p ;
void add ( int n ) ;
void display ( struct node *q ) ;
int main( )
{
      p = NULL ;
      add ( 100 ) ;
      add ( 500 ) ;
      add ( 80 ) ;
      add ( 140 ) ;
      display ( &p ) ;
      return 0 ;
}
void add ( int n )
{
      struct node *t, *t1 ;
      t = malloc ( sizeof ( struct node ) ) ;
      t -> data = n ;
      t -> link = NULL ;
      if ( p == NULL )
            p = t ;
      else
      {
            t -> link = p ;
```

```
        p = t ;
    }
}
void display ( struct node *q )
{
    while ( q != NULL )
    {
        printf ( " %d", q -> data ) ;
        q = q -> link ;
    }
}
```

(a) The program will report an error.

(b) The program will cause an exception.

(c) The program will print output as garbage value.

(d) The program will print output as 100.

Question 48

What will be the output of the following program?

```
# include <stdio.h>
struct node
{
    int data ;
    struct node *link ;
} ;
struct node *p ;
void add ( int n ) ;
void display ( struct node *q ) ;
int main( )
{
    p = NULL ;
```

```
    add ( 10 ) ;
    add ( 5 ) ;
    add ( 8 ) ;
    add ( 14 ) ;
    display ( p ) ;
    return 0 ;
}
void add ( int n )
{
    struct node *t, *t1 ;
    t = malloc ( sizeof ( struct node ) ) ;
    t -> data = n ;
    t -> link = NULL ;
    if ( p == NULL )
        p = t ;
    else
    {
        t -> link = p ;
        p = t ;
    }
}
void display ( struct node *q )
{
    while ( q != NULL )
    {
        printf ( " %d", q -> data ) ;
        q = q -> link ;
    }
}
```

(a) 10 5 8 14

(b) 5 8 14 10

(c) 5 10 8 14

(d) 14 8 5 10

Question 49

Which of the following statement is correct about the program given below?

```
# include <stdio.h>
# include <malloc.h>
void add ( struct node **, char * ) ;
void dis ( struct node * ) ;
struct node
{
    struct node *pre ;
    char data[ 25 ] ;
    struct node *next ;
} ;
extern int flag = 0 ;
struct node *p ;
int main( )
{
    p = NULL ;
    add ( &p, "jack" ) ;
    add ( &p, "and" ) ;
    add ( &p, "jill" ) ;
    add ( &p, "jerry" ) ;
    dis ( p ) ;
    return 0 ;
}
void add ( struct node **s, char *z )
{
    struct node *r, *t ;
    if ( *s == NULL )
    {
        *s = ( struct node * ) malloc ( sizeof ( struct node ) ) ;
        ( *s ) -> pre = NULL ;
```

```
        strcpy ( ( *s ) -> data, z ) ;
        ( *s ) -> next = NULL ;
    }
    else
    {
        t = *s ;
        while ( t -> next != NULL )
            t = t -> next ;
        r = ( struct node * ) malloc ( sizeof ( struct node ) ) ;
        r -> pre = t ;
        strcpy ( r -> data, z ) ;
        r -> next = NULL ;
        t -> next = r ;
    }
}
void dis ( struct node *q )
{
    char *p ;
    while ( q -> next != NULL )
    {
        p = q -> next -> data ;
        printf ( "%s ", strcat ( q -> data, p ) ) ;
        q = q -> next ;
    }
}
```

(a) The program will print the output as JACKand andJILL andjerry.

(b) The program will print the output as JACKand andJILL jerry.

(c) The program will print the output as JACKand andJILL JILLjerry.

(d) The program will report an error.

Question 50

Which of the following statement is correct about the program given below?

```
# include <stdio.h>
# include <malloc.h>
extern int flag = 0 ;
void fun ( struct node **, struct node **, char * ) ;
void dis ( struct node * ) ;
struct node
{
     char data[ 25 ] ;
     struct node *list ;
} ;
struct node *f, *r ;
int main( )
{
     f = r = NULL ;
     fun ( &f, &r, "BOMBAY" ) ;
     fun ( &f, &r, "NAGPUR" ) ;
     dis ( f ) ;
     return 0 ;
}
void fun ( struct node **q, struct node **r, char *p )
{
     struct node *temp ;
     char *s –" and" ;
     int flag ;
     temp = ( struct node * ) malloc ( sizeof ( struct node ) ) ;
     strcpy ( temp -> data, p ) ;
     if ( flag == 0 )
     {
          strcat ( temp -> data, s ) ;
          flag++ ;
     }
     temp -> list = NULL ;
```

```
        if ( *q == NULL )
                *q = temp ;
        else
                ( *r ) -> list = temp ;
        ( *r ) = temp ;
        ( *r ) -> list = *q ;
}
void dis ( struct node *f )
{
        struct node *q = f, *p = NULL ;
        while ( q != p )
        {
                printf ( "%s ", q -> data ) ;
                q = q -> list ;
                p = f ;
        }
}
```

(a) The program will result in a compiler time error.

(b) The program will print the output as BOMBAY and NAGPUR.

(c) The program will print the output as BOMBAY and NAGPUR AND.

(d) The program will print the output as BOMBAY NAGPUR.

Question 51

Which of the following statement is correct about the program given below?

```
# include <stdio.h>
# include <malloc.h>
void add ( struct node **, struct node **, int ) ;
void dis ( struct node * ) ;
struct node
{
```

```
    int data ;
    struct node *link ;
} ;
struct node *f, *r ;
int main( )
{
    f = r = NULL ;
    add ( &f, &r, 101 ) ;
    add ( &f, &r, 201 ) ;
    dis ( f ) ;
    return 0 ;
}
void add ( struct node **f, struct node **r, int num )
{
    struct node *z ;
    z = ( struct node * ) malloc ( sizeof ( struct node ) ) ;
    z -> data = num ;
    z -> link = NULL ;
    If ( *f == NULL )
        *f = z ;
    else
        ( *r ) -> link = z ;
    *r = z ;
    ( *r ) -> link = *f ;
}
void dis ( struct node *f )
{
    struct node *q = f, *p = NULL ;
    while ( q != p )
    {
        printf ( "%d ", q -> data = ( ( q -> data + 5 * ( 2 + 10 ) ) - 11 ) ) ;
        q = q -> link ;
        p = f ;
    }
}
```

(a) The program will print the output as 101 201.

(b) The program will print the output as 161 261.

(c) The program will print the output as 150 250.

(d) The program will result in a compile time error.

Question 52

What will be the output of the following program?

```
# include <stdio.h>
# include <malloc.h>
void strname ( char * ) ;
void comp ( struct node ** ) ;
void dis ( struct node * ) ;
struct node
{
    char str[ 20 ] ;
    struct node *link ;
} ;
struct node *p, *start ;
int main( )
{
    p = NULL ;
    strname ( "amit" ) ;
    strname ( "suraj" ) ;
    strname ( "sameer" ) ;
    strname ( "basileo" ) ;
    strname ( "ali" ) ;
    comp ( &p ) ;
    dis ( start ) ;
    return 0 ;
}
```

```
void strname ( char *s )
{
    struct node *r, *t ;
    if ( p == NULL )
    {
        r = ( struct node * ) malloc ( sizeof ( struct node ) ) ;
        strcpy ( r -> str, s ) ;
        r -> link = NULL ;
        start = p = r ;
    }
    else
    {
        t = p ;
        r = ( struct node * ) malloc ( sizeof ( struct node ) ) ;
        strcpy ( r -> str, s ) ;
        r -> link = NULL ;
        while ( t -> link != NULL )
        {
            t = t -> link ;
        }
        t -> link = r ;
    }
}
void comp ( struct node **q )
{
    struct node *r ;
    char ch[ 20 ] ;
    while ( ( *q ) -> link != NULL )
    {
        r = ( *q ) -> link ;
        while ( r -> link != NULL )
        {
            if ( strcmp ( ( *q ) -> str, r -> str ) > 0 )
            {
                strcpy ( ch, ( *q ) -> str ) ;
```

```
                strcpy ( ( *q ) -> str, r -> str ) ;
                strcpy ( r -> str, ch ) ;
            }
            r = r -> link ;
        }
        ( *q ) = ( *q ) -> link ;
    }
}
void dis ( struct node *s )
{
    while ( s != NULL )
    {
        printf ( "%s ", s -> str ) ;
        s = s -> link ;
    }
}
```

(a) amit suraj sameer basileo ali

(b) ali basileo sameer suraj amit

(c) ali amit basileo sameer suraj

(d) amit basileo sameer suraj ali

Question 53

Which of the following statement is correct about the program given below?

```
# include <stdio.h>
# include <malloc.h>
# include <stdarg.h>
fun ( int,... ) ;
void dis ( struct node * ) ;
void add ( int ) ;
struct node
```

```
{
    int data ;
    struct node *link ;
} ;
struct node *s, *p ;
int main( )
{
    p = NULL ;
    s = p ;
    fun ( 3, "M.S. dhoni","sachin tendulkar", "india" ) ;
    dis ( p ) ;
    return 0 ;
}
fun ( int num,...)
{
    int i = 0 ;
    va_list start ;
    va_start ( start, num ) ;
    for ( i = 0 ; i < num ; i++ )
    {
        add ( strlen ( va_arg ( start, int ) ) ) ;
    }
}
void add ( int n )
{
    struct node *r, *t ;
    if ( s == NULL)
    {
        r = ( struct node * ) malloc ( sizeof ( struct node * ) ) ;
        r -> data = n ;
        r -> link = NULL ;
        s = r ;
        p = r ;
    }
    else
```

```
    {
        t = s ;
        r = ( struct node * ) malloc ( sizeof ( struct node * ) ) ;
        r -> data = n ;
        r -> link = NULL ;
        while ( t -> link != NULL )
        {
            t = t -> link ;
        }
        t -> link = r ;
    }
}
void dis ( struct node *q )
{
    while ( q != NULL )
    {
        printf ( "%d\n", q -> data += q -> data ) ;
        q = q -> link ;
    }
}
```

(a) The program will result in a compiler time error.

(b) The program will print the output as 31.

(c) The program will print the output as 10 16 5.

(d) The program will print the output as 20 32 10.

Question 54

Which of the following statement is correct about the program given below?

```
# include <stdio.h>
# include <malloc.h>
void dis ( struct node * ) ;
```

```
void add ( int ) ;
struct node
{
    int data ;
    struct node *next ;
    struct node *prev ;
} ;
struct node *p ;
int main( )
{
    p = NULL ;
    add ( 10 ) ;
    add ( 20 ) ;
    add ( 30 ) ;
    dis ( p ) ;
    return 0 ;
}
void add ( int num )
{
    struct node *t, *t1 ;
    t = ( struct node* ) malloc ( sizeof ( struct node ) ) ;
    t -> data = num ;
    t -> next = NULL ;
    if ( p == NULL)
    {
        p = t ;
        t -> prev = NULL ;
    }
    else
    {
        t1 = p ;
        while ( t1 -> next != NULL )
            t1 = t1 -> next ;
        t1 -> next = t ;
        t -> prev = t1 ;
```

```
    }
}
void dis ( struct node *z )
{
    while ( z -> next != NULL )
        z = z -> next ;
    while ( z != NULL )
    {
        printf ( "%d ", z -> data ) ;
        z = z -> prev ;
    }
}
```

(a) The program will print the output as 10 20 30.

(b) The program will result in a compile time error.

(c) The program will cause an exception.

(d) The program will print the output as 30 20 10.

Question 55

Which of the following statement is correct about the program given below?

```
# include <stdio.h>
# include <malloc.h>
extern int flag = 0 ;
void fun ( struct node **, struct node **, char * ) ;
void dis ( struct node * ) ;
struct node
{
    char data[ 25 ] ;
    struct node *list ;
} ;
struct node *f, *r ;
```

```
int main( )
{
    f = r = NULL ;
    fun ( &f, &r, "TOM" ) ;
    fun ( &f, &r, "HARRY" ) ;
    dis ( f ) ;
    return 0 ;
}
void fun ( struct node **q, struct node **r, char *p )
{
    struct node *temp ;
    char *s =" and" ;
    static int flag = 0 ;
    temp = ( struct node * ) malloc ( sizeof ( struct node ) ) ;
    strcpy ( temp -> data, p ) ;
    if ( flag == 0 )
    {
        strcat ( temp -> data, s ) ;
        flag++ ;
    }
    temp -> list = NULL ;
    if ( *q == NULL )
        *q = temp ;
    else
        *r -> list = temp ;
     *r = temp ;
     *r -> list = *q ;
}
void dis ( struct node *f )
{
    struct node *q = f, *p = NULL ;
    while ( q != p )
    {
        printf ( "%s ", q -> data ) ;
        q = q -> list ;
```

```
        p = f ;
    }
}
```

(a) The program will result in a compile time error.

(b) The program will print the output as TOM and HARRY.

(c) The program will print the output as TOM and HARRY and.

(d) The program will cause an exception.

Question 56

Which of the following statement is correct about the program given below?

```
# include <stdio.h>
# include <malloc.h>
void add ( struct node **, int ) ;
void dis ( struct node * ) ;
struct node
{
    struct node *pre ;
    int data ;
    struct node *next ;
} ;
struct node *p ;
int main( )
{
    p = NULL ;
    add ( &p, 100 ) ;
    add ( &p, 200 ) ;
    add ( &p, 300 ) ;
    add ( &p, 400 ) ;
    add ( &p, 500 ) ;
    dis ( p ) ;
```

```
    return 0 ;
}
void add ( struct node **s, int num )
{
    struct node *r, *t ;
    if ( *s == NULL )
    {
        *s = ( struct node * ) malloc ( sizeof ( struct node ) ) ;
        ( *s ) -> pre = NULL ;
        ( *s ) -> data = num ;
        ( *s ) -> next = NULL ;
    }
    else
    {
        t = *s ;
        while ( t -> next != NULL )
            t = t -> next ;
        r = ( struct node * ) malloc ( sizeof ( struct node ) ) ;
        r -> pre = t ;
        r -> data = num ;
        r -> next = NULL ;
        t -> next = r ;
    }
}
void dis ( struct node *q )
{
    while ( q != NULL )
    {
        printf ( "%d", ( q -> data / ( 10 ) * 2 ) ) ;
        q = q -> next ;
    }
}
```

(a) The program will result in a compile time error.

(b) The program will print the output as 20 40 60 80 100.

(c) The program will print the output as 5 10 15 20 25.

(d) The program will print the output as 100 200 300 400 500.

Question 57

Which of the following statement is correct about the program given below?

```
# include <stdio.h>
# include <malloc.h>
void add ( struct node **, char * ) ;
void dis ( struct node * ) ;
struct node
{
    struct node *pre ;
    char data[ 25 ] ;
    struct node *next ;
} ;
extern int flag = 0 ;
struct node *p ;
int main( )
{
    p = NULL ;
    add ( &p, "HELLO" ) ;
    add ( &p, "tom" ) ;
    add ( &p, "HELLO" ) ;
    add ( &p, "jerry" ) ;
    dis ( p ) ;
    return 0 ;
}
void add ( struct node **s, char *z )
{
    struct node *r, *t ;
    if ( *s == NULL )
```

```
    {
        *s = ( struct node * ) malloc ( sizeof ( struct node ) ) ;
        ( *s ) -> pre = NULL ;
        strcpy ( ( *s ) -> data , z ) ;
        ( *s ) -> next = NULL ;
    }
    else
    {
        t = *s ;
        while ( t -> next != NULL )
            t = t -> next ;
        r = ( struct node * ) malloc ( sizeof ( struct node ) ) ;
        r -> pre = t ;
        strcpy ( r -> data, z ) ;
        r -> next = NULL ;
        t -> next = r ;
    }
}
void dis ( struct node *q )
{
    int flag = 1 ;
    while ( q != NULL )
    {
        if ( flag % 2 == 0 )
        {
            printf ( "%s ", ( strlwr ( q -> data ) ) ) ;
            flag += 2 ;
        }
        else
        {
            printf ( "%s ", ( strupr ( q -> data ) ) ) ;
        }
        q = q -> next -> next ;
        flag++ ;
    }
```

```
}
```

(a) The program will print the output as HELLO hello.

(b) The program will print the output as HELLO tom HELLO jerry.

(c) The program will print the output as hello TOM HELLO JERRY.

(d) The program will result in a compile time error.

Question 58

What will be the output of the following program?

```
# include <stdio.h>
# include <malloc.h>
void add ( struct node **, char * ) ;
void dis ( struct node * ) ;
struct node
{
    struct node *pre ;
    char data[ 25 ] ;
    struct node *next ;
} ;
extern int flag = 0 ;
struct node *p ;
int main( )
{
    p = NULL ;
    add ( &p, "jack" ) ;
    add ( &p, "and" ) ;
    add ( &p, "jill" ) ;
    add ( &p, "jerry" ) ;
    dis ( p ) ;
    return 0 ;
}
```

```
void add ( struct node **s, char *z )
{
    struct node *r, *t ;
    if ( *s == NULL )
    {
        *s = ( struct node * ) malloc ( sizeof ( struct node ) ) ;
        ( *s ) -> pre = NULL ;
        strcpy ( ( *s ) -> data, z ) ;
        ( *s ) -> next = NULL ;
    }
    else
    {
        t = *s ;
        while ( t -> next != NULL )
            t = t -> next ;
        r = ( struct node * ) malloc ( sizeof ( struct node ) ) ;
        r -> pre = t ;
        strcpy ( r -> data, z ) ;
        r -> next = NULL ;
        t -> next = r ;
    }
}
void dis ( struct node *q )
{
    char *p ;
    while ( q -> next != NULL )
    {
        p = q -> next -> data ;
        printf ( "%d ", strlen ( strcat ( q -> data, p ) ) ) ;
        q = q -> next ;
    }
}
```

(a) 4 3 4 5

(b) 7 9

(c) 7 11 15

(d) 7 7 9

Question 59

Which of the following statement is correct about the program given below?

```
# include <stdio.h>
# include <malloc.h>
void add ( int ) ;
void dis ( struct node * ) ;
struct node
{
    int data ;
    struct node *next ;
    struct node *prev ;
} ;
struct node *p ;
int main( )
{
    p = NULL ;
    add ( 10 ) ;
    add ( 20 ) ;
    add ( 30 ) ;
    dis ( p ) ;
    return 0 ;
}
void add ( int num )
{
    struct node *t, *t1 ;
    t = ( struct node* ) malloc ( sizeof ( struct node ) ) ;
    t -> data = num ;
    t -> next = NULL ;
```

```
    if ( p == NULL )
    {
        p = t ;
        t -> prev = NULL ;
    }
    else
    {
        t1 = p ;
        while ( t1 -> next != NULL )
            t1 = t1 -> next ;
        t1 -> next = t ;
        t -> prev = t1 ;
    }
}
void dis ( struct node *z )
{
    while ( z != NULL )
    {
        printf ( "%d", z -> data ) ;
        z = z -> next ;
    }
    while ( z != NULL )
    {
        printf ( "%d ", z ->data ) ;
        z = z -> prev ;
    }
}
```

(a) The program will result in a compile time error.

(b) The program will cause an exception.

(c) The program will print the output as 10 20 30.

(d) The program will print the output as 30 20 10.

Question 60

What will be the output of the following program?

```
# include <stdio.h>
# include <malloc.h>
# include <stdarg.h>
fun ( int,... ) ;
void dis ( struct node * ) ;
void add ( int ) ;
struct node
{
    int data ;
    struct node *link ;
} ;
struct node *s, *p ;

int main( )
{
    int nos ;
    p = NULL ;
    s = p ;
    fun ( 3, "M.S.dhoni", "sachin tendulkar", "india" ) ;
    dis ( p ) ;
    return 0 ;
}
fun (int num,...)
{
    int i = 0 ;
    va_list start ;
    va_start ( start, num ) ;
    add ( ( strlen ( va_arg ( start, int ) ) ) + ( strlen ( va_arg ( start, int ) ) ) + ( strlen ( va_arg (
            start, int ) ) ) ) ;
}
void add ( int n )
```

```
{
    struct node *r, *t ;
    if ( s == NULL )
    {
        r = ( struct node * ) malloc ( sizeof ( struct node * ) ) ;
        r -> data = n ;
        r -> link = NULL ;
        s = r ;
        p = r ;
    }
    else
    {
        t = s ;
        r = ( struct node * ) malloc ( sizeof ( struct node * ) ) ;
        r -> data = n ;
        r -> link = NULL ;
        while ( t -> link != NULL )
        {
            t = t -> link ;
        }
        t -> link = r ;
    }
}
void dis ( struct node *q )
{
    while ( q !- NULL )
    {
        printf ( "%d", q -> data *= 2 ) ;
        q = q -> link ;
    }
}
```

(a) 60

(b) 66

(c) 33

(d) 30

Answers

Q. 1 – A	Q. 2 – B	Q. 3 – C
Q. 4 – D	Q. 5 – A	Q. 6 – B
Q. 7 – D	Q. 8 – D	Q. 9 – C
Q. 10 – C	Q. 11 – B	Q. 12 – D
Q. 13 – A	Q. 14 – C	Q. 15 – C
Q. 16 – A	Q. 17 – D	Q. 18 – A
Q. 19 – C	Q. 20 – C	Q. 21 – B
Q. 22 – D	Q. 23 – C	Q. 24 – A
Q. 25 – D	Q. 26 – D	Q. 27 – B
Q. 28 – A	Q. 29 – D	Q. 30 – A
Q. 31 – B	Q. 32 – C	Q. 33 – B
Q. 34 – D	Q. 35 – D	Q. 36 – D
Q. 37 – C	Q. 38 – C	Q. 39 – D
Q. 40 – C	Q. 41 – D	Q. 42 – A
Q. 43 – D	Q. 44 – B	Q. 45 – C
Q. 46 – C	Q. 47 – C	Q. 48 – D

Q. 49 – C	Q. 50 – D	Q. 51 – C
Q. 52 – D	Q. 53 – D	Q. 54 – D
Q. 55 – A	Q. 56 – B	Q. 57 – A
Q. 58 – D	Q. 59 – C	Q. 60 – A

4

Sparse Matrices

Question 1

Which of the following matrix has lots of elements with value 0?

(a) Symmetric matrix

(b) Skewed-symmetric matrix

(c) Sparse matrix

(d) Identical matrix

Question 2

Which of the following statements are correct?

I. In 3-tuple form, each non-zero element is stored in a row with first and second element of this row containing the row and column in which the element is present in the original matrix.

II. The third element in a row of 3-tuple stores the actual value of the non-zero element.

(a) Only I is correct.

(b) Only II is correct.

(c) Both I and II are correct.

(d) Both I and II are incorrect.

Question 3

What does the head node for a column list stores in the linked representation of a sparse matrix?

I. A pointer to the next column head node

II. A pointer to the first node in column list

III. Column number

(a) Only I and II

(b) Only II and III

(c) Only I and III

(d) I, II and III

Question 4

Which of the following is a common way of representing non-zero elements of a sparse matrix?

(a) 2-tuple

(b) 3-tuple

(c) 4-tuple

(d) None of the above

Question 5

Which of the following statements are correct?

I. In the linked list representation of a sparse matrix a separate list is maintained for each column as well as each row of the matrix.

II. A node in a list stores the row number, column number and the value of the non-zero element of the sparse matrix.

(a) Only I is correct.

(b) Only II is correct.

(c) Both I and II are correct.

(d) Both I and II are incorrect.

Question 6

Which of the following sparse matrix has the non-zero elements placed below the leading diagonal?

(a) Diagonal matrix

(b) Tridiagonal matrix

(c) Lower Triangular matrix

(d) Upper Triangular matrix

Question 7

Which of the following statements are correct?

I. A sparse matrix represented as a linked list can be considered as a chain of 3-tuple.

II. Using linked list to represent a sparse matrix is less efficient than using an array.

(a) Only I is correct.

(b) Only II is correct.

(c) Both I and II are correct.

(d) Both I and II are incorrect.

Question 8

Which of the following are the correct ways to store information of 3-tuple?

I. Arrays

II. Linked list

III. Graphs

(a) Only I and II

(b) Only I and III

(c) Only II and III

(d) I, II and III

Question 9

Which of the following statements are correct?

I. If a sparse matrix is represented as an array of 3-tuple on which addition or multiplication is carried out then it is possible to predict beforehand how many elements in the resultant matrix would be non-zero.

II. It is possible to predict the size of resultant matrix beforehand when the sparse matrix is represented as an array of 3-tuple.

(a) Only I is correct.

(b) Only II is correct.

(c) Both I and II are correct.

(d) Both I and II are incorrect.

Question 10

Which of the following statements are correct?

I. In a linked list representation of a sparse matrix, if the matrix is of size 3 x 3 then there would be 3 lists for 3 columns and 3 lists for 3 rows.

II. A head node for a row list stores a pointer to the node which comes last in the row list and a pointer to the previous row head node.

(a) Only I is correct.

(b) Only II is correct.

(c) Both I and II are correct.

(d) Both I and II are incorrect.

Question 11

Which of the following statements are correct?

I. A special node is used to store the information required for traversing the list of sparse matrix.

II. In an upper triangular sparse matrix the non-zero elements are stored on the leading diagonal of the matrix.

(a) Only I is correct.

(b) Only II is correct.

(c) Both I and II are correct.

(d) Both I and II are incorrect.

Question 12

Which of the following statements are correct?

I. A sparse matrix is a node having two pointers one pointing to the list of rows and the other pointing to the list of columns.

II. The sparse matrix node should contain two integers specifying the number of rows and the number of columns.

(a) Only I is correct.

(b) Only II is correct.

(c) Both I and II are correct.

(d) Both I and II are incorrect.

Question 13

Which of the following statements are correct?

I. For a diagonal n x n matrix, we need only n / n bytes assuming one bit for each entry.

II. For a m x n dimensional sparse matrix and 0 <= I < m, 0 <= j < n, the non-zero elements m[i][j] are mapped using only row major orientation.

(a) Only I is correct.

(b) Only II is correct.

(c) Both I and II are correct.

(d) Both I and II are incorrect.

Question 14

Which of the following statements are correct?

I. A matrix which is n x m with k non-zero entries is sparse if k << n x m.

II. A sparse matrix can be represented as a list of non-zero indexes and associated entries.

(a) Only I is correct.

(b) Only II is correct.

(c) Both I and II are correct.

(d) Both I and II are incorrect.

Question 15

Which of the following statements are correct?

I. While storing and multiplying sparse matrices, it is not necessary to modify the standard matrix multiplication algorithm.

II. While storing and manipulating sparse matrices, it is advantageous to make the use of sparse structure of the matrix.

(a) Only I is correct.

(b) Only II is correct.

(c) Both I and II are correct.

(d) Both I and II are incorrect.

Question 16

Which of the following statements are correct?

I. The native data structure for the sparse matrix is a one dimensional array.

II. For a n x m matrix we need at least (n * m) / 8 bytes to represent the matrix, assuming one bit for each entry.

(a) Only I is correct.

(b) Only II is correct.

(c) Both I and II are correct.

(d) Both I and II are incorrect.

Question 17

Which of the following statements are correct?

I. Depending on the number and distribution of non-zero entries different data structures can be used for sparse matrix.

II. An efficient structure for a tridiagonal matrix is to store the entries in the main diagonal as a one dimensional array.

(a) Only I is correct.

(b) Only II is correct.

(c) Both I and II are correct.

(d) Both I and II are incorrect.

Question 18

Which of the following statements are correct?

I. In order to create a linked list version of a sparse matrix, the elements of the matrix represented as triplets must be inserted repeatedly to a partially constructed sparse matrix by linked list.

II. It is mandatory to store the non-zero elements in the 3-tuple in some ordered fashion.

(a) Only I is correct.

(b) Only II is correct.

(c) Both I and II are correct.

(d) Both I and II are incorrect.

Question 19

Which of the following will correctly represent the matrix given below?

4	0	0	0
0	1	0	0
0	0	9	0
0	0	0	12

(a) Diagonal matrix

(b) Tridiagonal matrix

(c) Lower Triangular matrix

(d) Upper Triangular matrix

Question 20

Which of the following will correctly represent the matrix given below?

0	0	0	0
13	0	0	0
9	2	0	0
6	0	12	0

(a) Diagonal matrix

(b) Tridiagonal matrix

(c) Lower Triangular matrix

(d) Upper Triangular matrix

Question 21

Which of the following will correctly represent the matrix given below?

0	4	0	3
0	0	1	0
0	0	0	9
0	0	0	0

(a) Diagonal matrix

(b) Tridiagonal matrix

(c) Lower Triangular matrix

(d) Upper Triangular matrix

Question 22

Which of the following will correctly represent the matrix given below?

0	3	0	0
0	0	8	0
0	0	0	5
0	0	0	0

(a) Diagonal matrix

(b) Tridiagonal matrix

(c) Lower Triangular matrix

(d) Upper Triangular matrix

Question 23

What is the dimension of sparse matrix represented by the 3-tuple form given below?

```
int arr[ 5 ][ 3 ] = {
                    7, 7, 4,
                    0, 3, -5,
                    1, 1, 4,
                    1, 6, 7,
                    2, 4, 9
                };
```

(a) 5 x 3

(b) 7 x 7

(c) 7 x 4

(d) 3 x 5

Question 24

Which of the following is the correct sparse matrix representation of the 3-tuple for given below?

(a) int arr[8][3] = {

```
                    5, 5, 7,
                    0, 3, 5,
                    1, 1, 4,
                    2, 4, 9,
                    3, 1, 3,
                    3, 3, 2,
                    4, 0, 1,
                    4, 2, 2
                };
```

(b) int arr[5][5] = {

```
                    0, 0, 5, 0, 0,
```

```
                4, 0, 0, 0, 0,
                0, 0, 0, 9, 0,
                3, 0, 2, 0, 0,
                1, 2, 0, 0, 0
            } ;
```

(b) int arr[5][7] = {

```
                0, 0, 0, 0, 5,
                0, 0, 4, 0, 0,
                0, 0, 0, 0, 9,
                0, 0, 3, 0, 2,
                0, 1, 0, 2, 0
                0, 0, 0, 0, 0
                0, 0, 0, 0, 0
            } ;
```

(c) int arr[5][5] = {

```
                0, 0, 0, 5, 0,
                0, 4, 0, 0, 0,
                0, 0, 0, 0, 9,
                0, 3, 0, 2, 0,
                1, 0, 2, 0, 0
            } ;
```

(d) int arr[5][7] = {

```
                5, 0, 0, 0, 0,
                4, 0, 0, 0, 0,
                0, 0, 0, 0, 9,
                0, 3, 0, 2, 0,
                1, 0, 2, 0, 0
                0, 0, 0, 0, 0
                0, 0, 0, 0, 0
```

```
};
```

Question 25

What will be the 3-tuple form of non-zero elements present in the sparse matrix arr?

int arr[3][4] = { 4, 0, 0, 1,2, 0, 0, 9, 6, 1, 0, 0 } ;

(a) 3 4 6
0 0 4
0 3 1
1 0 2
1 3 9
2 0 6
2 1 1

(b) 3 4 6
0 0 4
3 0 1
0 1 2
3 1 9
0 2 6
1 2 1

(c) 3 4 6
0 0 4
3 0 1
1 0 2
1 3 9
2 0 6
2 1 1

(d) 3 4 6
0 0 4
0 3 1

```
1 0 2
1 3 9
2 0 6
1 2 1
```

Question 26

How many zeros are present in the sparse matrix of which 3-tuple form is given below?

```
int arr[ 7 ][ 3 ] = {
                        5, 5, 6,
                        0, 3, 5,
                        1, 1, 4,
                        2, 4, 9,
                        3, 1, 3,
                        3, 3, 2,
                        4, 0, 1
                    };
```

(a) 15

(b) 6

(c) 2

(d) 19

Question 27

Which of the following type of matrix is represented by the 3-tuple form given below?

```
int arr[ 4 ][ 3 ] = {
                        4, 4, 3,
                        0, 1, 3,
                        1, 2, 8,
```

```
        2, 3, 5
    } ;
```

(a) Diagonal matrix

(b) Tridiagonal matrix

(c) Lower Triangular matrix

(d) Upper Triangular matrix

Question 28

Which of the following is a correct declaration of structure node that can be used to store elements of a sparse matrix?

(a)
```
struct node
{
    int col ;
    int val ;
    struct node *right ;
} ;
```

(b)
```
struct node
{
    int row ;
    int col ;
    int val ;
    struct node *down ;
    struct node *right ;
} ;
```

(c)
```
struct node
{
    int row ;
    int col ;
    struct node *down ;
```

```
};
```

(d)
```
struct node
{
        int row ;
        int val ;
        struct node *down ;
};
```

Question 29

Which of the following code snippet is correct that can be added to the given code snippet to count the total number of non-zero element in a matrix?

```
int count ( int *pa, int r, int c )
{
        int count = 0, i, j ;
        for ( i = 0 ; i < r ; i++ )
        {
                for ( i = 0 ; i < r ; i++ )
                {
                        /*Add code here*/
                }
        }
        return count ;
}
```

(a)
```
if ( pa != 0 )
        count++ ;
pa++ ;
```

(b)
```
if ( *pa == 0 )
        count++ ;
pa++ ;
```

(c)
```
        count++ ;
pa++ ;
```

(d)
```
if ( *pa != 0 )
        count++ ;
pa++ ;
```

Question 30

Which of the following is a correct declaration of structure rheadnode to store the information of row headnode in a sparse matrix represented using a Linked List?

(a)
```
struct rheadnode
{
        int rowno ;
        struct node * right ;
        struct rheadnode *next ;
} ;
```

(b)
```
struct rheadnode
{
        int rowno ;
        struct rheadnode *next ;
} ;
```

(c)
```
struct rheadnode
{
        struct node * right ;
        struct rheadnode *next ;
} ;
```

(d)
```
struct rheadnode
{
        int rowno ;
        struct node * right ;
} ;
```

Question 31

Which of the following statement is correct about the code snippet given below?

```
int* fun ( int *pa, int r, int c )
{
      int rows, *p, i, j, k ;
      rows = count ( pa, r, c ) + 1 ;
      p = ( int* ) malloc ( rows * 3 * sizeof ( int ) ) ;
      p[ 0 ] = r ;
      p[ 1 ] = c ;
      p[ 2 ] = rows - 1 ;
      k = 3 ;
      for ( i = 0 ; i < r ; i++ )
      {
            for ( j = 0 ; j < c ; j++ )
            {
                  if ( *pa != 0 )
                  {
                        p[ k ] = i ; k++ ;
                        p[ k ] = j ; k++ ;
                        p[ k ] = *pa ; k++ ;
                  }
                  pa++ ;
            }
      }
      return p ;
}
```

(a) The code implements sparse matrix in a 3-tuple form.

(b) The code implements sparse matrix in a 2-tuple form.

(c) The code implements sparse matrix in a column major arrangement.

(d) The code implements sparse matrix in a row major arrangement.

Question 32

Which of the following is a correct declaration of structure of a special node that is used to store the information required for traversing the list used to represent a sparse matrix?

(a)
```
struct spmat
{
        int noofrows ;
        int noofcols ;
        struct cheadnode *firstcol ;
} ;
```

(b)
```
struct spmat
{
        struct rheadnode *firstrow ;
        int noofrows ;
        int noofcols ;
        struct cheadnode *firstcol ;
} ;
```

(c)
```
struct spmat
{
        struct rheadnode *firstrow ;
        struct cheadnode *firstcol ;
} ;
```

(d)
```
struct spmat
{
        struct rheadnode *firstrow ;
        int noofrows ;
        int noofcols ;
} ;
```

Question 33

Which of the following is the correct definition of function fun( ) that you will add to the code snippet given below to dynamically create the matrix of size MAX1 x MAX2?

```
# include <stdio.h>
# define MAX1 3
# define MAX2 3
struct sparse
{
    int *sp ;
    int row ;
} ;
void fun ( struct sparse * ) ;

int main( )
{
    struct sparse s1 ;
    fun ( &s1 ) ;
    return 0 ;
}
/* Add code here */
```

(a)
```
void fun ( struct sparse *s )
{
    int n, i ;
    s.sp = ( int * ) malloc ( MAX1 * MAX2 * sizeof ( int ) ) ;
    for ( i = 0 ; i < MAX1 * MAX2 ; i++ )
    {
        scanf ( "%d", &n ) ;
        * ( s.sp + i ) = n ;
    }
}
```

(b)
```
void fun ( struct sparse *s )
{
    int n, i ;
    s -> sp = ( int * ) malloc ( MAX1 * MAX2 * sizeof ( int ) ) ;
```

```
        for ( i = 0 ; i < MAX1 * MAX2 ; i++ )
        {
            scanf ( "%d", &n ) ;
            * ( s -> sp + i ) = n ;
        }
    }
```

(c)
```
    void fun ( struct sparse *s )
    {
        int n, i ;
        s -> sp = malloc ( MAX1 * MAX2 * sizeof ( int ) ) ;
        for ( i = 0 ; i < MAX1 * MAX2 ; i++ )
        {
            scanf ( "%d", &n ) ;
            s -> sp + i = n ;
        }
    }
```

(d)
```
    void fun ( struct sparse *s )
    {
        int n, i ;
        s.sp = malloc ( MAX1 * MAX2 * sizeof ( int ) ) ;
        for ( i = 0 ; i < MAX1 * MAX2 ; i++ )
        {
            scanf ( "%d", &n ) ;
            * ( s.sp + i ) = n ;
        }
    }
```

Question 34

Which of the following is the correct definition of function fun( ) that you will add to the code snippet given below to deallocate the memory?

```
# include <stdio.h>
```

```
# define MAX1 3
# define MAX2 3
struct sparse
{
    int *sp ;
    int row ;
} ;
void fun ( struct sparse * ) ;
int main( )
{
    struct sparse s1 ;
    s1.sp = ( int * ) malloc ( MAX1 * MAX2 * sizeof ( int ) ) ;
    fun ( &s1 ) ;
    return 0 ;
}
/* Add code here */
```

(a)
```
void fun ( struct sparse *s )
{
    free ( s ) ;
}
```

(b)
```
void fun ( struct sparse *s )
{
    free ( s -> sp ) ;
}
```

(c)
```
void fun ( struct sparse *s )
{
    free ( s.sp ) ;
}
```

(d) All of the above

Question 35

Which of the following is the correct definition of function fun( ) that you will add to the code snippet given below to store information about total number of rows, columns and non-zero values in a 3-tuple of sparse matrix?

```
# include <stdio.h>
# define MAX1 3
# define MAX2 3
struct sparse
{
    int *sp ;
    int row ;
    int *result ;
};
void fun ( struct sparse * ) ;
int main( )
{
    struct sparse s ;
    s.sp = ( int * ) malloc ( MAX1 * MAX2 * sizeof ( int ) ) ;
    return 0 ;
}
/* Add code here */
```

```
(a) void fun ( struct sparse *s )
    {
        * ( s -> sp + 0 ) = MAX1 ;
        * ( s -> sp + 1 ) = MAX2 ;
        * ( s -> sp + 2 ) = MAX1 * MAX2 ;
    }

(b) void fun ( struct sparse *s )
    {
        int cnt, i ;
        for ( i = 0 ; i < MAX1 * MAX2 ; i++ )
```

```
        {
            if ( * ( s.sp + i ) != 0 )
                cnt++ ;
        }
        * ( s.sp + 0 ) = MAX1 ;
        * ( s.sp + 1 ) = MAX2 ;
        * ( s.sp + 2 ) = cnt ;
    }
```

(c)
```
    void fun ( struct sparse *s )
    {
        int cnt = 0, i ;
        for ( i = 0 ; i < MAX1 * MAX2 ; i++ )
        {
            if ( * ( s -> sp + i ) != 0 )
                cnt++ ;
        }
        * ( s -> sp + 0 ) = MAX1 ;
        * ( s -> sp + 1 ) = MAX2 ;
        * ( s -> sp + 2 ) = cnt ;
    }
```

(d)
```
    void fun ( struct sparse *s )
    {
        * ( s.sp + 0 ) = MAX1 ;
        * ( s.sp + 1 ) = MAX2 ;
        * ( s.sp + 2 ) = MAX1 * MAX2 ;
    }
```

Question 36

Which of the following is the correct definition of function fun( ) that you will add to the code snippet given below to create an array that stores information about non-zero elements of a sparse matrix?

```
# include <stdio.h>
# define MAX1 3
# define MAX2 3
struct sparse
{
    int *sp ;
    int row ;
} ;
void fun ( struct sparse *, struct sparse ) ;
int main( )
{
    struct sparse s1, s2 ;
    s1.sp = ( int * ) malloc ( MAX1 * MAX2 * sizeof ( int ) ) ;
    s2.sp = ( int * ) malloc ( MAX1 * MAX2 * sizeof ( int ) ) ;
    fun ( &s2, s1 ) ;
    return 0 ;
}
/* Add code here */
```

(a)
```
void fun ( struct sparse *p, struct sparse s )
{
    int r = 0, c = -1, l = -1, i, cnt = 0 ;
    for ( i = 0 ; i < MAX1 * MAX2 ; i++ )
    {
        if ( * ( p -> sp + i ) != 0 )
            cnt++ ;
    }
    p -> row = cnt + 1 ;
    p -> sp = ( int * ) malloc ( p -> row * 3 * sizeof ( int ) ) ;
    * ( p -> sp + 0 ) = MAX1 ;
    * ( p -> sp + 1 ) = MAX2 ;
    * ( p -> sp + 2 ) = cnt ;
    l = 2 ;
    for ( i = 0 ; i < MAX1 * MAX2 ; i++ )
    {
```

```
            c++ ;
            if ( * ( s.sp + i ) != 0 )
            {
                l++ ;
                * ( p -> sp + l ) = r ;
                l++ ;
                * ( p -> sp + l ) = c ;
                l++ ;
                * ( p -> sp + l ) = * ( s.sp + i ) ;
            }
        }
    }
```

(b)
```
void fun ( struct sparse *p, struct sparse s )
{
    int r = 0, c = -1, l = -1, i, cnt = 0 ;
    for ( i = 0 ; i < MAX1 * MAX2 ; i++ )
    {
        if ( * ( p -> sp + i ) != 0 )
            cnt++ ;
    }
    p -> row = cnt + 1 ;
    p -> sp = ( int * ) malloc ( p -> row * 3 * sizeof ( int ) ) ;
    * ( p -> sp + 0 ) = MAX1 ;
    * ( p -> sp + 1 ) = MAX2 ;
    * ( p -> sp + 2 ) = cnt ;
    l = 2 ;
    for ( i = 0 ; i < MAX1 * MAX2 ; i++ )
    {
        c++ ;
        if ( ( ( i % MAX2 ) == 0 ) && ( i != 0 ) )
        {
            r++ ;
            c = 0 ;
        }
```

```
            if ( * ( s.sp + i ) != 0 )
            {
                l++ ;
                * ( p -> sp + l ) = r ;
                l++ ;
                * ( p -> sp + l ) = c ;
                l++ ;
                * ( p -> sp + l ) = * ( s.sp + i ) ;
            }
        }
    }
```

(c)

```
    void fun ( struct sparse *p, struct sparse s )
    {
        int r = 0, c = -1, l = -1, i, cnt = 0 ;
        for ( i = 0 ; i < MAX1 * MAX2 ; i++ )
        {
            if ( * ( p -> sp + i ) != 0 )
                cnt++ ;
        }
        * ( p -> sp + 0 ) = MAX1 ;
        * ( p -> sp + 1 ) = MAX2 ;
        * ( p -> sp + 2 ) = cnt ;
        l = 2 ;
        for ( i = 0 ; i < MAX1 * MAX2 ; i++ )
        {
            c++ ;
            if ( ( ( i % MAX2 ) == 0 ) && ( i != 0 ) )
            {
                r++ ;
                c = 0 ;
            }
            if ( * ( s.sp + i ) != 0 )
            {
                l++ ;
```

```
                * ( p -> sp + l ) = r ;
                l++ ;
                * ( p -> sp + l ) = c ;
                l++ ;
                * ( p -> sp + l ) = s.sp + i ;
            }
        }
    }
```

(d)
```
void fun ( struct sparse *p, struct sparse s )
{
    int r = 0, c = -1, l = -1, i, cnt = 0 ;
    for ( i = 0 ; i < MAX1 * MAX2 ; i++ )
    {
        if ( * ( p -> sp + i ) != 0 )
            cnt++ ;
    }
    * ( p -> sp + 0 ) = MAX1 ;
    * ( p -> sp + 1 ) = MAX2 ;
    * ( p -> sp + 2 ) = cnt ;
    l = 2 ;
    for ( i = 0 ; i < MAX1 * MAX2 ; i++ )
    {
        c++ ;
        if ( ( ( i % MAX2 ) == 0 ) && ( i != 0 ) )
        {
            r++ ;
            c = 0 ;
        }
        if ( * ( s.sp + i ) == 0 )
        {
            l++ ;
            * ( p -> sp + l ) = r ;
            l++ ;
            * ( p -> sp + l ) = c ;
```

```
            l++ ;
            * ( p -> sp + l ) = * ( s.sp + i ) ;
        }
    }
}
```

Question 37

Which of the following is the correct definition of function fun( ) that checks from 3-tuple form of a sparse matrix whether the original matrix is a square matrix?

(a)
```
struct sparse
{
    int *sp ;
    int row ;
} ;
void fun ( struct sparse *p )
{
    if ( ( p -> sp ) == ( p -> sp + 1 ) )
        printf ( "\nSquare Matrix" ) ;
}
```

(b)
```
struct sparse
{
    int *sp ;
    int row ;
} ;
void fun ( struct sparse *p )
{
    if ( ( p.sp ) == ( p.sp + 1 ) )
        printf ( "\nSquare Matrix" ) ;
}
```

(c)
```
struct sparse
{
    int *sp ;
```

```
        int row ;
    } ;
    void fun ( struct sparse *p )
    {
        if ( * ( p.sp ) == * ( p.sp + 1 ) )
            printf ( "\nSquare Matrix" ) ;
    }
```

(d)
```
    struct sparse
    {
        int *sp ;
        int row ;
    } ;
    void fun ( struct sparse *p )
    {
        if ( * ( p -> sp ) == * ( p -> sp + 1 ) )
            printf ( "\nSquare Matrix" ) ;
    }
```

Question 38

Which of the following is the correct code snippet that checks from 3-tuple form of sparse matrix whether the original matrix is a diagonal matrix?

(a)
```
    struct sparse
    {
        int *sp ;
        int row ;
    } ;
    void fun ( struct sparse *p )
    {
        if ( * ( p -> sp ) == * ( p -> sp + 1 ) )
        {
            for ( i = 3 ; i <= 9 ; i = i + 3 )
            {
                if ( ( * ( p -> sp + i ) ) != ( * ( p -> sp + i + 1 ) ) )
```

```
            {
                i = i + 6 ;
                break ;
            }
        }
        if ( i > 9 )
            printf ( "Diagonal matrix" ) ;
    }
}
```

(b)
```
struct sparse
{
    int *sp ;
    int row ;
} ;
void fun ( struct sparse *p )
{
    if ( * ( p -> sp ) == * ( p -> sp + 1 ) )
    {
        for ( i = 3 ; i <= 9 ; i = i + 3 )
        {
            if ( ( * ( p -> sp + i ) ) > ( * ( p -> sp + i + 1 ) ) )
            {
                i = i + 6 ;
                break ;
            }
        }
        if ( i > 9 )
            printf ( " Diagonal matrix" ) ;
    }
}
```

(c)
```
struct sparse
{
    int *sp ;
```

```
        int row ;
    } ;
    void fun ( struct sparse *p )
    {
        if ( * ( p -> sp ) == * ( p -> sp + 1 ) )
        {
            for ( i = 3 ; i <= 9 ; i = i + 3 )
            {
                if ( ( * ( p -> sp + i ) ) <= ( * ( p -> sp + i + 1 ) ) )
                {
                    i = i + 6 ;
                    break ;
                }
            }
            if ( i > 9 )
                printf ( " Diagonal matrix" ) ;
        }
    }
```

(d)
```
    struct sparse
    {
        int *sp ;
        int row ;
    } ;
    void fun ( struct sparse *p )
    {
        if ( * ( p -> sp ) == * ( p -> sp + 1 ) )
        {
            for ( i = 3 ; i <= 9 ; i = i + 3 )
            {
                if ( ( * ( p -> sp + i ) ) == ( * ( p -> sp + i + 1 ) ) )
                {
                    i = i + 6 ;
                    break ;
                }
```

```
        }
        if ( i > 9 )
            printf ( " Diagonal matrix" ) ;
    }
}
```

Question 39

Which of the following is the correct code snippet that checks from 3-tuple form of a sparse matrix whether the original array is a lower triangular matrix?

(a)
```
struct sparse
{
    int *sp ;
    int row ;
} ;
void fun ( struct sparse *p )
{
    if ( * ( p -> sp ) == * ( p -> sp + 1 ) )
    {
        for ( i = 3 ; i <= 9 ; i = i + 3 )
        {
            if ( ( * ( p -> sp + i ) ) != ( * ( p -> sp + i + 1 ) ) )
            {
                i = i + 6 ;
                break ;
            }
        }
        if ( i > 9 )
            printf ( "Lower triangular matrix" ) ;
    }
}
```

(b)
```
struct sparse
{
    int *sp ;
```

```
        int row ;
    } ;
    void fun ( struct sparse *p )
    {
        if ( * ( p -> sp ) == * ( p -> sp + 1 ) )
        {
            for ( i = 3 ; i <= 9 ; i = i + 3 )
            {
                if ( ( * ( p -> sp + i ) ) > ( * ( p -> sp + i + 1 ) ) )
                {
                    i = i + 6 ;
                    break ;
                }
            }
            if ( i > 9 )
                printf ( "Lower triangular matrix" ) ;
        }
    }
```

(c)
```
    struct sparse
    {
        int *sp ;
        int row ;
    } ;
    void fun ( struct sparse *p )
    {
        if ( * ( p -> sp ) == * ( p -> sp + 1 ) )
        {
            for ( i = 3 ; i <= 9 ; i = i + 3 )
            {
                if ( ( * ( p -> sp + i ) ) <= ( * ( p -> sp + i + 1 ) ) )
                {
                    i = i + 6 ;
                    break ;
                }
```

```
        }
        if ( i > 9 )
            printf ( "Lower triangular matrix" ) ;
    }
}
```

(d)
```
struct sparse
{
    int *sp ;
    int row ;
} ;
void fun ( struct sparse *p )
{
    if ( * ( p -> sp ) == * ( p -> sp + 1 ) )
    {
        for ( i = 3 ; i <= 9 ; i = i + 3 )
        {
            if ( ( * ( p -> sp + i ) ) == ( * ( p -> sp + i + 1 ) ) )
            {
                i = i + 6 ;
                break ;
            }
        }
        if ( i > 9 )
            printf ( "Lower triangular matrix" ) ;
    }
}
```

Question 40

Which of the following is the correct code snippet that checks from the 3-tuple form of a sparse matrix whether the original matrix is an upper triangular matrix?

(a)
```
struct sparse
{
    int *sp ;
```

```
        int row ;
    } ;
    void fun ( struct sparse *p )
    {
        if ( * ( p -> sp ) == * ( p -> sp + 1 ) )
        {
            for ( i = 3 ; i <= 9 ; i = i + 3 )
            {
                if ( ( * ( p -> sp + i ) ) != ( * ( p -> sp + i + 1 ) ) )
                {
                    i = i + 6 ;
                    break ;
                }
            }
            if ( i > 9 )
                printf ( "Upper triangular matrix" ) ;
        }
    }
```

(b)
```
    struct sparse
    {
        int *sp ;
        int row ;
    } ;
    void fun ( struct sparse *p )
    {
        if ( * ( p -> sp ) == * ( p -> sp + 1 ) )
        {
            for ( i = 3 ; i <= 9 ; i = i + 3 )
            {
                if ( ( * ( p -> sp + i ) ) > ( * ( p -> sp + i + 1 ) ) )
                {
                    i = i + 6 ;
                    break ;
                }
```

```
            }
            if ( i > 9 )
                printf ( "Upper triangular matrix" ) ;
        }
    }
```

(c)
```
    struct sparse
    {
        int *sp ;
        int row ;
    } ;
    void fun ( struct sparse *p )
    {
        if ( * ( p -> sp ) == * ( p -> sp + 1 ) )
        {
            for ( i = 3 ; i <= 9 ; i = i + 3 )
            {
                if ( ( * ( p -> sp + i ) ) <= ( * ( p -> sp + i + 1 ) ) )
                {
                    i = i + 6 ;
                    break ;
                }
            }
            if ( i > 9 )
                printf ( "Upper triangular matrix" ) ;
        }
    }
```

(d)
```
    struct sparse
    {
        int *sp ;
        int row ;
    } ;
    void fun ( struct sparse *p )
    {
```

```
        if ( * ( p -> sp ) == * ( p -> sp + 1 ) )
        {
            for ( i = 3 ; i <= 9 ; i = i + 3 )
            {
                if ( ( * ( p -> sp + i ) ) == ( * ( p -> sp + i + 1 ) ) )
                {
                    i = i + 6 ;
                    break ;
                }
            }
            if ( i > 9 )
                printf ( "Upper triangular matrix" ) ;
        }
    }
```

Question 41

Which of the following is the correct code snippet that checks from the 3-tuple form of a sparse matrix whether the original matrix is a tridiagonal matrix?

(a)
```
    struct sparse
    {
        int *sp ;
        int row ;
    } ;
    void fun ( struct sparse *p )
    {
        if ( * ( p -> sp ) == * ( p -> sp + 1 ) )
        {
            if ( * ( p -> sp + 2 ) == 2 )
            {
                for ( i = 3 ; i <= 9 ; i = i + 3 )
                {
                    if ( ( * ( p -> sp + i ) ) == ( * ( p -> sp + i + 1 ) - 1 ) )
                    {
                        i = i + 6 ;
```

```
                break ;
            }
        }
        if ( i > 9 )
            printf ( "Tridiagonal matrix" ) ;

        for ( i = 3 ; i <= 9 ; i = i + 3 )
        {
            if ( ( * ( p -> sp + i ) ) == ( * ( p -> sp + i + 1 ) + 1 ) )
            {
                i = i + 6 ;
                break ;
            }
        }
        if ( i > 9 )
            printf ( "Tridiagonal matrix" ) ;
    }
  }
}
```

(b)

```
struct sparse
{
    int *sp ;
    int row ;
} ;
void fun ( struct sparse *p )
{
    if ( * ( p -> sp ) == * ( p -> sp + 1 ) )
    {
        if ( * ( p -> sp + 2 ) == 2 )
        {
            for ( i = 3 ; i <= 9 ; i = i + 3 )
            {
                if ( ( * ( p -> sp + i ) ) > ( * ( p -> sp + i + 1 ) - 1 ) )
                {
```

```
                        i = i + 6 ;
                        break ;
                    }
                }
                if ( i > 9 )
                    printf ( "Tridiagonal matrix" ) ;

                for ( i = 3 ; i <= 9 ; i = i + 3 )
                {
                    if ( ( * ( p -> sp + i ) ) > ( * ( p -> sp + i + 1 ) + 1 ) )
                    {
                        i = i + 6 ;
                        break ;
                    }
                }
                if ( i > 9 )
                    printf ( "Tridiagonal matrix" ) ;
            }
        }
    }
```

(c)
```
    struct sparse
    {
        int *sp ;
        int row ;
    } ;
    void fun ( struct sparse *p )
    {
        if ( * ( p -> sp ) == * ( p -> sp + 1 ) )
        {
            if ( * ( p -> sp + 2 ) == 2 )
            {
                for ( i = 3 ; i <= 9 ; i = i + 3 )
                {
                    if ( ( * ( p -> sp + i ) ) < ( * ( p -> sp + i + 1 ) - 1 ) )
```

```
                {
                    i = i + 6 ;
                    break ;
                }
            }
            if ( i > 9 )
                printf ( "Tridiagonal matrix" ) ;

            for ( i = 3 ; i <= 9 ; i = i + 3 )
            {
                if ( ( * ( p -> sp + i ) ) < ( * ( p -> sp + i + 1 ) + 1 ) )
                {
                    i = i + 6 ;
                    break ;
                }
            }
            if ( i > 9 )
                printf ( "Tridiagonal matrix" ) ;
        }
    }
}
```

(d)
```
struct sparse
{
    int *sp ;
    int row ;
} ;
void fun ( struct sparse *p )
{
    if ( * ( p -> sp ) == * ( p -> sp + 1 ) )
    {
        if ( * ( p -> sp + 2 ) == 2 )
        {
            for ( i = 3 ; i <= 9 ; i = i + 3 )
            {
```

```
                    if ( ( * ( p -> sp + i ) ) != ( * ( p -> sp + i + 1 ) - 1 ) )
                    {
                        i = i + 6 ;
                        break ;
                    }
                }
                if ( i > 9 )
                    printf ( "Tridiagonal matrix" ) ;

                for ( i = 3 ; i <= 9 ; i = i + 3 )
                {
                    if ( ( * ( p -> sp + i ) ) != ( * ( p -> sp + i + 1 ) + 1 ) )
                    {
                        i = i + 6 ;
                        break ;
                    }
                }
                if ( i > 9 )
                    printf ( "Tridiagonal matrix" ) ;
            }
        }
    }
```

Question 42

What will be the output of the code snippet given below if the elements passed to the array are 4 0 0 0 0 1 0 0 0 0 9 0 0 0 0 12?

```
# include <stdio.h>
struct sparse
{
    int *sp ;
    int row ;
} ;
void fun ( struct sparse *, struct sparse, int ) ;
```

```
int main( )
{
    struct sparse s1, s2 ;
    int cnt = 0, i, n ;
    s1.sp = NULL ;
    s2.sp = NULL ;
    s1.sp = ( int * ) malloc ( 16 * sizeof ( int ) ) ;
    s2.sp = ( int * ) malloc ( 16 * sizeof ( int ) ) ;
    for ( i = 0 ; i < 16 ; i++ )
    {
        if ( * ( s1.sp + i ) != 0 )
            cnt++ ;
    }
    fun ( &s2, s1, cnt ) ;
    return 0 ;
}
void fun ( struct sparse *p, struct sparse s, int cnt )
{
    int r = 0, c = -1, l = -1, i ;
    p -> row = cnt + 1 ;
    p -> sp = ( int* ) malloc ( p -> row * 3 * sizeof ( int ) ) ;
    * ( p -> sp + 0 ) = 4 ;
    * ( p -> sp + 1 ) = 4 ;
    * ( p -> sp + 2 ) = p -> row - 1 ;
    l = 2 ;
    for ( i = 0 ; i < 16 ; i++ )
    {
        c++ ;
        if ( ( ( i % 4 ) == 0 ) && ( i != 0 ) )
        {
            r++ ;
            c = 0 ;
        }
        if ( * ( s.sp + i ) != 0 )
        {
```

```
                l++ ;
                * ( p -> sp + l ) = r ;
                l++ ;
                * ( p -> sp + l ) = c ;
                l++ ;
                * ( p -> sp + l ) = * ( s.sp + i ) ;
            }
        }
        for ( i = 0 ; i < p -> row * 3 ; i++ )
        {
            if ( ( i % 3 ) == 0 )
                printf ( "\n" ) ;
            printf ( "%d ", * ( p -> sp + i ) ) ;
        }
}
```

(a) 4 0 0 0
0 1 0 0
0 0 9 0
0 0 0 12

(b) 4 4 4
1 1 4
2 2 1
3 3 9
4 4 12

(c) 4 4 4
0 0 4
1 1 1
2 2 9
3 3 12

(d) 4 4 4
3 3 12

2 2 9
1 1 1
0 0 4

Question 43

What will be the output of the code snippet given below if all the elements of the array passed are 0?

```
# include <stdio.h>
struct sparse
{
	int *sp ;
	int row ;
} ;
void fun ( struct sparse *, struct sparse, int ) ;
int main( )
{
	struct sparse s1, s2 ;
	int cnt = 0, i, n ;
	s1.sp = NULL ;
	s2.sp = NULL ;
	s1.sp = ( int * ) malloc ( 9 * sizeof ( int ) ) ;
	s2.sp = ( int * ) malloc ( 9 * sizeof ( int ) ) ;
	for ( i = 0 ; i < 9 ; i++ )
	{
		if ( * ( s1.sp + i ) != 0 )
			cnt++ ;
	}
	fun ( &s2, s1, cnt ) ;
	return 0 ;
}
void fun ( struct sparse *p, struct sparse s, int cnt )
{
	int r = 0, c = -1, l = -1, i ;
```

```
    p -> row = cnt + 1 ;
    p -> sp = ( int* ) malloc ( p -> row * 3 * sizeof ( int ) ) ;
    * ( p -> sp + 0 ) = 3 ;
    * ( p -> sp + 1 ) = 3 ;
    * ( p -> sp + 2 ) = p -> row - 1 ;
    l = 2 ;
    for ( i = 0 ; i < 9 ; i++ )
    {
        c++ ;
        if ( ( ( i % 3 ) == 0 ) && ( i != 0 ) )
        {
            r++ ;
            c = 0 ;
        }
        if ( * ( s.sp + i ) != 0 )
        {
            l++ ;
            * ( p -> sp + l ) = r ;
            l++ ;
            * ( p -> sp + l ) = c ;
            l++ ;
            * ( p -> sp + l ) = * ( s.sp + i ) ;
        }
    }
    for ( i = 0 ; i < p -> row * 3 ; i++ )
    {
        if ( ( i % 3 ) == 0 )
            printf ( "\n" ) ;
        printf ( "%d ", * ( p -> sp + i ) ) ;
    }
}
```

(a) 0 0 0

(b) 3 3 0

(c) 0

(d) 9

Question 44

What will be the output of the code snippet given below if the elements passed to the array are 2 4 0 0 0 0 0 0 0?

```
# include <stdio.h>
struct sparse
{
    int *sp ;
    int row ;
} ;
void fun ( struct sparse *, struct sparse, int ) ;
int main( )
{
    struct sparse s1, s2 ;
    int cnt = 0, i, n ;
    s1.sp = NULL ;
    s2.sp = NULL ;
    s1.sp = ( int * ) malloc ( 9 * sizeof ( int ) ) ;
    s2.sp = ( int * ) malloc ( 9 * sizeof ( int ) ) ;
    for ( i = 0 ; i < 9 ; i++ )
    {
        if ( * ( s1.sp + i ) != 0 )
            cnt++ ;
    }
    fun ( &s2, s1, cnt ) ;
    return 0 ;
}
void fun ( struct sparse *p, struct sparse s, int cnt )
{
    int r = 0, c = -1, l = -1, i ;
```

```
        p -> row = cnt + 1 ;
        p -> sp = ( int* ) malloc ( p -> row * 3 * sizeof ( int ) ) ;
        * ( p -> sp + 0 ) = 3 ;
        * ( p -> sp + 1 ) = 3 ;
        * ( p -> sp + 2 ) = p -> row - 1 ;
        l = 2 ;
        for ( i = 0 ; i < 9 ; i++ )
        {
            c++ ;
            if ( ( ( i % 3 ) == 0 ) || ( i != 0 ) )
            {
                r++ ;
                c = 0 ;
            }
            if ( * ( s.sp + i ) != 0 )
            {
                l++ ;
                * ( p -> sp + l ) = r ;
                l++ ;
                * ( p -> sp + l ) = c ;
                l++ ;
                * ( p -> sp + l ) = * ( s.sp + i ) ;
            }
        }
        for ( i = 0 ; i < p -> row * 3 ; i++ )
        {
            if ( ( i % 3 ) == 0 )
                printf ( "\n" ) ;
            printf ( "%d ", * ( p -> sp + i ) ) ;
        }
}
```

(a) 3 3 2
1 0 2
2 0 4

(b) 2 4 0
0 0 0
0 0 0

(c) 3 3 2
0 0 2
0 1 4

(d) 3 3 2
1 1 2
1 2 4

Question 45

What will be the output of the code snippet given below if the elements passed to an array are 1 0 0 0 1 0 0 0 1?

```
# include <stdio.h>
struct sparse
{
    Int *sp ;
    int row ;
} ;
void fun ( struct sparse *, struct sparse, int ) ;
int main( )
{
    struct sparse s1, s2 ;
    int cnt = 0, i, n ;
    s1.sp = NULL ;
    s2.sp = NULL ;
    s1.sp = ( int * ) malloc ( 9 * sizeof ( int ) ) ;
    s2.sp = ( int * ) malloc ( 9 * sizeof ( int ) ) ;
    for ( i = 0 ; i < 9 ; i++ )
    {
```

```
            if ( * ( s1.sp + i ) != 0 )
                cnt++ ;
        }
        fun ( &s2, s1, cnt ) ;
        return 0 ;
}
void fun ( struct sparse *p, struct sparse s, int cnt )
{
        int r = 0, c = -1, l = -1, i ;
        p -> row = cnt + 1 ;
        p -> sp = ( int* ) malloc ( p -> row * 3 * sizeof ( int ) ) ;
        * ( p -> sp + 0 ) = 3 ;
        * ( p -> sp + 1 ) = 3 ;
        * ( p -> sp + 2 ) = p -> row - 1 ;
        l = 2 ;
        for ( i = 0 ; i < 9 ; i++ )
        {
            c++ ;
            if ( i != 0 )
            {
                r++ ;
                c = 0 ;
            }
            if ( * ( s.sp + i ) != 0 )
            {
                l++ ;
                * ( p -> sp + l ) = r ;
                l++ ;
                * ( p -> sp + l ) = c ;
                l++ ;
                * ( p -> sp + l ) = * ( s.sp + i ) ;
            }
        }
        for ( i = 0 ; i < p -> row * 3 ; i++ )
        {
```

```
        if ( ( i % 3 ) == 0 )
            printf ( "\n" ) ;
        printf ( "%d ", * ( p -> sp + i ) ) ;
    }
}
```

(a) 1 0 0
0 1 0
0 0 1

(b) 3 3 3
0 0 1
1 0 1
1 1 1

(c) 3 3 3
1 1 1
2 2 1
3 3 1

(d) 3 3 3
0 0 1
4 0 1
8 0 1

Question 46

What will be the output of the code snippet given below if the elements passed to an array are 9 0 0 1 0 8 5 0 0?

```
# include <stdio.h>
struct sparse
{
    int *sp ;
    int row ;
```

```
};
void fun ( struct sparse *, struct sparse, int ) ;
int main( )
{
      struct sparse s1, s2 ;
      int cnt = 0, i, n ;
      s1.sp = NULL ;
      s2.sp = NULL ;
      s1.sp = ( int * ) malloc ( 16 * sizeof ( int ) ) ;
      s2.sp = ( int * ) malloc ( 16 * sizeof ( int ) ) ;
      for ( i = 0 ; i < 9 ; i++ )
      {
            if ( * ( s1.sp + i ) != 0 )
                  cnt++ ;
      }
      fun ( &s2, s1, cnt ) ;
      return 0 ;
}
void fun ( struct sparse *p, struct sparse s, int cnt )
{
      int r = 0, c = -1, l = -1, i ;
      p -> row = cnt + 1 ;
      p -> sp = ( int* ) malloc ( p -> row * 3 * sizeof ( int ) ) ;
      * ( p -> sp + 0 ) = 3 ;
      * ( p -> sp + 1 ) = 3 ;
      * ( p -> sp + 2 ) = p -> row - 1 ;
      l = 2 ;
      for ( i = 0 ; i < 9 ; i++ )
      {
            c++ ;
            if ( * ( s.sp + i ) != 0 )
            {
                  l++ ;
                  * ( p -> sp + l ) = r ;
                  l++ ;
```

```
            * ( p -> sp + l ) = c ;
            l++ ;
            * ( p -> sp + l ) = * ( s.sp + i ) ;
        }
    }
    for ( i = 0 ; i < p -> row * 3 ; i++ )
    {
        if ( ( ( i % 3 ) == 0 ) && ( i != 0 ) )
            printf ( "\n" ) ;
        printf ( "%d ", * ( p -> sp + i ) ) ;
    }
}
```

(a) 9 0 0
1 0 8
5 0 0

(b) 3 3 4
0 0 9
1 0 1
1 2 8
2 0 5

(c) 3 3 4
0 0 9
0 3 1
0 5 8
0 6 5

(d) 3 3 4
1 1 9
2 1 1
2 3 8
3 1 5

Question 47

Which of the following statement is correct about the function fun( ) given below?

```
# include <stdio.h>
struct sparse
{
    int *sp ;
    int row ;
} ;
void fun ( struct sparse *p, struct sparse s )
{
    int x, q, pos1, pos2, col, elem, c, y, i ;
    p -> sp = ( int * ) malloc ( s.row * 3 * sizeof ( int ) ) ;
    p -> row = s.row ;
    * ( p -> sp + 0 ) = * ( s.sp + 1 ) ;
    * ( p -> sp + 1 ) = * ( s.sp + 0 ) ;
    * ( p -> sp + 2 ) = * ( s.sp + 2 ) ;
    col = * ( p -> sp + 1 ) ;
    elem = * ( p -> sp + 2 ) ;
    if ( elem <= 0 )
        return ;
    x = 1 ;
    for ( c = 0 ; c < col ; c++ )
    {
        for ( y = 1 ; y <= elem ; y++ )
        {
            q = y * 3 + 1 ;
            if ( * ( s.sp + q ) == c )
            {
                pos2 = x * 3 + 0 ;
                pos1 = y * 3 + 1 ;
                * ( p -> sp + pos2 ) = * ( s.sp + pos1 ) ;
                pos2 = x * 3 + 1 ;
                pos1 = y * 3 + 0 ;
```

```
                    * ( p -> sp + pos2 ) = * ( s.sp + pos1 ) ;
                    pos2 = x * 3 + 2 ;
                    pos1 = y * 3 + 2 ;
                    * ( p -> sp + pos2 ) = * ( s.sp + pos1 ) ;
                    x++ ;
                }
            }
        }
}
```

(a) The code creates a 3-tuple from the given sparse matrix.

(b) The code creates transpose of a 3-tuple.

(c) The code finds that the matrix is diagonal.

(d) The code finds that the matrix is tridiagonal.

Question 48

What will be the output of the code snippet given below if the elements of sparse matrix are 4 0 1 0 0 3 -2 0 0?

```
void fun ( struct sparse *p, struct sparse s )
{
    int x, q, pos1, pos2, col, elem, c, y, i ;
    p -> sp = ( int * ) malloc ( s.row * 3 * sizeof ( int ) ) ;
    p -> row = s.row ;
    * ( p -> sp + 0 ) = * ( s.sp + 1 ) ;
    * ( p -> sp + 1 ) = * ( s.sp + 0 ) ;
    * ( p -> sp + 2 ) = * ( s.sp + 2 ) ;
    col = * ( p -> sp + 1 ) ;
    elem = * ( p -> sp + 2 ) ;
    if ( elem <= 0 )
        return ;
    x = 1 ;
```

```
    for ( c = 0 ; c < col ; c++ )
    {
        for ( y = 1 ; y <= elem ; y++ )
        {
            q = y * 3 + 1 ;
            if ( * ( s.sp + q ) == c )
            {
                pos2 = x * 3 + 0 ;
                pos1 = y * 3 + 1 ;
                * ( p -> sp + pos2 ) = * ( s.sp + pos1 ) ;
                pos2 = x * 3 + 1 ;
                pos1 = y * 3 + 0 ;
                * ( p -> sp + pos2 ) = * ( s.sp + pos1 ) ;
                pos2 = x * 3 + 2 ;
                pos1 = y * 3 + 2 ;
                * ( p -> sp + pos2 ) = * ( s.sp + pos1 ) ;
                x++ ;
            }
        }
    }
    for ( i = 0 ; i < p -> row * 3 ; i++ )
    {
        if ( i % 3 == 0 )
            printf ( "\n" ) ;
        printf ( "%d ", * ( p -> sp + i ) ) ;
    }
}
```

(a) 3 3 4
0 0 4
0 2 -2
2 0 1
2 1 3

(b) 3 3 4

0 0 4
0 2 1
1 2 3
2 0 -2

(c) 4 0 1
0 0 3
-2 0 0

(d) 3 3 4
1 1 4
1 3 1
2 3 3
3 1 -2

Question 49

What will be the output of the code snippet given below if the elements of sparse matrix are 4 0 1 0 0 3 -2 0 0?

```
void fun ( struct sparse *p, struct sparse s )
{
    int x, q, pos1, pos2, col, elem, c, y, i ;
    p -> sp =  ( int * ) malloc ( s.row * 3 * sizeof ( int ) ) ;
    p -> row = s.row ;
    * ( p -> sp + 0 ) = * ( s.sp + 1 ) ;
    * ( p -> sp + 1 ) = * ( s.sp + 0 ) ;
    * ( p -> sp + 2 ) = * ( s.sp + 2 ) ;
    col = * ( p -> sp + 1 ) ;
    elem = * ( p -> sp + 2 ) ;
    if ( elem <= 0 )
        return ;
    x = 1 ;
    for ( c = 0 ; c < col ; c++ )
    {
```

```
            for ( y = 1 ; y <= elem ; y++ )
            {
                q = y * 3 + 1 ;
                if ( * ( s.sp + q ) == c )
                {
                    pos1 = x * 3 + 0 ;
                    pos2 = y * 3 + 1 ;
                    * ( p -> sp + pos2 ) = * ( s.sp + pos1 ) ;
                    pos1 = x * 3 + 1 ;
                    pos2 = y * 3 + 0 ;
                    * ( p -> sp + pos2 ) = * ( s.sp + pos1 ) ;
                    pos1 = x * 3 + 2 ;
                    pos2 = y * 3 + 2 ;
                    * ( p -> sp + pos2 ) = * ( s.sp + pos1 ) ;
                    x++ ;
                }
            }
        }
        for ( i = 0 ; i < p -> row * 3 ; i++ )
        {
            if ( i % 3 == 0 )
                printf ( "\n" ) ;
            printf ( "%d ", * ( p -> sp + i ) ) ;
        }
}
```

(a) 3 3 4
0 0 4
0 2 -2
2 0 1
2 1 3

(b) 3 3 4
0 0 4
0 2 1

1 2 3
2 0 -2

(c) 3 3 4
0 0 4
2 1 3
0 2 -2
2 0 1

(d) 3 3 4
1 1 4
1 3 1
2 3 3
3 1 -2

Question 50

Which of the following statement is correct about the code snippet given below?

```
typedef struct element
{
    int row, col, val ;
} element ;
typedef struct sparse
{
    int elem, r, c ;
    element data[ 10 ] ;
} spmat ;
void fun ( spmat *a )
{
    int i, j, count = 0 ;
    for ( i = 0 ; i < a -> c  ; i++ )
    {
        count = 0 ;
        for ( j = 0 ; j < a -> elem ; j++ )
```

```
            if ( a ->data [ j ].col == i )
                count++ ;
    }
}
```

(a) The code finds number of elements in each row.

(b) The code finds total number of elements in the matrix.

(c) The code finds number of elements in each column.

(d) The code finds total number of non-zero elements in the matrix.

Question 51

Which of the following statement is correct about the code snippet given below?

```
typedef struct element
{
    int row, col, val ;
} element ;
typedef struct sparse
{
    int elem, r, c ;
    element data[ 10 ] ;
} spmat ;
void fun ( spmat *a )
{
    int i, j, col[ 10 ] ;
    for ( i = 0 ; i < a -> c ; i++ )
        col[ i ] = 0 ;
    for ( i = 0 ; i < a -> elem ; i++ )
    {
        j = a -> data[ i ].col ;
        col[ j ] += 1 ;
    }
```

```
}
```

(a) col[i] stores the number of elements in the ith column.

(b) col[i] stores the number of non-zero elements in the ith column.

(c) col[i] stores the total number of non-zero elements in the matrix.

(d) col[i] stores the number of elements in the matrix.

Question 52

Which of the following statement is correct about the code snippet given below?

```
typedef struct element
{
    int row, col, val ;
} element ;
typedef struct sparse
{
    int elem, r, c ;
    element data[ 10 ] ;
} spmat ;
void fun ( spmat *a, spmat *b )
{
    int i ;
    b -> r = a -> c ;
    b -> c = a -> r ;
    b -> elem = a -> elem ;
    for ( i = 0 ; i < a -> elem ; i++ )
    {
        b -> data[ i ].row = a -> data[ i ].col ;
        b -> data[ i ].col = a -> data[ i ].row ;
        b -> data[ i ].val = a -> data[ i ].val ;
    }
}
```

(a) The code copies elements of matrix a into matrix b.

(b) The code finds transpose of a matrix.

(c) The code copies elements of matrix b into matrix a.

(d) The code finds that the matrix is orthogonal.

Question 53

Which of the following statement is correct about the code snippet given below?

```
typedef struct element
{
    int row, col, val ;
} element ;
typedef struct sparse
{
    int elem, r, c ;
    element data[ 10 ] ;
} spmat ;
void fun ( spmat *a, spmat *b )
{
    int i, j, k = 0 ;
    b -> r = a -> c ;
    b -> c = a -> r ;
    b -> elem = a -> elem ;
    for ( i = 0 ; i < a -> c ; i++ )
    {
        for ( j = 0 ; j < a -> elem ; j++ )
        {
            if ( a -> data[ j ].col == i )
            {
                b -> data[ k ].row = i ;
                b -> data[ k ].col = a -> data[ j ].row ;
```

```
                    b -> data[ k ].val = a -> data[ j ].val ;
                    k++ ;
                }
            }
        }
}
```

(a) The code finds that the matrix is orthogonal.

(b) The code finds that the matrix is tridiagonal.

(c) The code finds that the matrix is square.

(d) The code finds transpose of a matrix.

Question 54

Which of the following statement is correct about the code snippet given below?

```
typedef struct element
{
    int row, col, val ;
} element ;
typedef struct sparse
{
    int elem, r, c ;
    element data[ 10 ] ;
} spmat ;
void fun ( spmat *a, spmat *b )
{
    int i, j, s[ 10 ], col[ 10 ] ;
    for ( i = 0 ; i < a -> c ; i++ )
        col[ i ] = 0 ;
    for ( i = 0 ; i < a -> elem ; i++ )
        col[ a -> data[ i ].col ] += 1 ;
    s[ 0 ] = 0 ;
```

```
        for ( i = 1 ; i < a -> c ; i++ )
            s[ i ] = s[ i - 1 ] + col[ i - 1 ] ;
        for ( i = 0 ; i < a -> elem ; i++ )
        {
            j = a -> data[ i ].col ;
            b -> data[ s[ j ] ].row = a -> data[ i ].col ;
            b -> data[ s[ j ] ].col = a -> data[ i ].row ;
            b -> data[ s[ j ] ].val = a -> data[ i ].val ;
            s[ j ] += 1 ;
        }
        b -> r = a -> c ;
        b -> c = a -> r ;
        b -> elem = a -> elem ;
}
```

(a) The code finds whether the matrix is a orthogonal matrix.

(b) The code finds whether the matrix is a tridiagonal matrix.

(c) The code finds whether the matrix is a square matrix.

(d) The code finds transpose of the matrix.

Question 55

Which of the following statement is correct about the code snippet given below?

```
void fun ( struct sparse s )
{
    struct node *temp ;
    int r = s.smat -> noofrows ;
    int i ;
    for ( i = 0 ; i < r ; i++ )
    {
        temp = s.rhead[ i ] -> right ;
        if ( temp != NULL )
```

```
            {
                while ( temp -> right != NULL )
                {
                    printf ( "%d %d %d", temp -> row, temp -> col, temp -> val ) ;
                    temp = temp -> right ;
                }
                if ( temp -> row == i )
                    printf ( "%d %d %d", temp -> row, temp -> col, temp -> val ) ;
            }
        }
}
```

(a) The code displays linked list of zeros.

(b) The code displays the linked list of 3-tuple form.

(c) The code displays linked list of number of rows, columns and elements in 3-tuple form.

(d) The code displays linked list of number of rows, columns and elements in an original sparse matrix.

Question 56

Which of the following statement is correct about the code snippet given below?

```
void fun ( struct sparse *p )
{
    int i, c, r = p -> smat -> noofrows ;
    struct rheadnode *rh ;
    struct node *temp1, *temp2 ;
    for ( i = r - 1 ; i >= 0 ; i-- )
    {
        rh = p -> rhead[ i ] ;
        temp1 = rh -> right ;
        while ( temp1 != NULL )
        {
```

```
                temp2 = temp1 -> right ;
                free ( temp1 ) ;
                temp1 = temp2 ;
            }
        }
        for ( i = r - 1 ; i >= 0 ; i-- )
            free ( p -> rhead[ i ] ) ;
        c = p -> smat -> noofcols ;
        for ( i = c - 1 ; i >= 0 ; i-- )
            free ( p -> chead[ i ] ) ;
}
```

(a) The code deallocates memory of node by traversing row-wise.

(b) The code deallocates memory of row head nodes.

(c) The code deallocates memory of column head nodes.

(d) All of the above.

Question 57

Which of the following statement is correct about the code snippet given below?

```
void fun ( struct sparse *p )
{
    int i ;
    for ( i = 0 ; i < 3 ; i++ )
        p -> rows[ i ] = ( struct rowhead* ) malloc ( sizeof ( struct rowhead ) ) ;
    for ( i = 0 ; i < 2 ; i++ )
    {
        p -> rows[ i ] -> nextrow = p -> rows[ i + 1 ] ;
        p -> rows[ i ] -> right = NULL ;
        p -> rows[ i ] -> row_number = i ;
    }
    p -> rows[ i ] -> right = NULL ;
```

```
    p -> rows[ i ] -> nextrow = NULL ;
    for ( i = 0 ; i < 3 ; i++ )
        p -> cols[ i ] = ( struct column* ) malloc ( sizeof ( struct column ) ) ;
    for ( i = 0 ; i < 2 ; i++ )
    {
        p -> cols[ i ] -> nextcol = p -> cols[ i + 1 ] ;
        p -> cols[ i ] -> down = NULL ;
        p -> cols[ i ] -> col_number = i ;
    }
    p -> cols[ i ] -> down = NULL ;
    p -> cols[ i ] -> nextcol = NULL ;
    p -> smat = ( struct spmat* ) malloc ( sizeof ( struct spmat ) ) ;
    p -> smat -> firstrow = p -> rows[ 0 ] ;
    p -> smat -> firstcol = p -> cols[ 0 ] ;
    p -> smat -> noofrows = 3 ;
    p -> smat -> noofcols = 3 ;
}
```

(a) The code initializes linked list of sparse matrix.

(b) The code finds transpose of sparse matrix using linked list.

(c) The code finds orthogonal matrix using linked list.

(d) The code finds lower triangular matrix using linked list.

Question 58

Which of the following statement is correct about the code snippet given below?

```
void fun ( struct spmat *s, int rowno, int colno, int val )
{
    int i ;
    struct node *p, *q, *r ;
    struct rowhead *rw ;
    struct column *cl ;
```

```
p = ( struct node* ) malloc ( sizeof ( struct node ) ) ;
p -> row = rowno ;
p -> col = colno ;
p -> val = val ;
rw = s -> firstrow ;
for ( i = 0 ; i < rowno ; i ++ )
        r = rw -> nextrow ;
q = rw -> right ;
if ( q == NULL )
{
        rw -> right = p ;
        p -> right = NULL ;
}
else
{
        while ( ( q != NULL ) )
        {
                r = q ;
                q = q -> right ;
        }
        r -> right = p ;
        p -> right = q ;
}
cl = s -> firstcol ;
for ( i = 0 ; i < colno ; i++ )
        cl = cl -> nextcol ;
q = cl -> down ;
if ( q == NULL )
{
        cl -> down = p ;
        p -> down = NULL ;
}
else
{
        while ( ( q != NULL ) && ( q -> row < rowno ) )
```

```
        {
            r = q ;
            q = q -> down ;
        }
        r -> down = p ;
        p -> down = q ;
    }
}
```

(a) The code retrieves an element from given row and column number of matrix.

(b) The code deletes an element from given row and column number of matrix.

(c) The code inserts an element when the row number, column number and value are provided by user.

(d) The code deletes all the zeros from the matrix.

Question 59

Which of the following statement is correct about the code snippet given below where function fun1( ) and fun2( ) searches for an element present at i^{th} row and j^{th} column respectively?

```
void fun ( struct sprase *p, struct sparse a, struct sparse b )
{
    int sum, k = 1, position, posi, flaga, flagb, i, j ;
    p -> result = ( int * ) malloc ( 20 * 3 * sizeof ( int ) ) ;
    for ( i = 0 ; i < * ( a.sp + 0 * 3 + 0 ) ; i++ )
    {
        for ( j = 0 ; j < * ( b.sp + 0 * 3 + 1 ) ; j++ )
        {
            fun1 ( a.sp, i, &position, &flaga ) ;
            if ( flaga == 1 )
            {
                sum = 0 ;
```

```
                while ( * ( a.sp + position * 3 + 0 ) == i )
                {
                    fun2 ( b.sp, j, * ( a.sp + position * 3 + 1 ), &posi, &flagb ) ;
                    if ( flagb == 1 )
                        sum = sum + * ( a.sp + position * 3 + 2 ) * * ( b.sp + posi * 3 + 2 )
;
                    position += 1 ;
                }
                if ( sum != 0 )
                {
                    * ( p -> result + k * 3 + 0 ) = i ;
                    * ( p -> result + k * 3 + 1 ) = j ;
                    * ( p -> result + k * 3 + 2 ) = sum ;
                    k += 1 ;
                }
            }
        }
    }
    * ( p -> result + 0 * 3 + 0 ) = * ( a.sp + 0 * 3 + 0 ) ;
    * ( p -> result + 0 * 3 + 1 ) = * ( b.sp + 0 * 3 + 1 ) ;
    * ( p -> result + 0 * 3 + 2 ) = k - 1 ;
}
```

(a) The code finds addition of two sparse matrices.

(b) The code copies elements of sparse matrix a into sparse matrix b.

(c) The code finds sum of all elements in sparse matrix a.

(d) The code finds multiplication of two sparse matrices.

Question 60

What will be the output of the code snippet given below if the elements in 3-tuple are 3 3 4 0 1 4 0 2 1 1 2 1 2 0 1 and 3 3 3 0 0 2 1 0 1 1 2 2?

```
void fun1 ( int *sp, int ii, int *p, int *flag )
{
    int j ;
    *flag = 2 ;
    for ( j = 1 ; j <= * ( sp + 0 * 3 + 2 ) ; j++ )
    {
        if ( * ( sp + j * 3 + 0 ) == ii )
        {
            *p = j ;
            *flag = 1 ;
            return ;
        }
    }
}
void fun2 ( int *sp, int jj, int colofa, int *p, int *flag )
{
    int j ;
    *flag = 2 ;
    for ( j = 1 ; j <= * ( sp + 0 * 3 + 2 ) ; j++ )
    {
        if ( * ( sp + j * 3 + 1 ) == jj && * ( sp + j * 3 + 0 ) == colofa )
        {
            *p = j ;
            *flag = 1 ;
            return ;
        }
    }
}
void fun ( struct sprase *p, struct sparse a, struct sparse b )
{
    int sum, k = 1, position, posi, flaga, flagb, i, j ;
    p -> result = ( int * ) malloc ( 20 * 3 * sizeof ( int ) ) ;
    for ( i = 0 ; i < * ( a.sp + 0 * 3 + 0 ) ; i++ )
    {
        for ( j = 0 ; j < * ( b.sp + 0 * 3 + 1 ) ; j++ )
```

```
        {
            fun1 ( a.sp, i, &position, &flaga ) ;
            if ( flaga == 1 )
            {
                sum = 0 ;
                while ( * ( a.sp + position * 3 + 0 ) == i )
                {
                    fun2 ( b.sp, j, * ( a.sp + position * 3 + 1 ), &posi, &flagb ) ;
                    if ( flagb == 1 )
                        sum = sum + * ( a.sp + position * 3 + 2 ) * * ( b.sp + posi * 3 + 2) ;
                    position += 1 ;
                }
                if ( sum != 0 )
                {
                    * ( p -> result + k * 3 + 0 ) = i ;
                    * ( p -> result + k * 3 + 1 ) = j ;
                    * ( p -> result + k * 3 + 2 ) = sum ;
                    k += 1 ;
                }
            }
        }
    }
    * ( p -> result + 0 * 3 + 0 ) = * ( a.sp + 0 * 3 + 0 ) ;
    * ( p -> result + 0 * 3 + 1 ) = * ( b.sp + 0 * 3 + 1 ) ;
    * ( p -> result + 0 * 3 + 2 ) = k - 1 ;
}
```

(a) 3 3 4
0 1 4
0 2 1
1 2 1
2 0 1

(b) 3 3 3
0 0 4

0 2 8
2 0 2

(c) 3 3 3
0 0 2
1 0 1
1 2 2

(d) 3 3 4
1 2 4
1 3 1
2 3 1
3 1 1

Answers

Q. 1 – C	Q. 2 – C	Q. 3 – D
Q. 4 – B	Q. 5 – C	Q. 6 – C
Q. 7 – D	Q. 8 – A	Q. 9 – D
Q. 10 – A	Q. 11 – A	Q. 12 – C
Q. 13 – A	Q. 14 – C	Q. 15 – B
Q. 16 – B	Q. 17 – A	Q. 18 – A
Q. 19 – A	Q. 20 – C	Q. 21 – D
Q. 22 – B	Q. 23 – B	Q. 24 – C
Q. 25 – A	Q. 26 – D	Q. 27 – B
Q. 28 – B	Q. 29 – D	Q. 30 – A
Q. 31 – A	Q. 32 – B	Q. 33 – B
Q. 34 – B	Q. 35 – C	Q. 36 – B
Q. 37 – D	Q. 38 – A	Q. 39 – C
Q. 40 – B	Q. 41 – D	Q. 42 – C
Q. 43 – B	Q. 44 – A	Q. 45 – D
Q. 46 – C	Q. 47 – B	Q. 48 – A

Q. 49 – C	Q. 50 – C	Q. 51 – A
Q. 52 – B	Q. 53 – D	Q. 54 – D
Q. 55 – B	Q. 56 – D	Q. 57 – A
Q. 58 – C	Q. 59 – D	Q. 60 – B

5

Stacks

Question 1

What is a stack?

(a) A stack is a linear list in which insertion and deletion takes place at the same end.

(b) A stack is a linear list in which insertion and deletion takes place at the different ends.

(c) A stack is a non-linear list in which insertion and deletion takes place at the same end.

(d) A stack is a non-linear list in which insertion and deletion takes place at the different ends.

Question 2

Stack is a ________ structure.

(a) First In First Out

(b) First In Last Out

(c) Last In First Out

(d) Last in Last Out

Question 3

A stack is a data structure in which addition of new element or deletion of an existing element always takes place at an end called ______.

(a) Top

(b) Bottom

(c) Front

(d) Rear

Question 4

Adding an element to the stack means

(a) Placing an element at the front end

(b) Placing an element at the top

(c) Placing an element at the rear end

(d) None of the above

Question 5

Pushing an element to a stack means

(a) Removing an element from the stack

(b) Searching a given element in the stack

(c) Adding a new element to the stack

(d) Sorting the elements in the stack

Question 6

Popping an element from the stack means

(a) Removing an element from the stack

(b) Searching a given element in the stack

(c) Adding a new element to the stack

(d) Sorting the elements in the stack

Question 7

In _______ notation the operator precedes the two operands in a binary operation.

(a) Infix

(b) Postfix

(c) Prefix

(d) Top

Question 8

In ________ notation the operator follows the two operands in a binary operation.

(a) Prefix

(b) Postfix

(c) Infix

(d) None of the above

Question 9

Which of the following operator precedence is followed while evaluating an infix expression?

(a) Highest priority: Exponentiation ($)
Next highest priority: Multiplication (*) and Division (/)
Lowest priority: Addition (+) and Subtraction (-)

(b) Highest priority: Multiplication (*)
Next highest priority: Exponentiation ($) and Division (/)
Lowest priority: Addition (+) and Subtraction (-)

(c) Highest priority: Multiplication (*) and Division (/)
Next highest priority: Exponentiation ($)
Lowest priority: Addition (+) and Subtraction (-)

(d) Highest priority: Addition (+) and Subtraction (-)
Next highest priority: Exponentiation ($)
Lowest priority: Multiplication (*) and Division (/)

Question 10

Which of the following features does the prefix and postfix expressions have?

(a) The operands maintain the same order as in the equivalent infix expression.

(b) Parentheses are not needed to designate the expression unambiguously.

(c) While evaluating the expression the priority of the operators is irrelevant.

(d) All of the above.

Question 11

Which of the following statement is incorrect?

(a) The place where stacks are frequently used is in evaluation of arithmetic expression.

(b) A stack is generally implemented with two basic operations—push and pop.

(c) Parentheses are required while writing expressions in Polish notation.

(d) In prefix notation the operator comes before the operands.

Question 12

The implementation of stack can be done using ______ & _____.

(a) Linked list & Array.

(b) Array & Structure.

(c) String & Linked list.

(d) Structure and Linked list.

Question 13

Which of the element would get deleted first from the stack?

(a) The element at the bottom of the stack.

(b) The element at the top of the stack.

(c) The element in the middle of the stack.

(d) Any specified element.

Question 14

In the element which will be added first in the stack implemented as linked list, the link part would contain ______.

(a) The address of the next element added in the stack.

(b) The address of the previous element added in the stack.

(c) NULL.

(d) Both A and B.

Question 15

What is the type of the expression 2 + 3 * 4?

(a) Infix Expression

(b) Postfix Expression

(c) Prefix Expression

(d) Priority Expression

Question 16

What is the type of the expression 6 9 5 + - ?

(a) Infix Expression

(b) Postfix Expression

(c) Prefix Expression

(d) Priority Expression

Question 17

What is the type of the expression * 9 / 3 6?

(a) Infix Expression

(b) Postfix Expression

(c) Prefix Expression

(d) Priority Expression

Question 18

In ______ notation the operator comes between the two operands.

(a) Infix Expression

(b) Postfix Expression

(c) Prefix Expression

(d) Priority Expression

Question 19

In ______ notation the operator comes before the operands.

(a) Infix

(b) Prefix

(c) Postfix

(d) Priority

Question 20

In ______ notation the operator comes after the operands.

(a) Infix

(b) Prefix

(c) Postfix

(d) Priority

Question 21

Which of the following prefix expression is obtained on converting the infix expression

(A + B) / (C - D) ?

(a) / + A B – C D

(d) A B - C *

Question 28

Which of the following postfix expression is obtained on converting the infix expression (A + B) / C ?

(a) A B C + /

(b) A B / C +

(c) A B + C /

(d) A B C / +

Question 29

Which of the following infix expression is obtained on converting the prefix expression - + A B C?

(a) A – B + C

(b) B + C – A

(c) A + B – C

(d) C – A + B

Question 30

Which of the following infix expression is obtained on converting the postfix expression A B C + - ?

(a) A – B + C

(b) B + C – A

(c) A + B – C

(d) C – A + B

Question 31

Which of the following postfix expression is obtained on converting the infix expression

(A + B $ D) / (E - F) + G?

(a) A B D $ + E F - / G +

(b) A B D + $ E F / - G +

(c) A B D + $ E F - / G +

(d) A B D $ + E F / - G +

Question 32

Which of the following postfix expression is obtained on converting the infix expression

A * (B + D) / E - F * (G + H / K) ?

(a) A B D * + E / F G H K / + * -

(b) A B D * + E / F G H K + / * -

(c) A B D + * E / F G H K / + * -

(d) A B D + * E / F G H K / + - *

Question 33

Which of the following postfix expression is obtained on converting the infix expression

(A + B) * (C - D) $ E * F ?

(a) A B + C D - E * $ F *

(b) A B + C D - E $ * F *

(c) A B - C D + E $ * F *

(d) A B + C D - E * F $ *

Question 34

Which of the following prefix expression is obtained on converting the infix expression (A+B$D)/(E-F)+G?

(a) ++/A$BD−EFG

(b) /++A$BD−EFG

(c) +/+A-BD$EFG

(d) +/+A$BD−EFG

Question 35

Which of the following prefix expression is obtained on converting the infix expression A*(B+D)/E-F*(G+H/K)?

(a) */-A+BDE*F+G/HK

(b) /*-A+BDE+F*G/HK

(c) -/*A+BDE*F+G/HK

(d) /*-A+BDE*F+G/HK

Question 36

Which of the following prefix expression is obtained on converting the infix expression (A+B)*(C−D)$E*F?

(a) *+*AB$-CDEF

(b) **+AB$-CDEF

(c) +**AB$-CDEF

(d) **+AB-$CDEF

Question 37

Which of the following infix expression is obtained on converting the prefix expression

+ - $ A B C * * * D E F G?

(a) A - B $ C + D * E * F * G

(b) A $ B + C - D * E * F * G

(c) A $ B - C * D + E * F * G

(d) A $ B - C + D * E * F * G

Question 38

Which of the following infix expression is obtained on converting the postfix expression

A B $ C – D E * F * G * +?

(a) A - B $ C + D * E * F * G

(b) A $ B + C - D * E * F * G

(c) A $ B - C * D + E * F * G

(d) A $ B - C + D * E * F * G

Question 39

Which of the following infix expression is obtained on converting the postfix expression

A B $ C D * - E F * G * +?

(a) A - B $ C + D * E * F * G

(b) A $ B + C - D * E * F * G

(c) A $ B - C * D + E * F * G

(d) A $ B - C + D * E * F * G

Question 40

Which of the following infix expression is obtained on converting the postfix expression A B $ C D * - E F $ G / +?

(a) A $ B * C - D + E $ F / G

(b) A $ B - C * D + E $ F / G

(c) A $ B - C * D $ E + F / G

(d) A $ B - C * D / E $ F + G

Question 41

Which of the following postfix expression is obtained on converting the infix expression (A + B) * (C $ (D - E) + F) / G $ (H - J) ?

(a) A B + C D E - $ F + * G H J - $ /

(b) A B + C D E $ - F * * G H J - $ /

(c) A B + C D E $ - F + * G H J $ * /

(d) A B + C D E - $ F + * G H J - / $

Question 42

Which of the following infix expression is obtained on converting the prefix expression + - + A * $ B C D E * / F G H I?

(a) A + B - C * D - E + F / G * H I

(b) A + B $ C * D - E + F / G * H I

(c) A $ B + C * D - E + F / G * H I

(d) A + B $ C * D - E + F * G / H I

Question 43

Which of the following infix expression is obtained on converting the postfix expression

A B - C + D E F - + $?

(a) A + B - C $ D + E − F

(b) A - B + C $ D + E − F

(c) A - B $ C + D + E − F

(d) A - B + C + D $ E − F

Question 44

Which of the following infix expression is obtained on converting the postfix expression

A B C D E - + $ * E F * - ?

(a) A * B $ C + D - E - E * F

(b) A $ B * C + D - E - E * F

(c) A * B + C $ D - E - E * F

(d) A * B $ C - D + E - E * F

Question 45

Which of the following prefix expression is obtained on converting the infix expression

4 $ 2 * 3 - 3 + 8 / 4 / (1 + 1) ?

(a) + - * $ 4 2 3 3 / + 8 4 + 1 1

(b) + - * $ 4 2 3 3 / / 8 4 + 1 1

(c) + * - $ 4 2 3 3 / / 8 4 + 1 1

(d) - * + $ 4 2 3 3 / / 8 4 + 1 1

Question 46

Which of following postfix expression is obtained on converting the infix expression

4 $ 2 * 3 - 3 + 8 / 4 / (1 + 1) ?

(a) 4 2 $ 3 * 3 − 8 4 / 1 1 + +

(b) 4 2 $ 3 * 3 − 8 4 / 1 1 + /

(c) 4 2 $ 3 * 3 − 8 4 / 1 1 + / +

(d) 4 2 $ 3 * 3 − 8 4 / 1 1 +

Question 47

Which of the following infix expression is obtained on converting the prefix expression

/ * + A B + $ C - D E F $ G - H J?

(a) (A + B) $ (C * (D - E) + F) / G $ (H - J)

(b) (A + B) * (C $ (D + E) - F) / G $ (H - J)

(c) (A + B) * (C $ (D - E) + F) / G $ (H - J)

(d) (A + B) * (C $ (D - E) + F) $ G / (H - J)

Question 48

Which of the following prefix expression is obtained on converting the postfix expression

4 2 $ 3 * 3 - 8 4 / 1 1 + / + ?

(a) + - * $ 4 2 3 3 / / 8 4 + 1 1

(b) + * $ 4 2 3 3 / / 8 4 + 1 1

(c) + - $ 4 2 3 3 / / 8 4 + 1 1

(d) * $ + - 4 2 3 3 / / 8 4 + 1 1

Question 49

Which of the following prefix expression is obtained on converting the postfix expression

A B – C + D E F - + $?

(a) $ - + A B C + D - E F

(b) $ + - A B C - D + E F

(c) $ + - A B C + D - E F

(d) + - $ A B C + D - E F

Question 50

Which of the following prefix expression is obtained on converting the postfix expression

A B D + * E / F G H K / + * - ?

(a) - / * A + B D E * F + G / H K

(b) / * - A + B D E * F + G / H K

(c) / - * A + B D E * F + G / H K

(d) - * / A + B D E + F * G / H K

Question 51

Which of the following prefix expression is obtained on converting the postfix expression

4 5 + 2 3 + $ 7 3 + /?

(a) / + $ 4 5 + 2 3 + 7 3

(b) / $ + 4 3 + 5 3 + 7 3

(c) $ / + 4 5 / 2 3 + 7 3

(d) / $ + 4 5 + 2 3 + 7 3

Question 52

Which of the following prefix expression is obtained on converting the postfix expression

4 9 + 5 8 4 - $ * 3 /?

(a) / * + 4 9 $ 5 - 8 4 3

(b) + * / 4 9 $ 5 - 8 4 3

(c) / + * 4 9 $ 5 - 8 4 3

(d) / * + 9 5 - 4 $ 8 4 3

Question 53

Which of the following prefix expression is obtained on converting the postfix expression

A C + B D - $ E F + /?

(a) / + $ A C - B D + E F

(b) / - + A C $ B D + E F

(c) / $ + A C - B D + E F

(d) $ / - A C + B D + E F

Question 54

Which of the following prefix expression is obtained on converting the postfix expression

A B + C D + % C E – F G - * / ?

(a) / + % A B + C D * - C E - F G

(b) % + / A B + C D * - C E - F G

(c) % / + A B + C D - * C E - F G

(d) / % + A B + C D * - C E - F G

Question 55

Which of the following operation is performed by the program given below?

```
# include <stdio.h>
# include <conio.h>
# include <malloc.h>

struct node
{
    int data ;
    struct node *link ;
} ;
void push ( struct node **, int ) ;
void copy ( struct node *, struct node ** ) ;
void display ( struct node * ) ;

int main( )
{
    struct node *s, *p ;
    int i ;
    s = p = NULL ;
    push ( &s, 11 ) ;
    push ( &s, -3 ) ;
    push ( &s, 18 ) ;
    push ( &s, 29 ) ;
    push ( &s, 31 ) ;
    push ( &s, 16 ) ;
    printf ( "\nContent of the first stack: " ) ;
    display ( s ) ;
    copy ( s, &p ) ;
    printf ( "\nContent of the second stack: " ) ;
    display ( p ) ;
    return 0 ;
}
```

```
void push ( struct node **top, int item )
{
      struct node *temp ;
      temp = ( struct node * ) malloc ( sizeof ( struct node ) ) ;

      if ( temp == NULL )
            printf ( "\nStack is full" ) ;

      temp -> data = item ;
      temp -> link = *top ;
      *top = temp ;
}

void copy ( struct node *s, struct node **top )
{
      struct node *temp ;
      while ( s != NULL )
      {
            temp = ( struct node * ) malloc ( sizeof ( struct node ) ) ;

            if ( temp == NULL )
                  printf ( "\n stack is full" ) ;

            temp -> data = s -> data ;
            temp -> link = *top ;
            *top = temp ;
            s = s -> link ;
      }
}

void display ( struct node *top )
{
      printf ( "\n" ) ;
```

```
    while ( top != NULL )
    {
        printf ( "%d  ", top -> data ) ;
        top = top -> link ;
    }
}
```

(a) The program is implementing the stack operation using array.

(b) The program is implementing the stack operation using linked list.

(c) The program is copying the content of one stack to another.

(d) The program is implementing a queue using an array.

Question 56

Which of the following statement is correct about the program given below?

```
# include <stdio.h>
# include <conio.h>
# include <malloc.h>

struct node
{
    int data ;
    struct node *link ;
} ;
void push ( struct node **, int ) ;
int pop ( struct node ** ) ;
void delstack ( struct node ** ) ;

int main( )
{
    struct node *s = NULL ;
    int i ;
```

```
        push ( &s, 14 ) ;
        push ( &s, -3 ) ;
        push ( &s, 18 ) ;
        push ( &s, 33 ) ;
        push ( &s, 32 ) ;

        i = pop ( &s ) ;
        printf ( "Item Popped:%d", i ) ;
        return 0 ;
}
void push ( struct node **top, int item )
{
        struct node *temp ;
        temp = ( struct node * ) malloc ( sizeof ( struct node ) ) ;
        if ( temp == NULL )
                printf ( "\n Stack is full" ) ;
        temp -> data = item ;
        temp ->link = *top ;
        *top = temp ;
}
int pop ( struct node **top )
{
        struct node *temp ;
        int item ;
        if ( *top == NULL )
        {
                printf ( "Stack is empty" ) ;
                return NULL ;
        }
        temp = *top ;
        item = temp -> data ;
        *top = ( *top ) -> link ;
        free ( temp ) ;
        return ( item ) ;
}
```

(a) The program is implementing the stack using an array.

(b) The program is implementing the stack using a linked list.

(c) The program is implementing the infix to prefix conversion.

(d) The program is implementing the prefix to postfix conversion.

Question 57

Which of the following option is correct about the program given below?

```
# include <stdio.h>
# include <conio.h>
# define MAX 10

struct stack
{
    int arr[MAX] ;
    int top ;
} ;
void initstack ( struct stack * ) ;
void push ( struct stack *, int item ) ;
int pop ( struct stack * ) ;

int main( )
{
    struct stack s ;
    int i ;
    initstack ( &s ) ;
    push ( &s, 11 ) ;
    push ( &s, 14 ) ;
    push ( &s, 28 ) ;
    push ( &s, 51 ) ;
    push ( &s, 31 ) ;
```

```
        i = pop ( &s ) ;
        printf ( "\n Item popped: %d", i ) ;
        return 0 ;
}
void initstack( struct stack *s )
{
        s -> top = -1 ;
}
void push ( struct stack *s, int item )
{
        if ( s -> top == MAX - 1 )
        {
                printf ( "\n stack is full" ) ;
                return ;
        }
        s -> top++ ;
        s -> arr[s -> top] = item ;
}
int pop ( struct stack *s )
{
        int data ;
        if ( s -> top == -1 )
        {
                printf ( "Stack is empty" ) ;
                return NULL ;
        }
        data = s -> arr[s -> top] ;
        s -> top-- ;
        return data ;
}
```

(a) Error : 'Type mismatch in redeclaration of push'

(b) The program will give runtime error

(c) The program will give output Item Popped : 31

(d) The program will give output Item Popped : 51

Question 58

What will happen when the following program is executed?

```
# include <malloc.h>
struct node
{
    int data ;
    struct node *link
} ;
void push ( struct node **, int ) ;
int main( )
{
    struct node *s = NULL ;
    int i ;
    push ( &s, 14 ) ;
    push ( &s, -3 ) ;
    push ( &s, 18 ) ;
    push ( &s, 29 ) ;
    return 0 ;
}
void push ( struct node **top, int item )
{
    struct node *temp ;
    temp = ( struct node ) malloc ( sizeof ( struct node ) ) ;
    if ( temp == NULL )
        printf ( "Stack is full" ) ;
    temp -> data = item ;
    temp -> link = *top ;
    *top = temp ;
}
```

(a) Error: 'Type mismatch in redeclaration of push'

(b) Error: 'Declaration missing ;'

(c) Error: 'Illegal structure operation'

(d) Error: 'Incompatible type conversion'

Question 59

What will happen when the following program is executed?

```
# include <malloc.h>
struct node
{
    int data ;
    struct node *link ;
} ;
void push ( struct node **, int ) ;
int main( )
{
    struct node *s = NULL ;
    int i ;
    push ( &s, 14 ) ;
    push ( &s, -3 ) ;
    push ( &s, 18 ) ;
    push ( &s, 29 ) ;
    return 0 ;
}
void push ( struct node **top, int item )
{
    struct node *temp ;
    temp = ( struct node ) malloc ( sizeof ( struct node ) ) ;
    if ( temp == NULL )
        printf ( "Stack is full" ) ;
    temp -> data = item ;
```

```
    temp -> link = *top ;
    *top = temp ;
}
```

(a) Error: 'Incompatible type conversion'

(b) Error: 'Statement missing'

(c) Error: 'Illegal structure operation'

(d) Error: 'Illegal structure operation'

Question 60

Which of the following statement is correct about the program given below?

```
# include <malloc.h>
# define MAX 80
int main( )
{
    char str[MAX] ;
    char *t ;
    int c1, c2, i, j ;
    c1 = c2 = 0 ;
    printf ( "Enter the expression" ) ;
    gets ( str ) ;
    t= str ;
    while ( *t )
    {
        if ( *t == '(' )
            c1++ ;
        if ( *t == ')' )
            c2++;
        t++ ;
    }
    if ( c1 == c2 )
```

```
        printf ( "\nStrings of opening and closing parenthesis is well formed. " ) ;
    else
        printf ( "\nStrings of opening and closing parenthesis is not well formed. " ) ;
    return 0 ;
}
```

(a) It checks whether expression is a legal C expression or not.

(b) It checks whether a string of opening and closing parenthesis is well formed or not.

(c) It checks the number of variables in the string.

(d) None of the above.

Answers

Q. 1 – A	Q. 2 – C	Q. 3 – A
Q. 4 – B	Q. 5 – C	Q. 6 – A
Q. 7 – C	Q. 8 – B	Q. 9 – A
Q. 10 – D	Q. 11 – C	Q. 12 – A
Q. 13 – B	Q. 14 – C	Q. 15 – A
Q. 16 – B	Q. 17 – C	Q. 18 – A
Q. 19 – B	Q. 20 – C	Q. 21 – A
Q. 22 – A	Q. 23 – B	Q. 24 – A
Q. 25 – C	Q. 26 – D	Q. 27 – B
Q. 28 – C	Q. 29 – C	Q. 30 – A
Q. 31 – A	Q. 32 – C	Q. 33 – B
Q. 34 – D	Q. 35 – C	Q. 36 – B
Q. 37 – D	Q. 38 – D	Q. 39 – C
Q. 40 – B	Q. 41 – A	Q. 42 – B
Q. 43 – B	Q. 44 – A	Q. 45 – B
Q. 46 – C	Q. 47 – C	Q. 48 – A

Q. 49 – C	Q. 50 – A	Q. 51 – D
Q. 52 – A	Q. 53 – C	Q. 54 – D
Q. 55 – C	Q. 56 – B	Q. 57 – C
Q. 58 – B	Q. 59 – A	Q. 60 – B

6

Queues

Question 1

What is queue?

(a) A queue is a linear list in which addition and deletion takes place at different ends.

(b) A queue is a linear list in which addition and deletion takes place at same ends.

(c) A queue is a non-linear list in which addition and deletion takes place at different ends.

(d) A queue is a non-linear list in which addition and deletion takes place at same ends.

Question 2

The end at which new elements are added is called the _____.

(a) Rear

(b) Front

(c) Top

(d) Bottom

Question 3

The end at which old elements are deleted is called the _____.

(a) Top

(b) Bottom

(c) Rear

(d) Front

Question 4

A queue is a _________ list.

(a) Last-in-Last-Out (LILO)

(b) Last-in-First-out (LIFO)

(c) First-in-First-out (FIFO)

(d) First-in-Last-Out (FILO)

Question 5

What is deque?

(a) The word deque is a short form of double-ended queue and defines a data structure in which items can be added or deleted at either the front or rear end.

(b) The word deque is a short form of double-ended queue and defines a data structure in which items can be added or deleted at the front.

(c) The word deque is a short form of double-ended queue and defines a data structure in which items can be added or deleted at the rear end.

(d) The word deque is a short form of double-ended queue and defines a data structure in which items can be added or deleted neither at the front or rear end.

Question 6

What is a priority queue?

(a) A priority queue is a collection of elements where the elements are stored according to the increasing number.

(b) A priority queue is a collection of elements where the elements are stored according to their priority levels.

(c) A priority queue is a short form of double-ended queue and defines a data structure in which items can be added or deleted neither at the front or rear end.

(d) A priority queue is a short form of double-ended queue and defines a data structure in which items can be added or deleted at the rear end.

Question 7

A queue is called __________ when addition as well as deletion of elements can take place at both the ends.

(a) Circular queue

(b) Simple queue

(c) Double-ended queue

(d) Priority queue

Question 8

__________ deque restricts the insertion of elements at one end only, but the deletion of elements can be done at both the ends of a queue.

(a) Input restricted

(b) Output restricted

(c) Priority

(d) Circular

Question 9

__________ deque restricts the deletion of elements at one end only, and allows insertion to be done at both the ends of a deque.

(a) Input restricted

(b) Output restricted

(c) Priority

(d) Circular

Question 10

For a queue built using an array and containing n elements, the value of front would be ______ and rear would be ____.

(a) 1 and n

(b) 0 and n

(c) 0 and n – 1

(d) n – 1 and 0

Question 11

In a circular queue implemented using an array and holding 5 elements, if front is equal to 3 and rear is equal to 4, then the new element get placed at _____ position.

(a) 4

(b) 5

(c) 1

(d) 0

Question 12

What happens when an attempt is made to insert an element in nonempty queue?

(a) Underflow.

(b) Overflow.

(c) Onflow.

(d) Queuefull.

Question 13

What happens when an attempt is made to read an element from an empty queue?

(a) Underflow.

(b) Overflow.

(c) Onflow.

(d) Queuefull.

Question 14

Specify which of the following applications would be suitable for a First-In-First-Out queue.

(a) A program is to keep track of patients as they check into a clinic, assigning them to doctors on a first come, first served basis.

(b) An inventory of parts is to be processed by part number.

(c) A dictionary of words used by spelling checker is to be created.

(d) Customers are to take numbers at a bakery and be served in order when their numbers come up.

Question 15

Queue is a _________.

(a) Linear data structure.

(b) Non - linear data structure.

(c) Both (a) and (b).

(d) Structural data structure.

Question 16

Following are the variations of the deque:

(a) input - output - restricted deque.

(b) input - restricted deque.

(c) Output - restricted deque.

(d) Both (b) and (c).

Question 17

The elements are stored according to their priority in _________.

(a) Queue.

(b) Deque.

(c) priority queue.

(d) priority deque.

Question 18

Which of the following is not valid?

(a) priority queue

(b) priority deque

(c) circular deque

(d) Both (b) and (c)

Question 19

Which of the following represents the scenario given below :

In a circular queue, if the front and rear are in adjacent locations with rear following front.

(a) Overflow

(b) Underflow

(c) Queue is full

(d) Queue is empty

Question 20

Select the correct alternative for the following :

I. Elements in the queue must be in sorted order.

II. Elements in the queue can be accessed in random order.

III. In priority queue the elements are stored according to their priority.

(a) True, True, False.

(b) True, False, True.

(c) False, True, True.

(d) False, False, True.

Question 21

In circular queue deletion takes place at ______.

(a) Only one end.

(b) Both ends.

(c) First time one end and then both ends.

(d) None of the above.

Question 22

For implementing a queue how many pointers are we required to maintain?

(a) 1

(b) 2

(c) 3

(d) 4

Question 23

A deque is a generalization of :

(a) Stack

(b) Queue

(c) Array

(d) Both (a) and (b)

Question 24

A Queue can be implemented using

(a) Arrays

(b) Stack

(c) linked list

(d) Both (b) and (c)

Question 25

Which of the following rule is applied to maintain a priority queue?

(a) The element with a higher priority is processed before any element of lower priority.

(b) The elements with the same priority can be processed in any order.

(c) If there are elements with the same priority, then the element added first in the queue would get processed first.

(d) Both (a) and (c).

Question 26

A circular queue implemented using array would be reported as full only if

(a) last element of array Is occupied.

(b) last few elements are occupied.

(c) all elements are occupied.

(d) first and last elements are occupied.

Question 27

Which of the following is implemented using a queue?

(a) evaluation of postfix expression.

(b) recursion.

(c) storing register values before function call.

(d) receiving keys typed at the keyboard.

Question 28

Which of the following condition correctly checks the overflow condition in a deque if n is the number of elements in the deque?

(a) rear < n and front = 0

(b) rear = 0 and front >= n

(c) rear >= n and front = 0

(d) rear = 0 and front < n

Question 29

Which of the following conditions check the underflow condition in a deque if n is the number of elements in the deque?

(a) front > n and rear > n

(b) front > 0 and rear = 0

(c) front = 0 and rear > n

(d) front = 0 and rear = 0

Question 30

Which of the following conditions correctly check the overflow condition in a queue?

(a) rear >= size – 1

(b) rear = 0

(c) front >= size – 1

(d) front = 0

Question 31

Which of the following conditions correctly check the underflow condition in a queue?

(a) rear = size

(b) rear = -1

(c) front = -1

(d) front = size

Question 32

Implementation of a queue using a ______________ does not have any restrictions on the number of elements it can hold.

(a) Arrays

(b) Strings

(c) Linked list

(d) Stacks

Question 33

What will be the output of the program given below?

```
# include <stdio.h>
# include <conio.h>
# define MAX 5

void addq ( int *, int, int *, int * ) ;
int delq ( int *, int *, int * ) ;

int main( )
{
    int arr[MAX] ;
```

```
        int front = -1, rear = -1, i ;
        addq ( arr, 23, &front, &rear ) ;
        addq ( arr, 9, &front, &rear ) ;
        addq ( arr, 11, &front, &rear ) ;
        addq ( arr, -10, &front, &rear ) ;
        addq ( arr, 25, &front, &rear ) ;
        addq ( arr, 5, &front, &rear ) ;
        i = delq ( arr, &front, &rear ) ;
        printf ( "\nItem deleted: %d", i ) ;
        return 0 ;
}

void addq ( int *arr, int item, int *pfront, int *prear )
{
        if ( *prear == MAX - 1 )
        {
                printf ( "\nQueue is full." ) ;
                return ;
        }
        ( *prear )++ ;
        arr[*prear] = item ;
        if ( *pfront == -1 )
                *pfront = 0 ;
}

int delq ( int *arr, int *pfront, int *prear )
{
        int data ;
        if ( *pfront == -1 )
        {
                printf ( "\nQueue is Empty." ) ;
                return NULL ;
        }
        data = arr[*pfront] ;
        arr[*pfront] = 0 ;
```

```
    if ( *pfront == *prear )
        *pfront = *prear = -1 ;
    else
        ( *pfront )++ ;
    return  data ;
}
```

(a) Queue is full.
Item deleted: 16

(b) Queue is full.
Item deleted: 23

(c) Queue is full.

(d) Queue is empty.

Question 34

What will be the output of the following program given below?

```
# include <stdio.h>
# include <conio.h>
# define MAX 10

void addq ( int *, int, int *, int * ) ;
int delq ( int *, int *, int * ) ;

int main( )
{
    int arr[MAX] ;
    int i, front, rear ;
    front = rear = -1 ;
    for ( i = 0 ; i < MAX ; i++ )
        arr[i] = 0 ;
```

```
    addq ( arr, 45, &front, &rear ) ;
    addq ( arr, 12, &front, &rear ) ;
    addq ( arr, 78, &front, &rear ) ;
    addq ( arr, -9, &front, &rear ) ;
    addq ( arr, 53, &front, &rear ) ;

    i = delq ( arr, &front, &rear ) ;
    printf ( "Item deleted: %d", i ) ;
    return 0 ;
}
void addq ( int *arr, int item, int *pfront, int *prear )
{
    if ( ( *prear == MAX - 1 && *pfront == 0 ) || ( *prear + 1 == *pfront ) )
    {
        printf ( "\nQueue is full." ) ;
        return ;
    }
    if ( *prear == MAX - 1 )
        *prear = 0 ;
    else
        ( *prear )++ ;
    arr[*prear] = item ;
    if ( *pfront == -1 )
        *pfront = 0 ;
}
int delq ( int *arr, int *pfront, int *prear )
{
    int data ;
    if ( *pfront == -1 )
    {
        printf ( "\nQueue is empty." ) ;
        return NULL ;
    }
    data = arr[*prear] ;
```

```
    arr[*prear] = 0 ;
    if ( *pfront == *prear )
    {
        *pfront = -1 ;
        *prear = -1 ;
    }
    else
    {
        if ( *pfront == MAX - 1 )
            *pfront = 0 ;
        else
            ( *pfront )++ ;
    }
    return data ;
}
```

(a) Queue is empty

(b) Queue is full

(c) Item deleted: 45

(d) Item deleted: 53

Question 35

Which of the following operation is performed by the function addq given below?

```
void addq ( int *arr, int item, int *pfront, int *prear )
{
    int i, k ;

    if ( *pfront == 0 && *prear == MAX - 1 )
    {
        printf ( "\nDeque is full.\n" ) ;
        return ;
```

```
    }

    if ( *pfront == -1 )
    {
        *prear = *pfront = 0 ;
        arr[*prear] = item ;
        return ;
    }

    if ( *prear == MAX - 1 )
    {
        k = *pfront - 1 ;
        for ( i = *pfront - 1 ; i < *prear ; i++ )
        {
            k = i ;
            if ( k == MAX - 1 )
                arr[k] = 0 ;
            else
                arr[k] = arr[i + 1] ;
        }
        ( *prear )-- ;
        ( *pfront )-- ;
    }
    ( *prear )++ ;
    arr[*prear] = item ;
}
```

(a) The function addq inserts a new element at the beginning of the queue.

(b) The function addq inserts a new element at the end of the queue.

(c) The function addq deletes an element from the beginning of the queue.

(d) The function addq deletes an element from the end of the queue.

Question 36

Which of the following operation is performed by the following function?

```
void addq ( int *arr, int item, int *pfront, int *prear )
{
    int i, k, c ;

    if ( *pfront == 0 && *prear == MAX - 1 )
    {
        printf ( "\nDeque is full.\n" ) ;
        return ;
    }

    if ( *pfront == -1 )
    {
        *pfront = *prear = 0 ;
        arr[*pfront] = item ;
        return ;
    }

    if ( *prear != MAX - 1 )
    {
        c = count ( arr ) ;
        k = *prear + 1 ;
        for ( i = 1 ; i <= c ; i++ )
        {
            arr[k] = arr[k - 1] ;
            k-- ;
        }
        arr[k] = item ;
        *pfront = k ;
        ( *prear )++ ;
    }
    else
```

```
    {
        ( *pfront )-- ;
        arr[*pfront] = item ;
    }
}
```

(a) The function addq inserts the element at the beginning of the queue.

(b) The function addq inserts the element at the end of the queue.

(c) The function addq deletes an element from the beginning of the queue.

(d) The function addq deletes an element from the end of the queue.

Question 37

Which of the following operation is performed by the following function?

```
void delqueue ( struct queue *q )
{
    struct node *temp ;

    if ( q -> front == NULL )
        return ;

    while ( q -> front != NULL )
    {
        temp = q -> front ;
        q -> front = q -> front -> link ;
        free ( temp ) ;
    }
}
```

(a) The function delqueue deletes the first element in the queue.

(b) The function delqueue frees the allocated memory.

(c) The function delqueue allocates the memory for the new element being added to the queue.

(d) The function delqueue counts the number of elements in the queue.

Question 38

What will be the output for the program given below if the program is executed successfully?

```
# include <stdio.h>
# include <conio.h>
# define MAX 10

void addq ( int *, int, int *, int * ) ;
int delq ( int *, int *, int * ) ;

int main( )
{
    int arr[MAX] ;
    int front = -1, rear = -1, i ;
    addq ( arr, 23, &front, &rear ) ;
    addq ( arr, 9, &front, &rear ) ;
    addq ( arr, 11, &front, &rear ) ;
    addq ( arr, -10, &front, &rear ) ;
    addq ( arr, 25, &front, &rear ) ;
    i = delq ( arr, &front, &rear ) ;
    printf ( "\nItem deleted: %d", i ) ;
    return 0 ;
}
void addq ( int *arr, int item, int *pfront, int *prear )
{
    if ( *prear == MAX - 1 )
    {
        printf ( "\nQueue is full." ) ;
```

```
        return ;
    }
    ( *prear )++ ;
    arr[*prear] = item ;
    if ( *pfront == -1 )
        *pfront = 0 ;
}
int delq ( int *arr, int *pfront, int *prear )
{
    int data ;

    if ( *pfront == -1 )
    {
        printf ( "\nQueue is Empty." ) ;
        return NULL ;
    }
    data = arr[*pfront] ;
    arr[*pfront] = 0 ;
    if ( *pfront == *prear )
        *pfront = *prear = -1 ;
    else
        ( *pfront )++ ;
    return data ;
}
```

(a) Queue is full

(b) Queue is empty

(c) Item deleted: 16

(d) Item deleted: 23

Question 39

What will happen when the program given below is executed?

```
# include <stdio.h>
# include <conio.h>
# define MAX 5
void addq ( int *, int, int *, int * ) ;

int main( )
{
    int arr[MAX] ;
    int front = -1, rear = -1, i ;
    addq ( arr, 23, &front, &rear ) ;
    addq ( arr, 9, &front, &rear ) ;
    addq ( arr, 11, &front, &rear ) ;
    addq ( arr, -10, &front, &rear ) ;
    addq ( arr, 25, &front, &rear ) ;
    addq ( arr, 5, &front, &rear ) ;
    return 0 ;
}
void addq ( int *arr, int item, int *pfront, int *prear )
{
    if ( *prear == MAX - 1 )
    {
        printf ( "\nQueue is full." ) ;
        return ;
    }
    ( *prear )++ ;
    arr[*prear] = item ;
    if ( *pfront == -1 )
        *pfront = 0 ;
}
```

(a) The program will give run time error.

(b) The program will give compile time error.

(c) The program will print: 23.

(d) Output: Queue is full.

Question 40

Which of the following operations is performed by the program given below?

```
# include <stdio.h>
# include <conio.h>
# define MAX 5

struct data
{
    char job[MAX] ;
    int prno ;
    int ord ;
} ;
struct pque
{
    struct data d[MAX] ;
    int front ;
    int rear ;
} ;

void initpque ( struct pque * ) ;
void add ( struct pque *, struct data ) ;
struct data delete ( struct pque * ) ;

int main( )
{
    struct pque q ;
    struct data dt, temp ;
    int i, j = 0 ;
    initpque ( &q ) ;
    printf ( "Enter Job description ( max 4 chars ) and its priority\n" ) ;
    printf ( "Lower the priority number, higher the priority\n" ) ;
```

```
    printf ( "Job Priority\n" ) ;
    for ( i = 0 ; i < MAX ; i++ )
    {
        scanf ( "%s %d", &dt.job, &dt.prno ) ;
        dt.ord = j++ ;
        add ( &q, dt ) ;
    }
    printf ( "\n" ) ;
    printf ( "Process jobs priority wise\n" ) ;
    printf ( "Job\tPriority\n" ) ;
    for ( i = 0 ; i < MAX ; i++ )
    {
        temp = delete ( &q ) ;
        printf ( "%s\t%d\n", temp.job, temp.prno ) ;
    }
    printf ( "\n" ) ;
    return 0 ;
}
void initpque ( struct pque *pq )
{
    int i ;
    pq -> front = pq -> rear = -1 ;
    for ( i = 0 ; i < MAX ; i++ )
    {
        strcpy ( pq -> d[i].job, '\0' ) ;
        pq -> d[i].prno = pq -> d[i].ord = 0 ;
    }
}
void add ( struct pque *pq, struct data dt )
{
    struct data temp ;
    int i, j ;
    if ( pq -> rear == MAX - 1 )
    {
        printf ( "\nQueue is full." ) ;
```

```
            return ;
        }
        pq -> rear++ ;
        pq -> d[pq -> rear] = dt ;
        if ( pq -> front == -1 )
            pq -> front = 0 ;
        for ( i = pq -> front ; i <= pq -> rear ; i++ )
        {
            for ( j = i + 1 ; j <= pq -> rear ; j++ )
            {
                if ( pq -> d[i].prno > pq -> d[j].prno )
                {
                    temp = pq -> d[i] ;
                    pq -> d[i] = pq -> d[j] ;
                    pq -> d[j] = temp ;
                }
                else
                {
                    if ( pq -> d[i].prno == pq -> d[j].prno )
                    {
                        if ( pq -> d[i].ord > pq -> d[j].ord )
                        {
                            temp = pq -> d[i] ;
                            pq -> d[i] = pq -> d[j] ;
                            pq -> d[j] = temp ;
                        }
                    }
                }
            }
        }
}
struct data  delete ( struct pque *pq )
{
    struct data  t ;
    strcpy ( t.job, "" ) ;
```

```
    t.prno = 0 ;
    t.ord = 0 ;
    if ( pq -> front == -1 )
    {
        printf ( "\nQueue is Empty.\n" ) ;
        return t ;
    }
    t = pq -> d[pq -> front] ;
    pq -> d[pq -> front] = t ;
    if ( pq -> front == pq -> rear )
        pq -> front = pq -> rear = -1 ;
    else
        pq -> front++ ;
    return  t ;
}
```

(a) The program implements a deque using linked list.

(b) The program copies the contents of one queue to another queue using linked list.

(c) The program implements a circular queue using arrays.

(d) The program determines the priority of the entered job by the user.

Question 41

What will be the output of the following program?

```
# include <stdio.h>
# include <conio.h>
# define MAX 5
void addq ( int *, int, int *, int * ) ;
int delq ( int *, int *, int * ) ;

int main( )
{
```

```
    int arr[MAX] ;
    int front = -1, rear = -1, i ;
    addq ( arr, 23, &front, &rear ) ;
    addq ( arr, 9, &front, &rear ) ;
    addq ( arr, 11, &front, &rear ) ;
    addq ( arr, -10, &front, &rear ) ;
    addq ( arr, 25, &front, &rear ) ;
    addq ( arr, 16, &front, &rear ) ;
    i = delq ( arr, &front, &rear ) ;
    printf ( "\nItem deleted: %d", i ) ;
    i = delq ( arr, &front, &rear ) ;
    printf ( "\nItem deleted: %d", i ) ;
    i = delq ( arr, &front, &rear ) ;
    printf ( "\nItem deleted: %d", i ) ;
    return 0 ;
}
void addq ( int *arr, int item, int *pfront, int *prear )
{
    if ( *prear == MAX - 1 )
    {
        printf ( "\nQueue is full." ) ;
        return ;
    }
    ( *prear )++ ;
    arr[*prear] = item ;
    if ( *pfront == -1 )
        *pfront = 0 ;
}
int delq ( int *arr, int *pfront, int *prear )
{
    int data ;
    if ( *pfront == -1 )
    {
        printf ( "\nQueue is Empty." ) ;
        return NULL ;
```

```
    }
    data = arr[*pfront] ;
    arr[*pfront] = 0 ;
    if ( *pfront == *prear )
        *pfront = *prear = -1 ;
    else
        ( *pfront )++ ;
    return data ;
}
```

(a) Queue is full.
Item deleted: 23
Item deleted: 9
Item deleted: 11

(b) Item deleted: 23
Item deleted: 9
Item deleted: 11

(c) Item deleted: 16
Item deleted: 25
Item deleted: -10

(d) Item deleted: -10
Item deleted: 25
Item deleted: 16

Question 42

What will be the output of the program given below?

```
# include <stdio.h>
# include <conio.h>
struct node
{
```

```
    int data ;
    struct node *link ;
} ;
struct queue
{
    struct node *front ;
    struct node *rear ;
} ;
void initqueue ( struct queue * ) ;
void addq ( struct queue *, int ) ;
int delq ( struct queue * ) ;
void delqueue ( struct queue * ) ;

int main( )
{
    struct queue a ;
    int i ;
    initqueue ( &a ) ;
    addq ( &a, 11 ) ;
    addq ( &a, -8 ) ;
    addq ( &a, 23 ) ;
    addq ( &a, 19 ) ;
    addq ( &a, 15 ) ;
    addq ( &a, 16 ) ;
    addq ( &a, 28 ) ;
    i = delq ( &a ) ;
    printf ( "\nItem extracted: %d", i ) ;
    i = delq ( &a ) ;
    printf ( "\nItem extracted: %d", i ) ;
    i = delq ( &a ) ;
    printf ( "\nItem extracted: %d", i ) ;
    return 0 ;
}
void initqueue ( struct queue *q )
{
```

```
    q -> front = q -> rear = NULL ;
}
void addq ( struct queue *q, int item )
{
    struct node *temp ;
    temp = ( struct node * ) malloc ( sizeof ( struct node ) ) ;
    if ( temp == NULL )
        printf ( "\nQueue is full." ) ;
    temp -> data = item ;
    temp -> link = NULL ;
    if ( q -> front == NULL )
    {
        q -> rear = q -> front = temp ;
        return ;
    }
    q -> rear -> link = temp ;
    q -> rear = q -> rear -> link ;
}
int delq ( struct queue * q )
{
    struct node *temp ;
    int item ;
    if ( q -> front == NULL )
    {
        printf ( "\nQueue is empty." ) ;
        return NULL ;
    }
    item = q -> front  -> data ;
    temp = q -> front ;
    q -> front = q -> front -> link ;
    free ( temp ) ;
    return item ;
}
```

(a) Item extracted: 11

Item extracted: -8
Item extracted: 23

(b) Item extracted: 28
Item extracted: 16
Item extracted: 15

(c) Queue is empty

(d) Queue is full

Question 43

What will be the output for the program given below?

```
# include <stdio.h>
# include <conio.h>
# define MAX 10
void addqatbeg ( int *, int, int *, int * ) ;
void addqatend ( int *, int, int *, int * ) ;
void display ( int * ) ;

int main( )
{
    int arr[MAX] ;
    int front, rear, i, n ;
    front = rear = -1 ;
    for ( i = 0 ; i < MAX ; i++ )
        arr[i] = 0 ;

    addqatend ( arr, 17, &front, &rear ) ;
    addqatbeg ( arr, 10, &front, &rear ) ;
    addqatend ( arr, 8, &front, &rear ) ;
    addqatbeg ( arr, -9, &front, &rear ) ;
    addqatend ( arr, 13, &front, &rear ) ;
    addqatbeg ( arr, 28, &front, &rear ) ;
```

```
    addqatend ( arr, 14, &front, &rear ) ;
    addqatbeg ( arr, 5, &front, &rear ) ;
    addqatend ( arr, 25, &front, &rear ) ;
    addqatbeg ( arr, 6, &front, &rear ) ;
    addqatend ( arr, 21, &front, &rear ) ;
    addqatbeg ( arr, 11, &front, &rear ) ;
    display ( arr ) ;
    return 0 ;
}
void addqatbeg ( int *arr, int item, int *pfront, int *prear )
{
    int i, k, c ;
    if ( *pfront == 0 && *prear == MAX - 1 )
    {
        printf ( "\nDeque is full.\n" ) ;
        return ;
    }
    if ( *pfront == -1 )
    {
        *pfront = *prear = 0 ;
        arr[*pfront] = item ;
        return ;
    }
    if ( *prear != MAX - 1 )
    {
        c = count ( arr ) ;
        k = *prear + 1 ;
        for ( i = 1 ; i <= c ; i++ )
        {
            arr[k] = arr[k - 1] ;
            k-- ;
        }
        arr[k] = item ;
        *pfront = k ;
        ( *prear )++ ;
```

```
    }
    else
    {
        ( *pfront )-- ;
        arr[*pfront] = item ;
    }
}
void addqatend ( int *arr, int item, int *pfront, int *prear )
{
    int i, k ;
    if ( *pfront == 0 && *prear == MAX - 1 )
    {
        printf ( "\nDeque is full.\n" ) ;
        return ;
    }
    if ( *pfront == -1 )
    {
        *prear = *pfront = 0 ;
        arr[*prear] = item ;
        return ;
    }
    if ( *prear == MAX - 1 )
    {
        k = *pfront - 1 ;
        for ( i = *pfront - 1 ; i < *prear ; i++ )
        {
            k = i ;
            if ( k == MAX - 1 )
                arr[k] = 0 ;
            else
                arr[k] = arr[i + 1] ;
        }
        ( *prear )-- ;
        ( *pfront )-- ;
    }
```

```
        ( *prear )++ ;
        arr[*prear] = item ;
}
void display ( int *arr )
{
        int i ;

        for ( i = 0 ; i < MAX ; i++ )
                printf ( "\t%d", arr[i] ) ;
}
int count ( int *arr )
{
        int c = 0, i ;

        for ( i = 0 ; i < MAX ; i++ )
        {
                if ( arr[i] != 0 )
                        c++ ;
        }
        return c ;
}
```

(a) Deque is full.
Deque is full.
17 8 13 14 25 6 5 28 -9 10

(b) Deque is full.
Deque is full.
6 5 28 -9 10 17 8 13 14 25

(c) Deque is full.

(d) Deque is empty.

Question 44

Which of the following operations is performed by the program given below?

```
# include <stdio.h>
# include <conio.h>
# define MAX 5

void addq ( int *, int, int *, int * ) ;
int delq ( int *, int *, int * ) ;

int main( )
{
    int arr[MAX] ;
    int front = -1, rear = -1, i ;
    addq ( arr, 23, &front, &rear ) ;
    addq ( arr, 9, &front, &rear ) ;
    addq ( arr, 11, &front, &rear ) ;
    addq ( arr, -10, &front, &rear ) ;
    addq ( arr, 25, &front, &rear ) ;
    addq ( arr, 5, &front, &rear ) ;
    i = delq ( arr, &front, &rear ) ;
    printf ( "\nItem deleted: %d", i ) ;
    return 0 ;
}
void addq ( int *arr, int item, int *pfront, int *prear  )
{
    if ( *prear == MAX - 1 )
    {
        printf ( "\nQueue is full." ) ;
        return ;
    }
    ( *prear )++ ;
    arr[*prear] = item ;
    if ( *pfront == -1 )
```

```
        *pfront = 0 ;
}
int delq ( int *arr, int *pfront, int *prear )
{
    int data ;
    if ( *pfront == -1 )
    {
        printf ( "\nQueue is Empty." ) ;
        return NULL ;
    }
    data = arr[*pfront] ;
    arr[*pfront] = 0 ;
    if ( *pfront == *prear )
        *pfront = *prear = -1 ;
    else
        ( *pfront )++ ;
    return  data ;
}
```

(a) Implementation of stack using linked list

(b) Implementation of stack using arrays

(c) Implementation of queues using arrays

(d) Implementation of queues using linked list

Question 45

Which of the following statements will be correct for the program given below?

```
# include <stdio.h>
# include <conio.h>
struct node
{
    int data ;
```

```
    struct node *link ;
} ;
struct queue
{
    struct node *front ;
    struct node *rear ;
} ;
void initqueue ( struct queue * ) ;
void addq ( struct queue *, int ) ;
int main( )
{
    struct queue a ;
    int i ;
    initqueue ( a ) ;
    addq ( &a, 11 ) ;
    addq ( &a, -8 ) ;
    addq ( &a, 23 ) ;
    addq ( &a, 19 ) ;
    addq ( &a, 15 ) ;
    addq ( &a, 16 ) ;
    addq ( &a, 28 ) ;
    return 0 ;
}
void initqueue ( struct queue *q )
{
    q -> front = q -> rear = NULL ;
}
void addq ( struct queue *q, int item )
{
    struct node *temp ;
    temp = ( struct node * ) malloc ( sizeof ( struct node ) ) ;
    if ( temp == NULL )
        printf ( "\nQueue is full." ) ;
    temp -> data = item ;
    temp -> link = NULL ;
```

```
    if ( q -> front == NULL )
    {
        q -> rear = q -> front = temp ;
        return ;
    }
    q -> rear -> link = temp ;
    q -> rear = q -> rear -> link ;
}
```

(a) The program will execute successfully.

(b) The program will give run time error.

(c) The compiler will report an Error: Type mismatch in parameter 1 in call to 'initqueue'.

(d) The compiler will report an Error: Type mismatch in parameter 1 in call to 'addq'.

Question 46

Which of the following statements will be correct for the program given below?

```
# include <stdio.h>
# include <conio.h>
struct node
{
    int data ;
    struct node *link ;
} ;
struct queue
{
    struct node *front ;
    struct node *rear ;
} ;
void initqueue ( struct queue * ) ;
void addq ( struct queue *, int ) ;
int delq ( struct queue * ) ;
```

```
int main( )
{
      struct queue a ;
      int i ;
      initqueue ( &a ) ;
      addq ( &a, 11 ) ;
      addq ( &a, -8 ) ;
      addq ( &a, 23 ) ;
      addq ( &a, 19 ) ;
      addq ( &a, 15 ) ;
      addq ( &a, 16 ) ;
      addq ( &a, 28 ) ;
      i = delq ( &a ) ;
      printf ( "\nItem extracted: %d", i ) ;
      i = delq ( &a ) ;
      printf ( "\nItem extracted: %d", i ) ;
      return 0 ;
}

void initqueue ( struct queue *q )
{
      q -> front = q -> rear = NULL ;
}
void addq ( struct queue *q, int item )
{
      struct node *temp ;
      temp = ( struct node * ) malloc ( sizeof ( struct node ) ) ;
      if ( temp == NULL )
            printf ( "\nQueue is full." ) ;
      temp -> data = item ;
      temp -> link = NULL ;
      if ( q -> front == NULL )
      {
            q -> rear = q -> front = temp ;
            return ;
```

```
    }
    q -> rear -> link = temp ;
    q -> rear = q -> rear -> link ;
}

int delq ( struct queue *q )
{
    struct node *temp ;
    int item ;
    if ( q -> front == NULL )
    {
        printf ( "\nQueue is empty." ) ;
        return NULL ;
    }
    item = q -> front  -> data ;
    temp = q -> front ;
    q -> front = q -> front -> link ;
    free ( temp ) ;
    return item ;
}
```

(a) The program will be executed successfully.

(b) The program will give run time error.

(c) The program will print output: Item extracted: 11
Item extracted: -8

(d) The program will print output: Item extracted: 28
Item extracted: 16

Question 47

Which of the following statements is correct for the program given below?

```
# include <stdio.h>
```

```
# include <conio.h>
struct node
{
    int data ;
    struct node *link ;
} ;
struct queue
{
    struct node *front ;
    struct node *rear ;
} ;
void initqueue ( struct queue * ) ;
void addq ( struct queue *, int ) ;
int delq ( struct queue * ) ;

int main( )
{
    struct queue a ;
    int i ;
    initqueue ( &a ) ;
    addq ( &a, 11 ) ;
    addq ( &a, -8 ) ;
    addq ( &a, 23 ) ;
    addq ( &a, 19 ) ;
    addq ( &a, 15 ) ;
    addq ( &a, 16 ) ;
    addq ( &a, 28 ) ;
    i = delq ( &a ) ;
    printf ( "\nItem extracted: %d", i ) ;
    i = delq ( &a ) ;
    printf ( "\nItem extracted: %d", i ) ;
    return 0 ;
}

void initqueue ( struct queue *q )
```

```
{
    q -> front = q -> rear = NULL ;
}

void addq ( struct queue *q, int item )
{
    struct node *temp ;
    temp = ( struct node ) malloc ( sizeof ( struct node ) ) ;
    if ( temp == NULL )
        printf ( "\nQueue is full." ) ;
    temp -> data = item ;
    temp -> link = NULL ;
    if ( q -> front == NULL )
    {
        q -> rear = q -> front = temp ;
        return ;
    }
    q -> rear -> link = temp ;
    q -> rear = q -> rear -> link ;
}

int delq ( struct queue *q )
{
    struct node *temp ;
    int item ;
    if ( q -> front == NULL )
    {
        printf ( "\nQueue is empty." ) ;
        return NULL ;
    }
    item = q -> front  -> data ;
    temp = q -> front ;
    q -> front = q -> front -> link ;
    free ( temp ) ;
    return item ;
```

```
}
```

(a) Error: 'Incompatible type conversion'.

(b) Error: Type mismatch in parameter 1 in call to 'delq'.

(c) Error: Too many types in declaration.

(d) The program will run successfully.

Question 48

Which of the following operation does the delqueue( ) function perform in the conde given below?

```
# include <stdio.h>
# include <conio.h>
struct node
{
    int data ;
    struct node *link ;
};
struct queue
{
    struct node *front ;
    struct node *rear ;
};
void initqueue ( struct queue * ) ;
void addq ( struct queue *, int ) ;
void delqueue ( struct queue * ) ;

int main( )
{
    struct queue a ;
    int i ;
    initqueue ( &a ) ;
```

```
        addq ( &a, 11 ) ;
        addq ( &a, -8 ) ;
        addq ( &a, 23 ) ;
        addq ( &a, 19 ) ;
        delqueue ( &a ) ;
        return 0 ;
}
void initqueue ( struct queue *q )
{
        q -> front = q -> rear = NULL ;
}
void addq ( struct queue *q, int item )
{
        struct node *temp ;
        temp = ( struct node * ) malloc ( sizeof ( struct node ) ) ;
        if ( temp == NULL )
                printf ( "\nQueue is full." ) ;
        temp -> data = item ;
        temp -> link = NULL ;
        if ( q -> front == NULL )
        {
                q -> rear = q -> front = temp ;
                return ;
        }
        q -> rear -> link = temp ;
        q -> rear = q -> rear -> link ;
}
void delqueue ( struct queue *q )
{
        struct node *temp ;
        if ( q -> front == NULL )
                return ;
        while ( q -> front != NULL )
        {
                temp = q -> front ;
```

```
        q -> front = q -> front -> link ;
        free ( temp ) ;
    }
}
```

(a) It allocates the memory to add the elements in the queue.

(b) It de-allocates the memory allocated for an existing element in the queue.

(c) It deletes the elements in the queue.

(d) It initializes the elements in the queue.

Question 49

What will be the output for the program given below?

```
# include <stdio.h>
# include <conio.h>
# define MAX 10
void addq ( int *, int, int *, int * ) ;
void display ( int * ) ;

int main( )
{
    int arr[MAX] ;
    int i, front, rear ;
    front = rear = -1 ;
    for ( i = 0 ; i < MAX ; i++ )
        arr[i] = 0 ;
    addq ( arr, 14, &front, &rear ) ;
    addq ( arr, 22, &front, &rear ) ;
    addq ( arr, 13, &front, &rear ) ;
    addq ( arr, -6, &front, &rear ) ;
    addq ( arr, 25, &front, &rear ) ;
    printf ( "\nElements in the circular queue: " ) ;
    display ( arr ) ;
```

```
    return 0 ;
}
void addq ( int *arr, int item, int *pfront, int *prear )
{
    if ( ( *prear == MAX - 1 && *pfront == 0 ) || ( *prear + 1 == *pfront ) )
    {
        printf ( "\nQueue is full." ) ;
        return ;
    }
    if ( *prear == MAX - 1 )
        *prear = 0 ;
    else
        ( *prear )++ ;
    arr[*prear] = item ;
    if ( *pfront == -1 )
        *pfront = 0 ;
}
void display ( int * arr )
{
    int i ;
    printf ( "\n" ) ;
    for ( i = 0 ; i < MAX ; i++ )
        printf ( "%d\t", arr[i] ) ;
    printf ( "\n" ) ;
}
```

(a) 14 22 13 -6 25 0 0 0 0 0

(b) 0 14 22 13 -6 25 0 0 0 0

(c) 0 0 0 0 0 14 22 13 -6 25

(d) 14 22 13 -6 25 14 22 13 -6 25

Question 50

What will be the value of rear and front when the following program is executed?

```
# include <stdio.h>
# include <conio.h>
# define MAX 5

void addq ( int *, int, int *, int * ) ;
int delq ( int *, int *, int * ) ;
int main( )
{
      int arr[MAX] ;
      int front = -1, rear = -1, i ;
      addq ( arr, 23, &front, &rear ) ;
      addq ( arr, 9, &front, &rear ) ;
      addq ( arr, 11, &front, &rear ) ;
      addq ( arr, -10, &front, &rear ) ;
      addq ( arr, 25, &front, &rear ) ;
      addq ( arr, 5, &front, &rear ) ;
      i = delq ( arr, &front, &rear ) ;
      printf ( "\nItem deleted: %d", i ) ;
      return 0 ;
}
void addq ( int *arr, int item, int *pfront, int *prear  )
{
      if ( *prear == MAX - 1 )
      {
            printf ( "\nQueue is full." ) ;
            return ;
      }
      ( *prear )++ ;
      arr[*prear] = item ;
      if ( *pfront == -1 )
            *pfront = 0 ;
```

```
}
int delq ( int *arr, int *pfront, int *prear )
{
    int data ;
    if ( *pfront == -1 )
    {
        printf ( "\nQueue is Empty." ) ;
        return NULL ;
    }
    data = arr[*pfront] ;
    arr[*pfront] = 0 ;
    if ( *pfront == *prear )
        *pfront = *prear = -1 ;
    else
        ( *pfront )++ ;
    return data ;
}
```

(a) rear = 4 and front = 1

(b) rear = 0 and front = 4

(c) rear = 4 and front = 4

(d) rear = 5 and front = 1

Question 51

What will be the output for the program given below?

```
# include <stdio.h>
# include <conio.h>
# define MAX 10
void addq ( int *, int, int *, int * ) ;
int delq ( int *, int *, int * ) ;
void display ( int * ) ;
```

```
int main( )
{
	int arr[MAX] ;
	int i, front, rear ;
	front = rear = -1 ;
	for ( i = 0 ; i < MAX ; i++ )
		arr[i] = 0 ;
	addq ( arr, 14, &front, &rear ) ;
	addq ( arr, 22, &front, &rear ) ;
	addq ( arr, 13, &front, &rear ) ;
	addq ( arr, -6, &front, &rear ) ;
	addq ( arr, 25, &front, &rear ) ;
	i = delq ( arr, &front, &rear ) ;
	i = delq ( arr, &front, &rear ) ;
	printf ( "\nElements in the circular queue: " ) ;
	display ( arr ) ;
	return 0 ;
}

void addq ( int *arr, int item, int *pfront, int *prear )
{
	if ( ( *prear == MAX - 1 && *pfront == 0 ) || ( *prear + 1 == *pfront ) )
	{
		printf ( "\nQueue is full." ) ;
		return ;
	}
	if ( *prear == MAX - 1 )
		*prear = 0 ;
	else
		( *prear )++ ;
	arr[*prear] = item ;
	if ( *pfront == -1 )
		*pfront = 0 ;
}
```

```
int delq ( int *arr, int *pfront, int *prear )
{
    int data ;
    if ( *pfront == -1 )
    {
        printf ( "\nQueue is empty." ) ;
        return NULL ;
    }
    data = arr[*pfront] ;
    arr[*pfront] = 0 ;
    if ( *pfront == *prear )
    {
        *pfront = -1 ;
        *prear = -1 ;
    }
    else
    {
        if ( *pfront == MAX - 1 )
            *pfront = 0 ;
        else
            ( *pfront )++ ;
    }
    return data ;
}

void display ( int * arr )
{
    int i ;
    printf ( "\n" ) ;
    for ( i = 0 ; i < MAX ; i++ )
        printf ( "%d\t", arr[i] ) ;
    printf ( "\n" ) ;
}
```

(a) 14 22 13 -6 25 0 0 0 0 0

(b) 0 0 0 0 0 14 22 13 -6 25

(c) 0 0 14 22 13 -6 25 0 0 0

(d) 0 0 13 -6 25 0 0 0 0 0

Question 52

What will be the output for the program given below?

```
# include <stdio.h>
# include <conio.h>
# define MAX 10
void addq ( int *, int, int *, int * ) ;
int delq ( int *, int *, int * ) ;
void display ( int * ) ;

int main( )
{
    int arr[MAX] ;
    int i, front, rear ;
    front = rear = -1 ;
    for ( i = 0 ; i < MAX ; i++ )
        arr[i] = 0 ;
    addq ( arr, 14, &front, &rear ) ;
    addq ( arr, 22, &front, &rear ) ;
    addq ( arr, 13, &front, &rear ) ;
    addq ( arr, -6, &front, &rear ) ;
    addq ( arr, 25, &front, &rear ) ;
    i = delq ( arr, &front, &rear ) ;
    i = delq ( arr, &front, &rear ) ;
    addq ( arr, 21, &front, &rear ) ;
    addq ( arr, 17, &front, &rear ) ;
    addq ( arr, 18, &front, &rear ) ;
```

```
    addq ( arr, 9, &front, &rear ) ;
    addq ( arr, 20, &front, &rear ) ;
    printf ( "Elements in the circular queue after addition: " ) ;
    display ( arr ) ;
    return 0 ;
}
void addq ( int *arr, int item, int *pfront, int *prear )
{
    if ( ( *prear == MAX - 1 && *pfront == 0 ) || ( *prear + 1 == *pfront ) )
    {
        printf ( "\nQueue is full." ) ;
        return ;
    }
    if ( *prear == MAX - 1 )
        *prear = 0 ;
    else
        ( *prear )++ ;
    arr[*prear] = item ;
    if ( *pfront == -1 )
        *pfront = 0 ;
}
int delq ( int *arr, int *pfront, int *prear )
{
    int data ;
    if ( *pfront == -1 )
    {
        printf ( "\nQueue is empty." ) ;
        return NULL ;
    }
    data = arr[*pfront] ;
    arr[*pfront] = 0 ;
    if ( *pfront == *prear )
    {
        *pfront = -1 ;
        *prear = -1 ;
```

```
    }
    else
    {
        if ( *pfront == MAX - 1 )
            *pfront = 0 ;
        else
            ( *pfront )++ ;
    }
    return data ;
}
void display ( int * arr )
{
    int i ;
    printf ( "\n" ) ;
    for ( i = 0 ; i < MAX ; i++ )
        printf ( "%d\t", arr[i] ) ;
    printf ( "\n" ) ;
}
```

(a) 21 17 18 9 20 3 -6 25 0 0

(b) 21 17 18 9 20 0 0 13 -6 25

(c) 0 0 13 -6 25 21 17 18 9 20

(d) 13 -6 25 21 17 18 9 20 0 0

Question 53

What will be the output of the following program given below?

```
# include <stdio.h>
# include <conio.h>
# define MAX 10
void addqatbeg ( int *, int, int *, int * ) ;
void addqatend ( int *, int, int *, int * ) ;
```

```
int count ( int * ) ;

int main( )
{
    int arr[MAX] ;
    int front, rear, i, n ;
    front = rear = -1 ;
    for ( i = 0 ; i < MAX ; i++ )
        arr[i] = 0 ;
    addqatend ( arr, 17, &front, &rear ) ;
    addqatbeg ( arr, 10, &front, &rear ) ;
    addqatend ( arr, 8, &front, &rear ) ;
    addqatbeg ( arr, -9, &front, &rear ) ;
    addqatend ( arr, 13, &front, &rear ) ;
    addqatbeg ( arr, 28, &front, &rear ) ;
    addqatend ( arr, 14, &front, &rear ) ;
    n = count ( arr ) ;
    printf ( "\nTotal number of elements in deque: %d", n ) ;
    return 0 ;
}
void addqatbeg ( int *arr, int item, int *pfront, int *prear )
{
    int i, k, c ;
    if ( *pfront == 0 && *prear == MAX - 1 )
    {
        printf ( "\nDeque is full.\n" ) ;
        return ;
    }
    if ( *pfront == -1 )
    {
        *pfront = *prear = 0 ;
        arr[*pfront] = item ;
        return ;
    }
    if ( *prear != MAX - 1 )
```

```
    {
        c = count ( arr ) ;
        k = *prear + 1 ;
        for ( i = 1 ; i <= c ; i++ )
        {
            arr[k] = arr[k - 1] ;
            k-- ;
        }
        arr[k] = item ;
        *pfront = k ;
        ( *prear )++ ;
    }
    else
    {
        ( *pfront )-- ;
        arr[*pfront] = item ;
    }
}
void addqatend ( int *arr, int item, int *pfront, int *prear )
{
    int i, k ;
    if ( *pfront == 0 && *prear == MAX - 1 )
    {
        printf ( "\nDeque is full.\n" ) ;
        return ;
    }
    if ( *pfront == -1 )
    {
        *prear = *pfront = 0 ;
        arr[*prear] = item ;
        return ;
    }
    if ( *prear == MAX - 1 )
    {
        k = *pfront - 1 ;
```

```
        for ( i = *pfront - 1 ; i < *prear ; i++ )
        {
            k = i ;
            if ( k == MAX - 1 )
                arr[k] = 0 ;
            else
                arr[k] = arr[i + 1] ;
        }
        ( *prear )-- ;
        ( *pfront )-- ;
    }
    ( *prear )++ ;
    arr[*prear] = item ;
}
int count ( int *arr )
{
    int c = 0, i ;
    for ( i = 0 ; i < MAX ; i++ )
    {
        if ( arr[i] != 0 )
            c++ ;
    }
    return c ;
}
```

(a) Deque is full

(b) Deque is empty

(c) Total number of elements in deque: 7

(d) Total number of elements in deque: 10

Question 54

What will be the output for the program given below?

```
# include <stdio.h>
# include <conio.h>
# define MAX 10
void addqatbeg ( int *, int, int *, int * ) ;
void addqatend ( int *, int, int *, int * ) ;
void display ( int * ) ;
int count ( int * ) ;

int main( )
{
      int arr[MAX] ;
      int front, rear, i, n ;
      front = rear = -1 ;
      for ( i = 0 ; i < MAX ; i++ )
            arr[i] = 0 ;
      addqatend ( arr, 13, &front, &rear ) ;
      addqatbeg ( arr, 28, &front, &rear ) ;
      addqatend ( arr, 14, &front, &rear ) ;
      addqatbeg ( arr, 5, &front, &rear ) ;
      addqatend ( arr, 25, &front, &rear ) ;
      addqatbeg ( arr, 6, &front, &rear ) ;
      addqatend ( arr, 21, &front, &rear ) ;
      addqatbeg ( arr, 11, &front, &rear ) ;
      display ( arr ) ;
      return 0 ;
}
void addqatbeg ( int *arr, int item, int *pfront, int *prear )
{
      int i, k, c ;

      if ( *pfront == 0 && *prear == MAX - 1 )
      {
            printf ( "\nDeque is full.\n" ) ;
            return ;
```

```
    }

    if ( *pfront == -1 )
    {
        *pfront = *prear = 0 ;
        arr[*pfront] = item ;
        return ;
    }

    if ( *prear != MAX - 1 )
    {
        c = count ( arr ) ;
        k = *prear + 1 ;
        for ( i = 1 ; i <= c ; i++ )
        {
            arr[k] = arr[k - 1] ;
            k-- ;
        }
        arr[k] = item ;
        *pfront = k ;
        ( *prear )++ ;
    }
    else
    {
        ( *pfront )-- ;
        arr[*pfront] = item ;
    }
}
void addqatend ( int *arr, int item, int *pfront, int *prear )
{
    int i, k ;
    if ( *pfront == 0 && *prear == MAX - 1 )
    {
        printf ( "\nDeque is full.\n" ) ;
        return ;
```

```
        }
        if ( *pfront == -1 )
        {
            *prear = *pfront = 0 ;
            arr[*prear] = item ;
            return ;
        }
        if ( *prear == MAX - 1 )
        {
            k = *pfront - 1 ;
            for ( i = *pfront - 1 ; i < *prear ; i++ )
            {
                k = i ;
                if ( k == MAX - 1 )
                    arr[k] = 0 ;
                else
                    arr[k] = arr[i + 1] ;
            }
            ( *prear )-- ;
            ( *pfront )-- ;
        }
        ( *prear )++ ;
        arr[*prear] = item ;
}
void display ( int *arr )
{
    int i ;
    for ( i = 0 ; i < MAX ; i++ )
        printf ( "%d\t", arr[i] ) ;
}
int count ( int *arr )
{
    int c = 0, i ;
    for ( i = 0 ; i < MAX ; i++ )
    {
```

```
        if ( arr[i] != 0 )
            c++ ;
    }
    return c ;
}
```

(a) 11 6 5 28 13 14 25 21 0 0

(b) 0 11 6 5 28 13 14 25 21 0

(c) 0 0 11 6 5 28 13 14 25 21

(d) 11 6 5 28 13 14 25 21 25 21

Question 55

What will be the output for the program given below?

```
# include <stdio.h>
# include <conio.h>
# define MAX 10
void addq ( int *, int, int *, int * ) ;
int delq ( int *, int *, int * ) ;
void display ( int * ) ;

int main( )
{
    int arr[MAX] ;
    int i, front, rear ;
    front = rear = -1 ;
    for ( i = 0 ; i < MAX ; i++ )
        arr[i] = 0 ;
    addq ( arr, 14, &front, &rear ) ;
    addq ( arr, 22, &front, &rear ) ;
    addq ( arr, 13, &front, &rear ) ;
    addq ( arr, -6, &front, &rear ) ;
```

```
    addq ( arr, 25, &front, &rear ) ;
    i = delq ( arr, &front, &rear ) ;
    i = delq ( arr, &front, &rear ) ;
    addq ( arr, 21, &front, &rear ) ;
    addq ( arr, 17, &front, &rear ) ;
    addq ( arr, 18, &front, &rear ) ;
    addq ( arr, 9, &front, &rear ) ;
    addq ( arr, 20, &front, &rear ) ;
    addq ( arr, 32, &front, &rear ) ;

    printf ( "Elements in the circular queue after addition: " ) ;
    display ( arr ) ;
    return 0 ;
}
void addq ( int *arr, int item, int *pfront, int *prear )
{
    if ( ( *prear == MAX - 1 && *pfront == 0 ) || ( *prear + 1 == *pfront ) )
    {
        printf ( "\nQueue is full." ) ;
        return ;
    }
    if ( *prear == MAX - 1 )
        *prear = 0 ;
    else
        ( *prear )++ ;
    arr[*prear] = item ;
    if ( *pfront == -1 )
        *pfront = 0 ;
}
int delq ( int *arr, int *pfront, int *prear )
{
    int data ;
    if ( *pfront == -1 )
    {
        printf ( "\nQueue is empty." ) ;
```

```
        return NULL ;
    }
    data = arr[*pfront] ;
    arr[*pfront] = 0 ;
    if ( *pfront == *prear )
    {
        *pfront = -1 ;
        *prear = -1 ;
    }
    else
    {
        if ( *pfront == MAX - 1 )
            *pfront = 0 ;
        else
            ( *pfront )++ ;
    }
    return data ;
}
void display ( int * arr )
{
    int i ;
    printf ( "\n" ) ;
    for ( i = 0 ; i < MAX ; i++ )
        printf ( "%d\t", arr[i] ) ;
    printf ( "\n" ) ;
}
```

(a) 0 32 13 -6 25 21 17 18 9 20

(b) 32 0 13 -6 25 21 17 18 9 20

(c) 32 13 -6 25 21 17 18 9 20 0

(d) 13 -6 25 21 17 18 9 20 0 32

Question 56

What will be the output for the program given below?

```
# include <stdio.h>
# include <conio.h>
# define MAX 10
void addqatbeg ( int *, int, int *, int * ) ;
void addqatend ( int *, int, int *, int * ) ;
int delqatbeg ( int *, int *, int * ) ;
void display ( int * ) ;
int count ( int * ) ;

int main( )
{
    int arr[MAX] ;
    int front, rear, i, n ;
    front = rear = -1 ;
    for ( i = 0 ; i < MAX ; i++ )
        arr[i] = 0 ;
    addqatend ( arr, 13, &front, &rear ) ;
    addqatbeg ( arr, 28, &front, &rear ) ;
    addqatend ( arr, 14, &front, &rear ) ;
    addqatbeg ( arr, 5, &front, &rear ) ;
    addqatend ( arr, 25, &front, &rear ) ;
    addqatbeg ( arr, 6, &front, &rear ) ;
    addqatend ( arr, 21, &front, &rear ) ;
    addqatbeg ( arr, 11, &front, &rear ) ;
    i = delqatbeg ( arr, &front, &rear ) ;
    printf ( "\nItem extracted: %d", i ) ;
    return 0 ;
}

void addqatbeg ( int *arr, int item, int *pfront, int *prear )
{
```

```
    int i, k, c ;
    if ( *pfront == 0 && *prear == MAX - 1 )
    {
        printf ( "\nDeque is full.\n" ) ;
        return ;
    }
    if ( *pfront == -1 )
    {
        *pfront = *prear = 0 ;
        arr[*pfront] = item ;
        return ;
    }
    if ( *prear != MAX - 1 )
    {
        c = count ( arr ) ;
        k = *prear + 1 ;
        for ( i = 1 ; i <= c ; i++ )
        {
            arr[k] = arr[k - 1] ;
            k-- ;
        }
        arr[k] = item ;
        *pfront = k ;
        ( *prear )++ ;
    }
    else
    {
        ( *pfront )-- ;
        arr[*pfront] = item ;
    }
}
void addqatend ( int *arr, int item, int *pfront, int *prear )
{
    int i, k ;
    if ( *pfront == 0 && *prear == MAX - 1 )
```

```
    {
        printf ( "\nDeque is full.\n" ) ;
        return ;
    }
    if ( *pfront == -1 )
    {
        *prear = *pfront = 0 ;
        arr[*prear] = item ;
        return ;
    }
    if ( *prear == MAX - 1 )
    {
        k = *pfront - 1 ;
        for ( i = *pfront - 1 ; i < *prear ; i++ )
        {
            k = i ;
            if ( k == MAX - 1 )
                arr[k] = 0 ;
            else
                arr[k] = arr[i + 1] ;
        }
        ( *prear )-- ;
        ( *pfront )-- ;
    }
    ( *prear )++ ;
    arr[*prear] = item ;
}

int delqatbeg ( int *arr, int *pfront, int *prear )
{
    int item ;

    if ( *pfront == -1 )
    {
        printf ( "\nDeque is empty.\n" ) ;
```

```
        return 0 ;
    }

    item = arr[*pfront] ;
    arr[*pfront] = 0 ;

    if ( *pfront == *prear )
        *pfront = *prear = -1 ;
    else
        ( *pfront )++ ;

    return item ;
}

int count ( int *arr )
{
    int c = 0, i ;

    for ( i = 0 ; i < MAX ; i++ )
    {
        if ( arr[i] != 0 )
            c++ ;
    }
    return c ;
}
```

(a) Item extracted: 13

(b) Item extracted: 11

(c) Deque is full

(d) Deque is empty

Question 57

Which of the following statements will be correct for the program given below?

```
# include <stdio.h>
# include <conio.h>
# define MAX 10
void addq ( int *, int, int *, int * ) ;
int delq ( int *, int *, int * ) ;
void display ( int * ) ;
int count ( int * ) ;

int main( )
{
    int arr[MAX] ;
    int front, rear, i, n ;
    front = rear = -1 ;
    for ( i = 0 ; i < MAX ; i++ )
        arr[i] = 0 ;
    addq ( arr, 1, &front, &rear ) ;
    addq ( arr, 2, &front, &rear ) ;
    addq ( arr, 4, &front, &rear ) ;
    addq ( arr, 5, &front, &rear ) ;
    addq ( arr, 25, &front, &rear ) ;
    addq ( arr, 6, &front, &rear ) ;
    addq ( arr, 31, &front, &rear ) ;
    addq ( arr, 91, &front, &rear ) ;
    i = delq ( arr, &front, &rear ) ;
    printf ( "\nItem extracted: %d", i ) ;
    return 0 ;
}
void addq ( int *arr, int item, int *pfront, int *prear )
{
    int i, k ;
    if ( *pfront == 0 && *prear == MAX - 1 )
```

```
    {
        printf ( "\nDeque is full.\n" ) ;
        return ;
    }
    if ( *pfront == -1 )
    {
        *prear = *pfront = 0 ;
        arr[*prear] = item ;
        return ;
    }
    if ( *prear == MAX - 1 )
    {
        k = *pfront - 1 ;
        for ( i = *pfront - 1 ; i < *prear ; i++ )
        {
            k = i ;
            if ( k == MAX - 1 )
                arr[k] = 0 ;
            else
                arr[k] = arr[i + 1] ;
        }
        ( *prear )-- ;
        ( *pfront )-- ;
    }
    ( *prear )++ ;
    arr[*prear] = item ;
}
int delq ( int *arr, int *pfront, int *prear )
{
    int item ;
    if ( *pfront == -1 )
    {
        printf ( "\nDeque is empty.\n" ) ;
        return 0 ;
    }
```

```
    *item = arr[*pfront] ;
    arr[*pfront] = 0 ;
    if ( *pfront == *prear )
        *pfront = *prear = -1 ;
    else
        ( *pfront )++ ;
    return item ;
}
int count ( int *arr )
{
    int c = 0, i ;
    for ( i = 0 ; i < MAX ; i++ )
    {
        if ( arr[i] != 0 )
            c++ ;
    }
    return c ;
}
```

(a) Error: Invalid indirection.

(b) Error: Type mismatch in parameter 1 in call to addq.

(c) Error: Type mismatch in parameter 3 in call to delq.

(d) Error: Type mismatch in parameter 1 in call to count.

Question 58

What will happen when the program given below is executed?

```
# include <stdio.h>
# include <conio.h>
# define MAX 10
void addq ( int *, int, int *, int * ) ;
int delq ( int *, int *, int * ) ;
```

```
void display ( int * ) ;
int count ( int * ) ;

int main( )
{
	int arr[MAX] ;
	int front, rear, i, n ;
	front = rear = -1 ;
	for ( i = 0 ; i < MAX ; i++ )
		arr[i] = 0 ;
	addq ( arr, 1, &front, &rear ) ;
	addq ( arr, 2, &front, &rear ) ;
	addq ( arr, 4, &front, &rear ) ;
	addq ( arr, 5, &front, &rear ) ;
	addq ( arr, 25, &front, &rear ) ;
	addq ( arr, 6, &front, &rear ) ;
	addq ( arr, 31, &front, &rear ) ;
	addq ( arr, 91, &front, &rear ) ;
	i = delq ( arr, &front, &rear ) ;
	printf ( "\nItem extracted: %d", i ) ;
	return 0 ;
}
void addq ( int *arr, int item, int *pfront, int *prear )
{
	int i, k ;
	if ( *pfront == 0 && *prear == MAX - 1 )
	{
		printf ( "\nDeque is full.\n" ) ;
		return ;
	}
	if ( *pfront == -1 )
	{
		*prear = *pfront = 0 ;
		arr[*prear] = item ;
		return ;
```

```
    }
    if ( *prear == MAX - 1 )
    {
        k = *pfront - 1 ;
        for ( i = *pfront - 1 ; i< *prear ; i++ )
        {
            k = i ;
            if ( k == MAX - 1 )
                arr[k] = 0 ;
            else
                arr[k] = arr[i + 1] ;
        }
        ( *prear )-- ;
        ( *pfront )-- ;
    }
    ( *prear )++ ;
    arr[*prear] = item ;
}
int delq ( int *arr, int *pfront, int *prear )
{
    int item ;

    if ( *pfront == -1 )
    {
        printf ( "\nDeque is empty.\n" ) ;
        return 0 ;
    }

    *item = arr[*pfront] ;
    arr[*pfront] = 0 ;

    if ( *pfront == *prear )
        *pfront = *prear = -1 ;
    else
        ( *pfront )++ ;
```

```
    return item ;
}
int count ( int *arr )
{
    int c = 0, i ;
    for ( i = 0 ; i < MAX ; i++ )
    {
        if ( arr[i] != 0 )
            c++ ;
    }
    return c ;
}
```

(a) The program will print output: "Item extracted: 1".

(b) The program will print output: "Item extracted: 91".

(c) The program will give run time error.

(d) The program will give compile time error.

Question 59

Which of the following statements will you add to the program given below to correctly initialize a dequeue?

```
# include <stdio.h>
# define MAX 5
struct data
{
    char job[MAX] ;
    int prno ;
    int ord ;
} ;
struct pque
{
```

```
        struct data d[MAX] ;
        int front ;
        int rear ;
} ;

void initpque ( struct pque * ) ;

int main( )
{
        struct pque q ;
        initpque ( &q ) ;
        return 0 ;
}
void initpque ( struct pque *pq )
{
        int i ;

        /* ADD STATEMENT HERE */
        for ( i = 0 ; i < MAX ; i++ )
        {
                pq -> d[i].job[ 0 ] = '\0' ;
                pq -> d[i].prno = pq -> d[i].ord = 0 ;
        }
}
```

(a) pq.front = pq.rear = -1 ;

(b) pq.front = pq -> rear = -1 ;

(c) pq -> front = pq.rear = -1 ;

(d) pq -> front = pq -> rear = -1 ;

Question 60

Which of the following is a limitation of a circular queue implemented using an array?

(a) The size of the array will limit the number of elements that can be maintained in the queue.

(b) Even if there are slots available in the queue, the queue will be reported as full.

(c) Even if there are elements in the queue, the queue will be reported as empty.

(d) On deletion of an element, the rest of the elements have to be shifted one position to the left.

Answers

Q. 1 – A	Q. 2 – A	Q. 3 – D
Q. 4 – C	Q. 5 – A	Q. 6 – B
Q. 7 – C	Q. 8 – A	Q. 9 – B
Q. 10 – C	Q. 11 – D	Q. 12 – B
Q. 13 – A	Q. 14 – A	Q. 15 – A
Q. 16 – D	Q. 17 – C	Q. 18 – D
Q. 19 – C	Q. 20 – D	Q. 21 – A
Q. 22 – B	Q. 23 – D	Q. 24 – D
Q. 25 – D	Q. 26 – C	Q. 27 – D
Q. 28 – C	Q. 29 – D	Q. 30 – A
Q. 31 – C	Q. 32 – C	Q. 33 – B
Q. 34 – D	Q. 35 – B	Q. 36 – A
Q. 37 – B	Q. 38 – D	Q. 39 – D
Q. 40 – D	Q. 41 – A	Q. 42 – A
Q. 43 – B	Q. 44 – C	Q. 45 – C
Q. 46 – C	Q. 47 – A	Q. 48 – B

Q. 49 – A	Q. 50 – A	Q. 51 – D
Q. 52 – C	Q. 53 – C	Q. 54 – A
Q. 55 – B	Q. 56 – B	Q. 57 – A
Q. 58 – A	Q. 59 – D	Q. 60 – A

7

Trees

Question 1

Which of the following is a non-linear data structure?

(a) Stack

(b) Queues

(c) Trees

(d) Linked List

Question 2

The children of a node in a tree are called as :

(a) Leaf nodes

(b) Right sub-tree

(c) Left sub-tree

(d) Siblings

Question 3

Each element present in a binary tree is called a ____ of that tree.

(a) Node

(b) Root

(c) Binary tree

(d) Left sub-tree

Question 4

The element that represents the base node of the tree is called the ____ of the tree.

(a) Node

(b) Root

(c) Binary Tree

(d) Right sub-tree

Question 5

A node that does not have any sons is called a __________.

(a) Node

(b) Leaf node

(c) Root

(d) Binary tree

Question 6

The root node of the tree has level __________.

(a) 0

(b) 1

(c) -1

(d) More than 1

Question 7

The number of nodes connected to a particular node of a tree is called the _____ of that node.

(a) Depth

(b) Degree

(c) Level

(d) Leaf

Question 8

The maximum level of any leaf node in the tree is called the _____ of the binary tree.

(a) Degree

(b) Root

(c) Depth

(d) Sibling

Question 9

What should be the value of the balance factor in an AVL tree?

(a) 0 and 1

(b) 1 and -1

(c) 0 and -1

(d) -1, 0 and 1

Question 10

The difference between the heights of left and right sub-trees of all the nodes in a binary search tree is at the most one. Such a binary search tree is called a __________.

(a) Threaded Binary Tree

(b) Balanced Binary Tree

(c) AVL Tree

(d) Both B and C

Question 11

When we traverse the tree from the root to the leaves the operation is known as:

(a) Descending

(b) Ascending

(c) Falling

(d) Climbing

Question 12

If n is the number given to the node then left child occurs at positions _________.

(a) 2n + 1

(b) 2n + 2

(c) 2n – 1

(d) 2n – 2

Question 13

If n is the number given to the node then its right child occurs at positions _____.

(a) 2n – 1

(b) 2n – 2

(c) 2n + 1

(d) 2n + 2

Question 14

Which of the following statements is correct?

(a) A binary tree whose non-leaf nodes has left and right child is a complete binary tree.

(b) To reconstruct a unique binary tree the in-order and pre-list are required.

(c) The balance factor of a node in an AVL tree is 1 if the height of the left sub-tree is one less than the height of the right sub tree.

(d) The number of nodes attached to a particular node in a tree is called the depth of the node.

Question 15

In a threaded binary tree the address of the in-order predecessor and in-order successor are stored in ____ and _____ child of the node respectively.

(a) Left, Right

(b) Right, Left

(c) Left, Left

(d) Right, Right

Question 16

In any node of B-tree of order n the minimum required values of children are ____ and ___ respectively.

(a) N, n

(b) n, n-1

(c) n+1, n

(d) n-1, n

Question 17

In a heap if the largest element is present at the root node then it is called as the ___ heap.

(a) Small

(b) Min

(c) Max

(d) Big

Question 18

When we are traversing the tree from the leaf node to the root node the operation is known as :

(a) Descending

(b) Ascending

(c) Falling

(d) Climbing

Question 19

Which one of the following form of expression is obtained when the expression tree is traversed in pre-order?

(a) Prefix

(b) Postfix

(c) Infix

(d) None of the above

Question 20

Which one of the following form of the expression is obtained when the expression tree is traversed in post-order?

(a) Prefix

(b) Postfix

(c) Infix

(d) None of the above

Question 21

What will be the output for the following program?

```
# include <stdio.h>
# include <conio.h>
# include <malloc.h>
```

```
struct node
{
    struct node *left ;
    char data ;
    struct node *right ;
} ;
struct node * buildtree ( int ) ;
void inorder ( struct node * ) ;
char arr[ ] = { 'A', 'B', 'C', 'D', 'E', 'F', 'G', '\0', '\0', 'H' } ;
int  lc[ ] = { 1,  3,  5,  -1,  9,  -1,  -1,  -1,  -1,  -1 } ;
int  rc[ ] = { 2,  4,  6,  -1,  -1,  -1,  -1,  -1,  -1,  -1 } ;

int main( )
{
    struct node *root ;
    root = buildtree ( 0 ) ;
    printf ( "In-order Traversal:\n" ) ;
    inorder ( root ) ;
    return 0 ;
}
struct node * buildtree ( int index )
{
    struct node *temp = NULL ;
    if ( index != -1 )
    {
        temp = ( struct node * ) malloc ( sizeof ( struct node ) ) ;
        temp -> left = buildtree ( lc[index] ) ;
        temp -> data = arr[index] ;
        temp -> right = buildtree ( rc[index] ) ;
    }
    return temp ;
}
void inorder ( struct node *root )
{
    if ( root != NULL )
```

```
    {
        inorder ( root -> left ) ;
        printf ( "%c\t", root -> data ) ;
        inorder ( root -> right ) ;
    }
}
```

(a) In-order Traversal :
D B E H A F C G

(b) In-order Traversal :
D B H E F A C G

(c) In-order Traversal :
D B H E A C F G

(d) In-order Traversal :
D B H E A F C G

Question 22

Which of the following will be the output of the program given below?

```
# include <stdio.h>
# include <conio.h>
# include <malloc.h>
struct node
{
    struct node *left ;
    char data ;
    struct node *right ;
} ;
struct node * buildtree ( int ) ;
void inorder ( struct node * ) ;
char a[ ] = {
```

```
            'G', 'C', 'B', 'A', 'D', 'F', 'E', '\0', '\0', 'H', '\0',
            '\0', '\0', '\0', '\0', '\0', '\0', '\0', '\0', '\0', '\0'
        } ;
int main( )
{
    struct node *root ;
    root = buildtree ( 0 ) ;
    printf ( "In-order Traversal:\n" ) ;
    inorder ( root ) ;
    return 0 ;
}
struct node * buildtree ( int n )
{
    struct node *temp = NULL ;
    if ( a[n] != '\0' )
    {
        temp = ( struct node * ) malloc ( sizeof ( struct node ) ) ;
        temp -> left = buildtree ( 2 * n + 1 ) ;
        temp -> data = a[n] ;
        temp -> right = buildtree ( 2 * n + 2 ) ;
    }
    return temp ;
}
void inorder ( struct node *root )
{
    if ( root != NULL )
    {
        inorder ( root -> left ) ;
        printf ( "%c\t", root -> data ) ;
        inorder ( root -> right ) ;
    }
}
```

(a) In-order Traversal :
E C H D G F B A

(b) In-order Traversal :
A C H D G F B E

(c) In-order Traversal :
G F B E A C H D

(d) In-order Traversal :
F B E A C H D G

Question 23

What will be the output for the program given below?

```
# include <stdio.h>
# include <conio.h>
# include <malloc.h>
struct btreenode
{
    struct btreenode *leftchild ;
    int data ;
    struct btreenode *rightchild ;
};
void insert ( struct btreenode **, int ) ;
void inorder ( struct btreenode * ) ;

int main( )
{
    struct btreenode *bt ;
    int req, i = 1, num ;
    bt = NULL ;
    insert ( &bt, 23 ) ;
    insert ( &bt, 12 ) ;
    insert ( &bt, 45 ) ;
    insert ( &bt, 77 ) ;
```

```
    insert ( &bt, 11 ) ;
    printf ( "\nIn-order   Traversal: " ) ;
    inorder ( bt ) ;
    return 0 ;
}
void insert ( struct btreenode **sr, int num )
{
    if ( *sr == NULL )
    {
        *sr = malloc ( sizeof ( struct btreenode ) ) ;
        ( *sr ) -> leftchild = NULL ;
        ( *sr ) -> data = num ;
        ( *sr ) -> rightchild = NULL ;
        return ;
    }
    else
    {
        if ( num < ( *sr ) -> data )
            insert ( &( ( *sr ) -> leftchild ), num ) ;
        else
            insert ( &( ( *sr ) -> rightchild ), num ) ;
    }
    return ;
}
void inorder ( struct btreenode *sr )
{
    if ( sr != NULL )
    {
        inorder ( sr -> leftchild ) ;
        printf ( "\t%d", sr -> data ) ;
        inorder ( sr -> rightchild ) ;
    }
    else
        return ;
}
```

(a) In-order Traversal : 11 77 23 12 45

(b) In-order Traversal : 45 77 23 11 12

(c) In-order Traversal : 11 12 23 45 77

(d) In-order Traversal : 77 45 23 12 11

Question 24

What will be the output of the program given below?

```
# include <stdio.h>
# include <conio.h>
# include <malloc.h>
struct btreenode
{
    struct btreenode *leftchild ;
    int data ;
    struct btreenode *rightchild ;
} ;
void insert ( struct btreenode **, int ) ;
void preorder ( struct btreenode * ) ;

int main( )
{
    struct btreenode *bt ;
    int req, i = 1, num ;
    bt = NULL ;
    insert ( &bt, 23 ) ;
    insert ( &bt, 12 ) ;
    insert ( &bt, 45 ) ;
    insert ( &bt, 77 ) ;
    insert ( &bt, 11 ) ;
    printf ( "\nPre-order  Traversal: " ) ;
```

```
        preorder ( bt ) ;
        return 0 ;
}
void insert ( struct btreenode **sr, int num )
{
        if ( *sr == NULL )
        {
                *sr = malloc ( sizeof ( struct btreenode ) ) ;
                ( *sr ) -> leftchild = NULL ;
                ( *sr ) -> data = num ;
                ( *sr ) -> rightchild = NULL ;
                return ;
        }
        else
        {
                if ( num < ( *sr ) -> data )
                        insert ( &( ( *sr ) -> leftchild ), num ) ;
                else
                        insert ( &( ( *sr ) -> rightchild ), num ) ;
        }
        return ;
}
void preorder ( struct btreenode *sr )
{
        if ( sr != NULL )
        {
                printf ( "\t%d", sr -> data ) ;
                preorder ( sr -> leftchild ) ;
                preorder ( sr -> rightchild ) ;
        }
        else
                return ;
}
```

(a) Pre-order Traversal: 77 45 23 12 11

(b) Pre-order Traversal: 11 12 23 45 77

(c) Pre-order Traversal: 45 77 11 23 12

(d) Pre-order Traversal: 23 12 11 45 77

Question 25

What will be the output of the program given below?

```
# include <stdio.h>
# include <conio.h>
# include <malloc.h>
struct btreenode
{
    struct btreenode *leftchild ;
    int data ;
    struct btreenode *rightchild ;
} ;
void insert ( struct btreenode **, int ) ;
void postorder ( struct btreenode * ) ;
int main( )
{
    struct btreenode *bt ;
    int req, i = 1, num ;
    bt = NULL ;
    insert ( &bt, 3 ) ;
    insert ( &bt, 9 ) ;
    insert ( &bt, 4 ) ;
    insert ( &bt, 1 ) ;
    insert ( &bt, 7 ) ;
    printf ( "\nPost-order Traversal: " ) ;
    postorder ( bt ) ;
    return 0 ;
}
void insert ( struct btreenode **sr, int num )
```

```
{
    if ( *sr == NULL )
    {
        *sr = malloc ( sizeof ( struct btreenode ) ) ;
        ( *sr ) -> leftchild = NULL ;
        ( *sr ) -> data = num ;
        ( *sr ) -> rightchild = NULL ;
        return ;
    }
    else
    {
        if ( num < ( *sr ) -> data )
            insert ( &( ( *sr ) -> leftchild ), num ) ;
        else
            insert ( &( ( *sr ) -> rightchild ), num ) ;
    }
    return ;
}
void postorder ( struct btreenode *sr )
{
    if ( sr != NULL )
    {
        postorder ( sr -> leftchild ) ;
        postorder ( sr -> rightchild ) ;
        printf ( "\t%d", sr -> data ) ;
    }
    else
        return ;
}
```

(a) Post-order Traversal : 1 3 4 7 9

(b) Post-order Traversal : 9 7 4 3 1

(c) Post-order Traversal : 1 7 4 3 9

(d) Post-order Traversal : 1 7 4 9 3

Question 26

Which of the following option is correct for the statements given below?

I. The nodes to the original tree are called internal nodes.

II. The new nodes that are added to binary tree, to make it an extended binary tree are called external nodes.

(a) Only I is correct.

(b) Only II is correct.

(c) Neither I nor II is correct.

(d) Both I and II are correct.

Question 27

Which of the following option is correct for the statements given below?

I. If a tree has n nodes then the number of branches it has is (n - 1).

II. Except the root node every node in a tree has exactly two parents.

III. Any two nodes of a tree are connected by only one single path.

(a) Only I and II are correct.

(b) Only II and III are correct.

(c) Only I and III are correct.

(d) All of the three are correct.

Question 28

Which of the following option is correct for the statements given below?

I. For a binary tree of height h the maximum number of nodes can be 2h+1 - 1.

II. Any binary tree with n internal nodes has (n - 1) external nodes.

(a) Only I is correct.

(b) Only II is correct.

(c) Neither I nor II is correct.

(d) Both I and II are correct.

Question 29

Which one of the following condition will you use in the delete( ) function given below to delete the node in a binary search tree which has two children?

```
# include <stdio.h>
# include <conio.h>
# include <malloc.h>
# define TRUE 1
# define FALSE 0
struct btreenode
{
    struct btreenode *leftchild ;
    int data ;
    struct btreenode *rightchild ;
} ;

void insert ( struct btreenode **, int ) ;
void delete ( struct btreenode **, int ) ;
void search ( struct btreenode **, int, struct btreenode **, struct btreenode **, int * ) ;
int main( )
{
    struct btreenode *bt ;
    int req, i = 0, num, a[ ] = { 11, 9, 13, 8, 10, 12, 14, 15, 7 } ;
    bt = NULL ;
    while ( i <= 8 )
    {
        insert ( &bt, a[i] ) ;
        i++ ;
    }
```

```
    delete ( &bt, 10 ) ;
    delete ( &bt, 14 ) ;
    delete ( &bt, 8 ) ;
    delete ( &bt, 13 ) ;
    return 0 ;
}
void insert ( struct btreenode **sr, int num )
{
    if ( *sr == NULL )
    {
        *sr = malloc ( sizeof ( struct btreenode ) ) ;
        ( *sr ) -> leftchild = NULL ;
        ( *sr ) -> data = num ;
        ( *sr ) -> rightchild = NULL ;
    }
    else
    {
        if ( num < ( *sr ) -> data )
            insert ( &( ( *sr ) -> leftchild ), num ) ;
        else
            insert ( &( ( *sr ) -> rightchild ), num ) ;
    }
}
void delete ( struct btreenode **root, int num )
{
    int found ;
    struct btreenode *parent, *x, *xsucc ;
    if ( *root == NULL )
    {
        printf ( "\nTree is empty" ) ;
        return ;
    }
    parent = x = NULL ;
    search ( root, num, &parent, &x, &found ) ;
    if ( found == FALSE )
```

```
    {
        printf ( "\nData to be deleted, not found" ) ;
        return ;
    }
    // Add code here
}
void search ( struct btreenode **root, int num, struct btreenode **par, struct btreenode
**x, int *found )
{
    struct btreenode *q ;
    q = *root ;
    *found = FALSE ;
    *par = NULL ;
    while ( q != NULL )
    {
        if ( q -> data == num )
        {
            *found = TRUE ;
            *x = q ;
            return ;
        }
        *par = q ;
        if ( q -> data > num )
            q = q -> leftchild ;
        else
            q = q -> rightchild ;
    }
}
```

(a)
```
    if ( x -> leftchild != NULL && x -> rightchild != NULL )
    {
        parent = x ;
        xsucc = x -> rightchild ;
        while ( xsucc -> leftchild != NULL )
        {
```

```
            parent = xsucc ;
            xsucc = xsucc -> leftchild ;
        }
        x -> data = xsucc -> data ;
        x = xsucc ;
    }
```

(b)
```
    if ( x -> leftchild == NULL && x -> rightchild == NULL )
    {
        if ( parent -> rightchild == x )
            parent -> rightchild = NULL ;
        else
            parent -> leftchild = NULL ;
        free ( x ) ;
        return ;
    }
```

(c)
```
    if ( x -> leftchild == NULL && x -> rightchild != NULL )
    {
        if ( parent -> leftchild == x )
            parent -> leftchild = x -> rightchild ;
        else
            parent -> rightchild = x -> rightchild ;
        free ( x ) ;
        return ;
    }
```

(d)
```
    if ( x -> leftchild != NULL && x -> rightchild == NULL )
    {
        if ( parent -> leftchild == x )
            parent -> leftchild = x -> leftchild ;
        else
            parent -> rightchild = x -> leftchild ;
        free ( x ) ;
        return ;
```

```
    }
```

Question 30

Which one of the following condition will you add to the delete( ) function to delete the node in a binary search tree which has no child?

```
# include <stdio.h>
# include <conio.h>
# include <malloc.h>
# define TRUE 1
# define FALSE 0
struct btreenode
{
    struct btreenode *leftchild ;
    int data ;
    struct btreenode *rightchild ;
} ;

void insert ( struct btreenode **, int ) ;
void delete ( struct btreenode **, int ) ;
void search ( struct btreenode **, int, struct btreenode **, struct btreenode **, int * ) ;

int main( )
{
    struct btreenode *bt ;
    int req, i = 0, num, a[ ] = { 11, 9, 13, 8, 10, 12, 14, 15, 7 } ;
    bt = NULL ;
    while ( i <= 8 )
    {
        insert ( &bt, a[i] ) ;
        i++ ;
    }
    delete ( &bt, 10 ) ;
    delete ( &bt, 14 ) ;
```

```
    delete ( &bt, 8 ) ;
    delete ( &bt, 13 ) ;
    return 0 ;
}
void insert ( struct btreenode **sr, int num )
{
    if ( *sr == NULL )
    {
        *sr = malloc ( sizeof ( struct btreenode ) ) ;
        ( *sr ) -> leftchild = NULL ;
        ( *sr ) -> data = num ;
        ( *sr ) -> rightchild = NULL ;
    }
    else
    {
        if ( num < ( *sr ) -> data )
            insert ( &( ( *sr ) -> leftchild ), num ) ;
        else
            insert ( &( ( *sr ) -> rightchild ), num ) ;
    }
}
void delete ( struct btreenode **root, int num )
{
    int found ;
    struct btreenode *parent, *x, *xsucc ;
    if ( *root == NULL )
    {
        printf ( "\nTree is empty" ) ;
        return ;
    }
    parent = x = NULL ;
    search ( root, num, &parent, &x, &found ) ;
    if ( found == FALSE )
    {
        printf ( "\nData to be deleted, not found" ) ;
```

```
        return ;
    }
    // Add code here
}
void search ( struct btreenode **root, int num, struct btreenode **par, struct btreenode
**x, int *found )
{
    struct btreenode *q ;
    q = *root ;
    *found = FALSE ;
    *par = NULL ;
    while ( q != NULL )
    {
        if ( q -> data == num )
        {
            *found = TRUE ;
            *x = q ;
            return ;
        }
        *par = q ;
        if ( q -> data > num )
            q = q -> leftchild ;
        else
            q = q -> rightchild ;
    }
}
```

(a)
```
if ( x -> leftchild != NULL && x -> rightchild != NULL )
{
    parent = x ;
    xsucc = x -> rightchild ;
    while ( xsucc -> leftchild != NULL )
    {
        parent = xsucc ;
        xsucc = xsucc -> leftchild ;
```

```
        }
        x -> data = xsucc -> data ;
        x = xsucc ;
    }
```

(b)
```
    if ( x -> leftchild == NULL && x -> rightchild == NULL )
    {
        if ( parent -> rightchild == x )
            parent -> rightchild = NULL ;
        else
            parent -> leftchild = NULL ;
        free ( x ) ;
        return ;
    }
```

(c)
```
    if ( x -> leftchild == NULL && x -> rightchild != NULL )
    {
        if ( parent -> leftchild == x )
            parent -> leftchild = x -> rightchild ;
        else
            parent -> rightchild = x -> rightchild ;
        free ( x ) ;
        return ;
    }
```

(d)
```
    if ( x -> leftchild != NULL && x -> rightchild == NULL )
    {
        if ( parent -> leftchild == x )
            parent -> leftchild = x -> leftchild ;
        else
            parent -> rightchild = x -> leftchild ;
        free ( x ) ;
        return ;
    }
```

Question 31

Which one of the following condition will you add to the delete( ) function to delete a node in a binary search tree which has only right-child?

```
# include <stdio.h>
# include <conio.h>
# include <malloc.h>
# define TRUE 1
# define FALSE 0
struct btreenode
{
    struct btreenode *leftchild ;
    int data ;
    struct btreenode *rightchild ;
} ;
void insert ( struct btreenode **, int ) ;
void delete ( struct btreenode **, int ) ;
void search ( struct btreenode **, int, struct btreenode **, struct btreenode **, int * ) ;

int main( )
{
    struct btreenode *bt ;
    int req, i = 0, num, a[ ] = { 11, 9, 13, 8, 10, 12, 14, 15, 7 } ;
    bt = NULL ;
    while ( i <= 8 )
    {
        insert ( &bt, a[i] ) ;
        i++ ;
    }
    delete ( &bt, 10 ) ;
    delete ( &bt, 14 ) ;
    delete ( &bt, 8 ) ;
    delete ( &bt, 13 ) ;
    return 0 ;
```

```
}
void insert ( struct btreenode **sr, int num )
{
    if ( *sr == NULL )
    {
        *sr = malloc ( sizeof ( struct btreenode ) ) ;
        ( *sr ) -> leftchild = NULL ;
        ( *sr ) -> data = num ;
        ( *sr ) -> rightchild = NULL ;
    }
    else
    {
        if ( num < ( *sr ) -> data )
            insert ( &( ( *sr ) -> leftchild ), num ) ;
        else
            insert ( &( ( *sr ) -> rightchild ), num ) ;
    }
}
void delete ( struct btreenode **root, int num )
{
    int found ;
    struct btreenode *parent, *x, *xsucc ;
    if ( *root == NULL )
    {
        printf ( "\nTree is empty" ) ;
        return ;
    }
    parent = x = NULL ;
    search ( root, num, &parent, &x, &found ) ;
    if ( found == FALSE )
    {
        printf ( "\nData to be deleted, not found" ) ;
        return ;
    }
    // Add code here
```

```
}
void search ( struct btreenode **root, int num, struct btreenode **par, struct btreenode
**x, int *found )
{
    struct btreenode *q ;
    q = *root ;
    *found = FALSE ;
    *par = NULL ;
    while ( q != NULL )
    {
        if ( q -> data == num )
        {
            *found = TRUE ;
            *x = q ;
            return ;
        }
        *par = q ;
        if ( q -> data > num )
            q = q -> leftchild ;
        else
            q = q -> rightchild ;
    }
}
```

(a)
```
if ( x -> leftchild != NULL && x -> rightchild != NULL )
{
    parent = x ;
    xsucc = x -> rightchild ;
    while ( xsucc -> leftchild != NULL )
    {
        parent = xsucc ;
        xsucc = xsucc -> leftchild ;
    }
    x -> data = xsucc -> data ;
    x = xsucc ;
```

```
    }
```

(b)
```
if ( x -> leftchild == NULL && x -> rightchild == NULL )
{
    if ( parent -> rightchild == x )
        parent -> rightchild = NULL ;
    else
        parent -> leftchild = NULL ;
    free ( x ) ;
    return ;
}
```

(c)
```
if ( x -> leftchild == NULL && x -> rightchild != NULL )
{
    if ( parent -> leftchild == x )
        parent -> leftchild = x -> rightchild ;
    else
        parent -> rightchild = x -> rightchild ;
    free ( x ) ;
    return ;
}
```

(d)
```
if ( x -> leftchild != NULL && x -> rightchild == NULL )
{
    if ( parent -> leftchild == x )
        parent -> leftchild = x -> leftchild ;
    else
        parent -> rightchild = x -> leftchild ;
    free ( x ) ;
    return ;
}
```

Question 32

Which of the following condition will you add to the delete( ) function to delete the node in a binary search tree which has a left-child?

```
# include <stdio.h>
# include <conio.h>
# include <malloc.h>
# define TRUE 1
# define FALSE 0
struct btreenode
{
        struct btreenode *leftchild ;
        int data ;
        struct btreenode *rightchild ;
} ;

void insert ( struct btreenode **, int ) ;
void delete ( struct btreenode **, int ) ;
void search ( struct btreenode **, int, struct btreenode **, struct btreenode **, int * ) ;

int main( )
{
        struct btreenode *bt ;
        int req, i = 0, num, a[ ] = { 11, 9, 13, 8, 10, 12, 14, 15, 7 } ;
        bt = NULL ;
        while ( i <= 8 )
        {
                insert ( &bt, a[i] ) ;
                i++ ;
        }
        delete ( &bt, 10 ) ;
        delete ( &bt, 14 ) ;
        delete ( &bt, 8 ) ;
        delete ( &bt, 13 ) ;
        return 0 ;
}
void insert ( struct btreenode **sr, int num )
```

```
{
    if ( *sr == NULL )
    {
        *sr = malloc ( sizeof ( struct btreenode ) ) ;
        ( *sr ) -> leftchild = NULL ;
        ( *sr ) -> data = num ;
        ( *sr ) -> rightchild = NULL ;
    }
    else
    {
        if ( num < ( *sr ) -> data )
            insert ( &( ( *sr ) -> leftchild ), num ) ;
        else
            insert ( &( ( *sr ) -> rightchild ), num ) ;
    }
}
void delete ( struct btreenode **root, int num )
{
    int found ;
    struct btreenode *parent, *x, *xsucc ;
    if ( *root == NULL )
    {
        printf ( "\nTree is empty" ) ;
        return ;
    }
    parent = x = NULL ;
    search ( root, num, &parent, &x, &found ) ;
    if ( found == FALSE )
    {
        printf ( "\nData to be deleted, not found" ) ;
        return ;
    }
    // Add code here
}
void search ( struct btreenode **root, int num, struct btreenode **par, struct btreenode
```

```
**x, int *found )
{
    struct btreenode *q ;
    q = *root ;
    *found = FALSE ;
    *par = NULL ;
    while ( q != NULL )
    {
        if ( q -> data == num )
        {
            *found = TRUE ;
            *x = q ;
            return ;
        }
        *par = q ;
        if ( q -> data > num )
            q = q -> leftchild ;
        else
            q = q -> rightchild ;
    }
}
```

(a)
```
if ( x -> leftchild != NULL && x -> rightchild != NULL )
{
    parent = x ;
    xsucc = x -> rightchild ;
    while ( xsucc -> leftchild != NULL )
    {
        parent = xsucc ;
        xsucc = xsucc -> leftchild ;
    }
    x -> data = xsucc -> data ;
    x = xsucc ;
}
```

(b)
```
if ( x -> leftchild == NULL && x -> rightchild == NULL )
{
    if ( parent -> rightchild == x )
        parent -> rightchild = NULL ;
    else
        parent -> leftchild = NULL ;
    free ( x ) ;
    return ;
}
```

(c)
```
if ( x -> leftchild == NULL && x -> rightchild != NULL )
{
    if ( parent -> leftchild == x )
        parent -> leftchild = x -> rightchild ;
    else
        parent -> rightchild = x -> rightchild ;
    free ( x ) ;
    return ;
}
```

(d)
```
if ( x -> leftchild != NULL && x -> rightchild == NULL )
{
    if ( parent -> leftchild == x )
        parent -> leftchild = x -> leftchild ;
    else
        parent -> rightchild = x -> leftchild ;
    free ( x ) ;
    return ;
}.
```

Question 33

Which of the following is the correct sequence of operations that should be performed to traverse a non-empty binary tree in in-order traversal?

(a) Visit the root.

Traverse the left sub-tree in pre-order.
Traverse the right sub-tree in pre-order.

(b) Traverse the left sub-tree in pre-order.
Visit the root.
Traverse the right sub-tree in pre-order.

(c) Traverse the left sub-tree in pre-order.
Traverse the right sub-tree in pre-order.
Visit the root.

(d) All of the above.

Question 34

Which of the following statements regarding trees are correct?

I. A binary tree consists of infinite set of elements.

II. Root is one of the sub-sets of binary tree.

(a) I is correct II is not correct.

(b) Both I and II are correct.

(c) II is correct I is not correct.

(d) Both I and II are not correct.

Question 35

Which of the following is the correct sequence of operations that should be performed to traverse a non-empty binary tree in pre-order traversal?

(a) Visit the root.
Traverse the left sub-tree in pre-order.
Traverse the right sub-tree in pre-order.

(b) Traverse the left sub-tree in pre-order.

Visit the root.
Traverse the right sub-tree in pre-order.

(c) Traverse the left sub-tree in pre-order.
Traverse the right sub-tree in pre-order.
Visit the root.

(d) All of the above.

Question 36

Which of the following statement is correct?

I. If the value of balfact of any node is -1, then the height of the right sub-tree of that node is one more than the height of its left sub-tree.

II. If the value of balfact of any node is 0 then the height of its left and right sub-tree is exactly same.

III. If the value of balfact of any node is 1 then the height of the left sub-tree of that node is one more than the height of its right sub-tree.

(a) Only I and II are correct.

(b) Only II and III are correct.

(c) Only I and III are correct.

(d) All the three are correct.

Question 37

Which of the following is the correct sequence of operations that should be performed to traverse a non-empty binary tree in post-order traversal?

(a) Visit the root.
Traverse the left sub-tree in pre-order.
Traverse the right sub-tree in pre-order.

(b) Traverse the left sub-tree in pre-order.
Visit the root.
Traverse the right sub-tree in pre-order.

(c) Traverse the left sub-tree in pre-order.
Traverse the right sub-tree in pre-order.
Visit the root.

(d) All of the above.

Question 38

Which of the following would be the correct structure that represents a node for a 2-3 tree?

(a)
```
struct node
{
    int count ;
    int data[3] ;
    struct node * child[4] ;
} ;
```

(b)
```
sturct node
{
    struct node *left ;
    int data ;
    struct node *right ;
} ;
```

(c)
```
struct node
{
    enum boolean left ;
    struct node *leftchild ;
    int data ;
    struct node *rightchild ;
    enum boolean right ;
} ;
```

(d)
```
struct node
{
    int data ;
    struct node *firstchild ;
    struct node *siblings ;
} ;
```

Question 39

Which of the following is the correct structure that represents a node of a threaded binary tree?

(a)
```
struct node
{
    int count ;
    int data[3] ;
    struct node * child[4] ;
} ;
```

(b)
```
sturct node
{
    struct node *left ;
    int data ;
    struct node *right ;
} ;
```

(c)
```
struct node
{
    enum boolean left ;
    struct node *leftchild ;
    int data ;
    struct node *rightchild ;
    enum boolean right ;
} ;
```

(d)
```
struct node
{
    int data ;
    struct node *firstchild ;
    struct node *siblings ;
};
```

Question 40

Which of the following would be the correct structure that represents a node of the general tree?

(a)
```
struct node
{
    int count ;
    int data[3] ;
    struct node * child[4] ;
};
```

(b)
```
sturct node
{
    struct node *left ;
    int data ;
    struct node *right ;
};
```

(c)
```
struct node
{
    enum boolean left ;
    struct node *leftchild ;
    int data ;
    struct node *rightchild ;
    enum boolean right ;
};
```

(d)
```
struct node
```

```
{
        int data ;
        struct node *firstchild ;
        struct node *siblings ;
} ;
```

Question 41

Which of the following statements is correct about the code given below?

```
# include <stdio.h>
# include <conio.h>
# include <malloc.h>
# define TRUE 1
# define FALSE 0

struct btreenode
{
        struct btreenode *leftchild ;
        int data ;
        struct btreenode *rightchild ;
} ;
int c = 0 ;
void insert ( struct btreenode **, int ) ;
void inorder ( struct btreenode * ) ;
void no_nodes ( struct btreenode * ) ;
int height ( struct btreenode * ) ;

int main( )
{
        struct btreenode *bt ;
        int num, h, req, i = 0 ;
        char ch ;
        bt = NULL ;
        printf ( "Specify the number of items to be inserted: " ) ;
```

```
    scanf ( "%d", &req ) ;
    while ( i++ < req )
    {
        printf ( "\nEnter the data: " ) ;
        scanf ( "%d", &num ) ;
        insert ( &bt, num ) ;
    }
    printf ( "\nBinary tree\n" ) ;
    inorder ( bt ) ;
    h = height ( bt ) ;
    printf ( "\n %d", h ) ;
    return 0 ;
}
void insert ( struct btreenode **sr, int num )
{
    if ( *sr == NULL )
    {
        *sr = malloc ( sizeof ( struct btreenode ) ) ;
        ( *sr ) -> leftchild = NULL ;
        ( *sr ) -> data = num ;
        ( *sr ) -> rightchild = NULL ;
    }
    else
    {
        if ( num < ( *sr ) -> data )
            insert ( &( ( *sr ) ->leftchild ), num ) ;
        else
            insert ( &( ( *sr ) ->rightchild ), num ) ;
    }
}
void inorder ( struct btreenode *sr )
{
    if ( sr != NULL )
    {
        inorder ( sr -> leftchild ) ;
```

```
        printf ( "%d\t", sr -> data ) ;
        inorder ( sr -> rightchild ) ;
    }
}
void no_nodes ( struct btreenode *sr )
{
    if ( sr != NULL )
    {
        c++ ;
        no_nodes ( sr -> leftchild ) ;
        no_nodes ( sr -> rightchild ) ;
    }
}
int height ( struct btreenode *sr )
{
    int h[ ] = { 0, 3, 7, 15, 31, 63, 127, 255, 511, 1023 } ;
    int i = 0, j ;
    no_nodes ( sr ) ;
    while ( i < 9 )
    {
        if ( c > h[i]  && c <= h[i+1] )
            return ( i + 1 ) ;
        else
            i++ ;
    }
    return 0 ;
}
```

(a) The program is to find the height of a binary tree.

(b) The program is to count the number of nodes in a binary tree.

(c) The program is to find number of nodes in a binary tree at each level.

(d) The program is to insert a node t as a left child of any node s in a threaded binary tree.

Question 42

Which of the following statements is correct about the code given below?

```
# include <stdio.h>
# include <conio.h>
# include <malloc.h>
struct btreenode
{
    struct btreenode *leftchild ;
    int data ;
    struct btreenode *rightchild ;
} ;
int c = 0 ;
void insert ( struct btreenode **, int ) ;
void inorder ( struct btreenode * ) ;
void no_nodes ( struct btreenode * ) ;

int main( )
{
    struct btreenode *bt ;
    int num, h, req, i = 0 ;
    char ch ;
    bt = NULL ;
    printf ( "Specify the number of items to be inserted: " ) ;
    scanf ( "%d", &req ) ;
    while ( i++ < req )
    {
        printf ( "\nEnter the data: " ) ;
        scanf ( "%d", &num ) ;
        insert ( &bt, num ) ;
    }
    printf ( "\nBinary tree\n" ) ;
    inorder ( bt ) ;
    no_nodes ( bt ) ;
```

```
    printf ( "\n %d", c ) ;
    return 0 ;
}
void insert ( struct btreenode **sr, int num )
{
    if ( *sr == NULL )
    {
        *sr = malloc ( sizeof ( struct btreenode ) ) ;
        ( *sr ) -> leftchild = NULL ;
        ( *sr ) -> data = num ;
        ( *sr ) -> rightchild = NULL ;
    }
    else
    {
        if ( num < ( *sr ) -> data )
            insert ( &( ( *sr ) -> leftchild ), num ) ;
        else
            insert ( &( ( *sr ) -> rightchild ), num ) ;
    }
}
void inorder ( struct btreenode *sr )
{
    if ( sr != NULL )
    {
        inorder ( sr -> leftchild ) ;
        printf ( "%d\t", sr -> data ) ;
        inorder ( sr -> rightchild ) ;
    }
}
void no_nodes ( struct btreenode *sr )
{
    if ( sr != NULL )
    {
        c++ ;
        no_nodes ( sr -> leftchild ) ;
```

```
            no_nodes ( sr -> rightchild ) ;
        }
}
```

(a) The program is to find the height of a binary tree.

(b) The program is to count the number of nodes in a binary tree.

(c) The program is to find the number of leaf-nodes in a binary tree.

(d) The program is to find number of nodes in a binary tree at each level.

Question 43

Which of the following statements is correct about the code given below?

```
# include <stdio.h>
# include <conio.h>
# include <malloc.h>
struct btreenode
{
      struct btreenode *leftchild ;
      int data ;
      struct btreenode *rightchild ;
} ;
int ln = 0 ;
void insert ( struct btreenode **, int ) ;
void inorder ( struct btreenode * ) ;
void no_nodes ( struct btreenode * ) ;

int main( )
{
      struct btreenode *bt ;
      int num, h, req, i = 0 ;
      char ch ;
      bt = NULL ;
```

```
    printf ( "Specify the number of items to be inserted: " ) ;
    scanf ( "%d", &req ) ;
    while ( i++ < req )
    {
        printf ( "\nEnter the data: " ) ;
        scanf ( "%d", &num ) ;
        insert ( &bt, num ) ;
    }
    printf ( "\nBinary tree\n" ) ;
    inorder ( bt ) ;
    no_nodes ( bt ) ;
    printf ( "\n %d ", ln ) ;
    return 0 ;
}
void insert ( struct btreenode **sr, int num )
{
    if ( *sr == NULL )
    {
        *sr = malloc ( sizeof ( struct btreenode ) ) ;
        ( *sr ) -> leftchild = NULL ;
        ( *sr ) -> data = num ;
        ( *sr ) -> rightchild = NULL ;
    }
    else
    {
        if ( num < ( *sr ) -> data )
            insert ( &( ( *sr ) ->leftchild ), num ) ;
        else
            insert ( &( ( *sr ) ->rightchild ), num ) ;
    }
}
void inorder ( struct btreenode *sr )
{
    if ( sr != NULL )
    {
```

```
        inorder ( sr -> leftchild ) ;
        printf ( "%d\t", sr -> data ) ;
        inorder ( sr -> rightchild ) ;
    }
}
void no_nodes ( struct btreenode *sr )
{
    if ( sr != NULL )
    {
        if ( sr -> leftchild == NULL && sr -> rightchild == NULL )
            ln++ ;
        no_nodes ( sr -> leftchild ) ;
        no_nodes ( sr -> rightchild ) ;
    }
}
```

(a) The program is to find the height of a binary tree.

(b) The program is to count the number of nodes in a binary tree.

(c) The program is to find the number of leaf-nodes in a binary tree.

(d) The program is to find number of nodes in a binary tree at each level.

Question 44

Which of the following statements is correct about the code given below?

```
# include <stdio.h>
# include <conio.h>
# include <malloc.h>
struct btreenode
{
    struct btreenode *leftchild ;
    int data ;
    struct btreenode *rightchild ;
} ;
```

```
void insert ( struct btreenode **, int ) ;
void inorder ( struct btreenode * ) ;
void mirror_insert ( struct btreenode **, int ) ;

int main( )
{
    struct btreenode *bt, *mbt ;
    int req, i = 0, num, a[ ] = { 11, 9, 13, 8, 10, 12, 14, 15, 7 } ;
    bt = mbt = NULL ;
    while ( i <= 8 )
    {
        insert ( &bt, a[i] ) ;
        i++ ;
    }
    inorder ( bt ) ;
    i = 0 ;
    while ( i <= 8 )
    {
        mirror_insert ( &mbt, a[i] ) ;
        i++ ;
    }
    inorder ( mbt ) ;
    return 0 ;
}
void insert ( struct btreenode **sr, int num )
{
    if ( *sr == NULL )
    {
        *sr = malloc ( sizeof ( struct btreenode ) ) ;
        ( *sr ) -> leftchild = NULL ;
        ( *sr ) -> data = num ;
        ( *sr ) -> rightchild = NULL ;
    }
    else
    {
```

```
        if ( num <  ( *sr ) -> data )
            insert ( &( ( *sr ) -> leftchild ), num ) ;
        else
            insert ( &( ( *sr ) ->rightchild ), num ) ;
    }
}
void inorder ( struct btreenode *sr )
{
    if ( sr != NULL )
    {
        inorder ( sr -> leftchild ) ;
        printf ( "\t%d", sr -> data ) ;
        inorder ( sr -> rightchild ) ;
    }
    else
        return ;
}
void mirror_insert ( struct btreenode **sr, int num )
{
    if ( *sr == NULL )
    {
        *sr = malloc ( sizeof ( struct btreenode ) ) ;
        ( *sr ) -> leftchild = NULL ;
        ( *sr ) -> data = num ;
        ( *sr ) -> rightchild = NULL ;
    }
    else
    {
        if ( num < ( *sr ) -> data )
            mirror_insert ( &( ( *sr ) -> rightchild ), num ) ;
        else
            mirror_insert ( &( ( *sr ) -> leftchild ), num ) ;
    }
}
```

(a) The program is to create another binary tree that is mirror image of the given tree.

(b) The program is to find whether two binary trees are mirror image of each other or not.

(c) The program is to find whether two binary trees are similar or not.

(d) The program is to find the height of the binary tree.

Question 45

Which of the following statements is correct about the code given below?

```
# include <stdio.h>
# include <conio.h>
# include <malloc.h>
# define MAX 50

struct btreenode
{
      struct btreenode *lc ;
      int data ;
      struct btreenode *rc ;
} ;
void insert ( struct btreenode **, int ) ;
void order ( struct btreenode * ) ;
void deleteall ( struct btreenode *p ) ;
int main( )
{
      struct btreenode *bt ;
      bt = NULL ;
      insert ( &bt, 10 ) ;
      insert ( &bt, 6 ) ;
      insert ( &bt, 8 ) ;
      insert ( &bt, 15 ) ;
      insert ( &bt, 20 ) ;
      order ( bt ) ;
```

```
    deleteall ( bt ) ;
    return 0 ;
}
void insert ( struct btreenode **p, int num )
{
    if ( *p == NULL )
    {
        *p = ( struct btreenode * ) malloc ( sizeof ( struct btreenode ) ) ;
        ( *p ) -> lc = NULL ;
        ( *p ) -> data = num ;
        ( *p ) -> rc = NULL ;
    }
    else
    {
        if ( num < ( *p ) -> data )
            insert ( &( ( *p ) -> lc ), num ) ;
        else
            insert ( &( ( *p ) -> rc ), num ) ;
    }
}
void order ( struct btreenode *pt )
{
    struct btreenode *stack[ MAX ] ;
    int top = -1 ;
    while ( 1 )
    {
        while ( pt != NULL )
        {
            top++ ;
            if ( top > MAX - 1 )
            {
                printf ( "Stack full." ) ;
                return ;
            }
            stack[ top ] = pt ;
```

```
            pt = pt -> lc ;
        }

        if ( top != -1 )
        {
            pt = stack[ top ] ;
            top-- ;
            printf ( "\t%d", pt ->data ) ;
            pt = pt -> rc ;
        }
        else
            break ;
    }
}
void deleteall ( struct btreenode *p )
{
    if ( p != NULL )
    {
        deleteall ( p -> lc ) ;
        deleteall ( p -> rc ) ;
        free ( p ) ;
    }
}
```

(a) The program is to implement the non-recursive form of inorder traversal.

(b) The program is to implement the non-recursive form of preorder traversal.

(c) The program is to implement the non-recursive form of postorder traversal.

(d) None of the above.

Question 46

Which of the following statement is correct about the code given below?

```
# include <stdio.h>
# include <conio.h>
# include <malloc.h>
# define MAX 50

struct btreenode
{
      struct btreenode *lc ;
      int data ;
      struct btreenode *rc ;
} ;
void insert ( struct btreenode **, int ) ;
void order ( struct btreenode * ) ;
void deleteall ( struct btreenode *p ) ;

int main( )
{
      struct btreenode *bt ;
      bt = NULL ;
      insert ( &bt, 10 ) ;
      insert ( &bt, 6 ) ;
      insert ( &bt, 8 ) ;
      insert ( &bt, 15 ) ;
      insert ( &bt, 20 ) ;
      order ( bt ) ;
      deleteall ( bt ) ;
      return 0 ;
}
void insert ( struct btreenode **p, int num )
{
      if ( *p == NULL )
      {
            *p = ( struct btreenode * ) malloc ( sizeof ( struct btreenode ) ) ;
            ( *p ) -> lc = NULL ;
            ( *p ) -> data = num ;
```

```
        ( *p ) -> rc = NULL ;
    }
    else
    {
        if ( num < ( *p ) -> data )
            insert ( &( ( *p ) -> lc ), num ) ;
        else
            insert ( &( ( *p ) -> rc ), num ) ;
    }
}
void order ( struct btreenode *pt )
{
    struct btreenode *stack[ MAX ] ;
    int top = -1 ;
    while ( 1 )
    {
        while ( pt != NULL )
        {
            printf ( "\t%d", pt -> data ) ;
            top++ ;
            if ( top > MAX - 1 )
            {
                printf ( "Stack is full." ) ;
                return ;
            }
            stack[ top ] = pt ;
            pt = pt -> lc ;
        }
        if ( top != -1 )
        {
            pt = stack[ top ] ;
            top-- ;
            pt = pt -> rc ;
        }
        else
```

```
            break ;
        }
}
void deleteall ( struct btreenode *p )
{
        if ( p != NULL )
        {
                deleteall ( p -> lc ) ;
                deleteall ( p -> rc ) ;
                free ( p ) ;
        }
}
```

(a) The program is to implement the non-recursive form of inorder traversal.

(b) The program is to implement the non-recursive form of preorder traversal.

(c) The program is to implement the non-recursive form of postorder traversal.

(d) None of the above.

Question 47

Which of the following statements is correct about the code given below?

```
# include <stdio.h>
# include <conio.h>
# include <malloc.h>
# define MAX 50

struct btreenode
{
        struct btreenode *lc ;
        int data ;
        struct btreenode *rc ;
} ;
```

```
void insert ( struct btreenode **, int ) ;
void order ( struct btreenode * ) ;
void deleteall ( struct btreenode *p ) ;

int main( )
{
    struct btreenode *bt ;
    bt = NULL ;
    insert ( &bt, 10 ) ;
    insert ( &bt, 6 ) ;
    insert ( &bt, 8 ) ;
    insert ( &bt, 15 ) ;
    insert ( &bt, 20 ) ;
    order ( bt ) ;
    deleteall ( bt ) ;
    return 0 ;
}
void insert ( struct btreenode **p, int num )
{
    if ( *p == NULL )
    {
        *p = ( struct btreenode * ) malloc ( sizeof ( struct btreenode ) ) ;
        ( *p ) -> lc = NULL ;
        ( *p ) -> data = num ;
        ( *p ) -> rc = NULL ;
    }
    else
    {
        if ( num < ( *p ) -> data )
            insert ( &( ( *p ) -> lc ), num ) ;
        else
            insert ( &( ( *p ) -> rc ), num ) ;
    }
}
void order ( struct btreenode *pt )
```

```
{
    struct btreenode *stack[ MAX ] ;
    int top = -1, l = 0, lr[ MAX ] ;
    int d ;
    while ( 1 )
    {
        while ( pt != NULL && l == 0 )
        {
            top++ ;
            if ( top > MAX - 1 )
            {
                printf ( "Stack full." ) ;
                return ;
            }
            stack[ top ] = pt ;
            lr[ top ] = 0 ;
            pt = pt -> lc ;
        }
        if ( top != -1 )
        {
            pt = stack[ top ] ;
            d = lr[ top ] ;
            top-- ;
            if ( d == 0 )
            {
                top++ ;
                stack[ top ] = pt ;
                lr[ top ] = 1 ;
                pt = pt -> rc ;
                l = 0 ;
            }
            else
            {
                printf ( "\t%d", pt -> data ) ;
                l = 1;
```

```
            }
        }
        else
            break ;
    }
}
void deleteall ( struct btreenode *p )
{
    if ( p != NULL )
    {
        deleteall ( p -> lc ) ;
        deleteall ( p -> rc ) ;
        free ( p ) ;
    }
}
```

(a) The program is to implement the non-recursive form of inorder traversal.

(b) The program is to implement the non-recursive form of preorder traversal.

(c) The program is to implement the non-recursive form of postorder traversal.

(d) None of the above.

Question 48

Which of the following statements is correct about the code given below?

```
# include <stdio.h>
# include <conio.h>
# include <malloc.h>
# define FALSE 0
# define TRUE 1

struct btnode
{
```

```
        struct btnode *lc ;
        int data ;
        struct btnode *rc ;
} ;
int level = 0 ;
void insert ( struct btnode **, int ) ;
void search ( struct btnode **, int, struct btnode  **, struct btnode **, int * ) ;
int main( )
{
        struct btnode *bt, *parent, *x ;
        int req, found, num ;
        bt = NULL ;
        insert ( &bt, 11 ) ;
        insert ( &bt, 9 ) ;
        insert ( &bt, 13 ) ;
        insert ( &bt, 8 ) ;
        insert ( &bt, 10 ) ;
        insert ( &bt, 12 ) ;
        insert ( &bt, 14 ) ;
        insert ( &bt, 15 ) ;
        insert ( &bt, 7 ) ;
        printf ( "Enter the number to be present in the binary tree" ) ;
        scanf ( "%d", &num ) ;
        search ( &bt, num, &parent, &x, &found ) ;
        if ( found == TRUE )
                printf ( "Data is present in the file at level %d", level ) ;
        else
                printf ( "Data is not present in the file" ) ;
        return 0 ;
}
void insert ( struct btnode **sr, int num )
{
        if ( *sr == NULL )
        {
                *sr = ( struct btnode * ) malloc ( sizeof ( struct btnode ) ) ;
```

```
            ( *sr ) -> lc = NULL ;
            ( *sr ) -> data = num ;
            ( *sr ) -> rc = NULL ;
      }
      else
      {
            if ( ( *sr ) -> data > num )
                  insert ( &( ( *sr ) -> lc ), num ) ;
            else
                  insert ( &( ( *sr ) -> rc ), num ) ;
      }
}
void search ( struct btnode **sr, int num, struct btnode  **par, struct btnode **x, int *found
)
{
      struct btnode *q ;
      q = *sr ;
      *found = FALSE ;
      *par = NULL ;
      while ( q != NULL )
      {
            if ( q -> data == num )
            {
                  *found = TRUE ;
                  *x = q ;
                  return ;
            }
            *par = q ;
            if ( q -> data > num )
            {
                  q = q -> lc ;
                  level++ ;
            }
            else
            {
```

```
                q = q -> rc ;
                level++ ;
            }
        }
}
```

(a) The program is to find whether the number is present in a binary tree at a particular level.

(b) The program is to traverse a binary tree level by level.

(c) The program is to find the number of nodes in a binary tree at each level.

(d) The program is to determine the level of the binary tree.

Question 49

Which of the following function is correct to complete the code given below?

```
# include <stdio.h>
# include <conio.h>
# include <malloc.h>
# define TRUE 1
# define FALSE 0

struct btnode
{
    struct btnode *lc ;
    int data ;
    struct btnode *rc ;
} ;
void insert ( struct btnode **, int ) ;
void compare ( struct btnode *, struct btnode *, int * ) ;

int main( )
{
```

```
    struct btnode *bt1, *bt2 ;
    int i ;
    bt1 = bt2 = NULL ;
    insert ( &bt1, 5 ) ;
    insert ( &bt1, 3 ) ;
    insert ( &bt1, 10 ) ;
    insert ( &bt1, 4 ) ;
    insert ( &bt1, 2 ) ;

    insert ( &bt2, 5 ) ;
    insert ( &bt2, 3 ) ;
    insert ( &bt2, 10 ) ;
    insert ( &bt2, 4 ) ;
    insert ( &bt2, 2 ) ;
    compare ( bt1, bt2, &i ) ;
    if ( i == TRUE )
        printf ( "SIMILAR" ) ;
    else
        printf ( "NOT SIMILAR" ) ;
    return 0 ;
}
void insert ( struct btnode **p, int num )
{
    if ( *p == NULL )
    {
        *p = ( struct btnode * ) malloc ( sizeof ( struct btnode ) ) ;

        ( *p ) -> lc = NULL ;
        ( *p ) -> data = num ;
        ( *p ) -> rc = NULL ;
    }
    else
    {
        if ( num < ( *p ) -> data )
            insert ( &( ( *p ) -> lc ), num ) ;
```

```
        else
            insert ( &( ( *p ) -> lc ), num ) ;
    }
}
```

(a)
```
void compare ( struct btnode p, struct btnode *q, int *flag )
{
    *flag = FALSE ;
    if ( p == NULL && q == NULL )
        *flag = TRUE ;
    if ( p != NULL && q != NULL )
    {
        if ( p -> data != q -> data )
            *flag = FALSE ;
        else
        {
            compare ( p -> lc, q -> lc, flag ) ;
            if ( *flag != FALSE )
                compare ( p -> rc, q -> rc, flag ) ;
        }
    }
}
```

(b)
```
void compare ( struct btnode *p, struct btnode *q, int *flag )
{
    *flag = FALSE ;
    if ( p == NULL && q == NULL )
        *flag = TRUE ;
    if ( p != NULL && q != NULL )
    {
        if ( p -> data != q -> data )
            *flag = FALSE ;
        else
        {
            if ( *flag != FALSE )
```

```
                    compare ( p -> rc, q -> rc, flag ) ;
            }
        }
    }
```

(c)
```
    void compare ( struct btnode *p, struct btnode *q, int *flag )
    {
        *flag = FALSE ;
        if ( p == NULL && q == NULL )
            *flag = TRUE ;
        if ( p != NULL && q != NULL )
        {
            if ( p -> data != q -> data )
                *flag = FALSE ;
            else
            {
                compare ( p -> lc, q -> lc, flag ) ;
                if ( *flag != FALSE )
                    ;
            }
        }
    }
```

(d)
```
    void compare ( struct btnode *p, struct btnode *q, int *flag )
    {
        *flag = FALSE ;
        if ( p == NULL && q == NULL )
            *flag = TRUE ;
        if ( p != NULL && q != NULL )
        {
            if ( p -> data != q -> data )
                *flag = FALSE ;
            else
            {
                compare ( p -> lc, q -> lc, flag ) ;
```

```
                if ( *flag != FALSE )
                    compare ( p -> rc, q -> rc, flag ) ;
            }
        }
    }
```

Question 50

Which of the following statements is correct about the code given below?

```
# include <stdio.h>
# include <conio.h>
# include <malloc.h>
# define TRUE 1
# define FALSE 0

struct btnode
{
    struct btnode *lc ;
    int data ;
    struct btnode *rc ;
} ;
void insert ( struct btnode **, int ) ;
void mirror ( struct btnode *p, struct btnode *q, int *flag ) ;

int main( )
{
    struct btnode *bt1, *bt2 ;
    int i ;
    bt1 = bt2 = NULL ;
    insert ( &bt1, 5 ) ;
    insert ( &bt1, 3 ) ;
    insert ( &bt1, 10 ) ;
    insert ( &bt1, 4 ) ;
    insert ( &bt1, 2 ) ;
```

```
    insert ( &bt2, 5 ) ;
    insert ( &bt2, 3 ) ;
    insert ( &bt2, 10 ) ;
    insert ( &bt2, 4 ) ;
    insert ( &bt2, 2 ) ;

    mirror ( bt1, bt2, &i ) ;
    if ( i == TRUE )
        printf ( "\nBoth Binary trees are mirror images of each other" ) ;
    else
        printf ( "\nBoth Binary trees arenot mirror images of each other" ) ;
    return 0 ;
}
void insert ( struct btnode **p, int num )
{
    if ( *p == NULL )
    {
        *p = ( struct btnode * ) malloc ( sizeof ( struct btnode ) ) ;

        ( *p ) -> lc = NULL ;
        ( *p ) -> data = num ;
        ( *p ) -> rc = NULL ;
    }
    else
    {
        if ( num < ( *p ) -> data )
            insert ( &( ( *p ) -> lc ), num ) ;
        else
            insert ( &( ( *p ) -> lc ), num ) ;
    }
}
void mirror ( struct btnode *p, struct btnode *q, int *flag )
{
    *flag = FALSE ;
```

```
    if ( p ==  NULL && q == NULL )
        *flag =TRUE ;

    if ( p != NULL && q != NULL )
    {
        if ( p -> data != q -> data )
            *flag = FALSE ;
        else
        {
            mirror ( p -> lc, q -> rc, flag ) ;
            if ( *flag != FALSE )
                mirror ( p -> rc, q -> lc, flag ) ;
        }
    }
}
```

(a) The program is to find whether the two binary trees are similar.

(b) The program is to find whether the two binary trees are mirror images of each other.

(c) The program is to find number of nodes in a binary tree at each level.

(d) The program is to find the number of leaf nodes in a binary tree.

Question 51

Which of the following statements is correct about the code given below?

```
# include <stdio.h>
# include <conio.h>
# include <malloc.h>

struct btnode
{
    struct btnode *lc ;
```

```
    int data ;
    struct btnode *rc ;
} ;
void insert ( struct btnode **, int ) ;
void search ( struct btnode **, int ) ;
int level = 0 ;
static int c[10] ;

int main( )
{
    struct btnode *bt, *parent, *x ;
    int req, found, num, i = 0, a[ ] = { 11, 9, 13, 8, 10, 12, 14, 15, 7 } ;
    int count ;
    int k ;
    bt = NULL ;
    while ( i <= 8 )
    {
        insert ( &bt, a[i] ) ;
        i++ ;
    }
    for( i = 0 ; i <= 8 ; i++ )
    search ( &bt, a[i] ) ;
    printf ( "Level\tNo of Nodes" ) ;
    for( i = 0 ; i <= 8 ; i++ )
    {
        count = 0 ;
        for( k = i ; k<= 8 ; k++ )
        {
            if ( c[i] == c[k] )
            {
                count++ ;
                if ( count > 1 )
                    c[k] = -1 ;
            }
```

```
        }
        if ( c[i] != -1 )
        printf ( "\n%d\t%d",c[i], count ) ;
    }
    return 0 ;
}
void insert ( struct btnode **sr, int num )
{
    if ( *sr == NULL )
    {
        *sr = ( struct btnode * ) malloc ( sizeof ( struct btnode ) ) ;
        ( *sr ) -> lc = NULL ;
        ( *sr ) -> data = num ;
        ( *sr ) -> rc = NULL ;
    }
    else
    {
        if ( ( *sr ) -> data > num )
            insert ( &( ( *sr ) -> lc ), num ) ;
        else
            insert ( &( ( *sr ) -> rc ), num ) ;
    }
}
int j ;
void search ( struct btnode **sr, int num )
{
    struct btnode *q ;
    q = *sr ;
    while ( q != NULL )
    {
        if ( q -> data == num )
        {
            j++ ;
            return ;
        }
```

```
        if ( q -> data > num )
        {
            q = q -> lc ;
            c[j]++ ;
        }
        else
        {
            q = q -> rc ;
            c[j]++ ;
        }
    }
}
```

(a) The program is to find the number at a particular level.

(b) The program is to finds the number of nodes in a binary tree at each level.

(c) The program is to finds the number of leaf-nodes at each level.

(d) The program is to find the total number of nodes in a binary tree.

Question 52

Which of the following statements is correct about the code given below?

```
# include <stdio.h>
# include <conio.h>
# include <malloc.h>
# define MAX 10

struct btreenode
{
    struct btreenode *lc ;
    int data ;
    struct btreenode *rc ;
} ;
```

```
void traverse ( struct btreenode * ) ;
void insert ( struct btreenode **, int ) ;

int main( )
{
    struct btreenode *bt ;
    int req, num, i = 0 ;
    bt = NULL ;
    printf ( "Specify the number of items to be inserted: " ) ;
    scanf ( "%d", &req ) ;

    while ( i++ < req )
    {
        printf ( "Enter the data: " ) ;
        scanf ( "%d", &num ) ;
        insert ( &bt, num ) ;
    }
    printf ( "\n\nTraversal of binary tree :\n" ) ;
    traverse ( bt ) ;
    return 0 ;
}
void insert ( struct btreenode **p, int num )
{
    if ( *p == NULL )
    {
        *p = ( struct btreenode * ) malloc ( sizeof ( struct btreenode ) ) ;
        ( *p ) -> lc = NULL ;
        ( *p ) -> data = num ;
        ( *p ) -> rc = NULL ;
    }
    else
    {
        if ( ( *p ) -> data > num )
            insert ( &( ( *p ) -> lc ), num ) ;
        else
```

```
            insert ( &( ( *p ) -> rc ), num ) ;
      }
}
void traverse ( struct btreenode *p )
{
      struct btreenode *stack[MAX] ;
      int top = -1 ;
      while ( 1 )
      {
            while ( p != NULL )
            {
                  top++ ;
                  if ( top > MAX - 1 )
                  {
                        printf ( "Stack full." ) ;
                        return ;
                  }
                  stack[top] = p ;
                  p = p -> lc ;
            }
            if ( top != -1 )
            {
                  p = stack[ top ] ;
                  top-- ;
                  printf ( "%d\t", p -> data ) ;
                  p = p -> rc ;
            }
            else
                  break ;
      }
}
```

(a) The program is to traverse a binary tree at a particular level by level from right towards left.

(b) The program is to traverse a binary tree at a particular level by level from left towards right.

(c) The program is to create the mirror image of the binary tree.

(d) The program is to find the number of nodes at a particular level.

Question 53

Which of the following statements is correct about the code given below?

```
# include <stdio.h>
# include <conio.h>
# include <malloc.h>

enum boolean
{
	false = 0,
	true = 1
} ;
struct thtree
{
	enum boolean isleft ;
	struct thtree *left ;
	int data ;
	struct thtree *right ;
	enum boolean isright ;
} ;
void insert ( struct thtree **, int ) ;
void inorder ( struct thtree * ) ;

int main( )
{
	struct thtree *th_head ;
	th_head = NULL ;
	insert ( &th_head, 12 ) ;
```

```
    insert ( &th_head, 9 ) ;
    insert ( &th_head, 13 ) ;
    insert ( &th_head, 8 ) ;
    insert ( &th_head, 15 ) ;

    printf ( "Threaded binary tree:\n" ) ;
    inorder ( th_head ) ;
    return 0 ;
}
void insert ( struct thtree **s, int num )
{
    struct thtree *p, *z, *head = *s ;
    z = malloc ( sizeof ( struct thtree ) ) ;
    z -> isleft = true ;
    z -> data = num ;
    z -> isright = true ;
    if ( *s == NULL )
    {
        head = malloc ( sizeof ( struct thtree ) ) ;
        head -> isleft = false ;
        head -> left = z ;
        head -> data = -9999 ;
        head -> right = head ;
        head -> isright = true ;
        *s = head ;
        z -> left = head ;
        z -> right = head ;
    }
    else
    {
        p = head -> left ;
        while ( p != head )
        {
            if ( p -> isleft != true )
                p = p -> left ;
```

```
            else
            {
                z -> left = p -> left ;
                p -> left = z ;
                p -> isleft = false ;
                p -> isright = true ;
                z -> right = p ;
                return ;
            }
        }
    }
}
void inorder ( struct thtree *root )
{
    struct thtree *p ;
    p = root -> left ;
    while ( p != root )
    {
        while ( p -> isleft == false )
            p = p -> left ;
        printf ( "%d\t", p -> data ) ;
        while ( p -> isright == true )
        {
            p = p -> right ;
            if ( p == root )
                break ;
            printf ( "%d\t", p -> data ) ;
        }
        p = p -> right ;
    }
}
```

(a) The program is to insert a node t as a right child of any node s in a binary tree.

(b) The program is to insert a node t as a right child of any node s in a threaded binary tree.

(c) The program is to insert a node t as a left child of any node s in a threaded binary tree.

(d) The program is to insert a node t as a left child of any node s in a binary tree.

Question 54

Which of the following statements is correct about the code given below?

```
# include <stdio.h>
# include <conio.h>
# include <dos.h>
# include <dir.h>
# include <string.h>
# include <malloc.h>
struct btreenode
{
    struct btreenode *leftchild ;
    char data[13] ;
    char *loc ;
    struct btreenode *rightchild ;
} *bt = NULL ;

void disktree( ) ;
int insert ( struct btreenode  **, char*, char* ) ;

int main( )
{
    char current_dir[32] ;
    getcwd ( current_dir, 32 ) ;
    chdir ( "\\" ) ;
    disktree( ) ;
    chdir ( current_dir ) ;
    return 0 ;
}
void disktree( )
```

```
{
    struct ffblk file ;
    int flag ;
    char loc[80] ;
    getcwd ( loc, 80 ) ;
    flag =  findfirst ( "*.*", &file, FA_NORMAL | FA_RDONLY | FA_HIDDEN |
                        FA_SYSTEM | FA_LABEL | FA_DIREC | FA_ARCH ) ;

    while ( flag == 0 )
    {
        if ( file.ff_name[0] != '.' )
        {
            if ( file.ff_attrib == FA_DIREC && file.ff_fsize == 0 )
            {
                chdir ( file.ff_name ) ;
                disktree( ) ;
                chdir ( loc ) ;
            }
            else
                insert ( &bt, loc, file.ff_name ) ;
        }
        flag = findnext ( &file ) ;
    }
}
int insert ( struct btreenode  **sr, char* l, char* f )
{
    char *p ;
    int flag ;

    if ( *sr == NULL )
    {
        *sr = ( struct btreenode * ) malloc ( sizeof ( struct btreenode ) ) ;
        if ( *sr == NULL )
        {
            printf ( "\nOut of memory." ) ;
```

```
        exit ( 1 ) ;
    }
    ( *sr ) -> leftchild = NULL ;
    ( *sr ) -> rightchild = NULL ;
    strcpy ( ( *sr ) -> data, f ) ;
    p = ( char * ) malloc ( ( strlen ( l ) + 1 ) ) ;

    if ( p == NULL )
    {
        printf ( "\nOut of memory." ) ;
        exit ( 1 ) ;
    }
    strcpy ( p, l ) ;
    ( *sr ) -> loc = p ;
}
else
{
    flag = strcmp ( ( *sr ) -> data, f ) ;

    if ( flag == 0 )
    {
        printf ( "org: %s", ( *sr ) -> loc ) ;

        if ( strlen ( ( *sr ) -> loc ) > 4 )
            printf ( "\\" ) ;

        printf ( "%s\n", ( *sr ) -> data ) ;
        printf ("dup: %s", l ) ;

        if ( strlen ( l ) > 4 )
            printf ( "\\" ) ;

        printf ( "%s\n\n", f ) ;
    }
    else if ( flag < 0 )
```

```
            insert ( &( ( *sr ) -> leftchild ), l, f ) ;
        else
            insert ( &( ( *sr ) -> rightchild ), l, f ) ;
    }
    return ;
}
```

(a) The program is to traverse a binary tree level by level.

(b) The program is to maintain a dictionary of words as a binary tree.

(c) The program is to find files with duplicate names using binary search tree.

(d) The program is to create a mirror image of a given tree.

Question 55

Which of the following rules must be followed to build a 2-3 tree?

I. All the non-leaf nodes in a 2-3 tree must always have two or three non-empty child nodes that are again 2-3 trees.

II. The level of all the leaf nodes must always be the same.

III. One single node can contain either one or two values.

IV. If any node has two children (left and right) then that node contains single data. The data occurring on left sub-tree of that node is less than the data of the node and the data occurring on right sub-tree of that node is greater than the data of the node.

V. If any node has three children (left, middle and right), then that node contains two data values, say i and j, where i < j. The data of all the nodes on the left sub-tree are less than i. The data of all the nodes on the middle sub-tree are greater than i but less than j and the data of all the nodes on the right sub-tree are greater than j.

(a) I, II and III are correct.

(b) II, III and IV are correct.

(c) I, II, III and IV are correct.

(d) All the statements from I to V are correct.

Question 56

Which of the following option must satisfies the condition by the B-tree of order n?

I. All the non-leaf nodes (except the root node) have at least n/2 children and at the most n children.

II. The non-leaf root node may have at the most n non-empty child and at least two child nodes.

III. A B-tree can exist with only one node i.e. the root node containing no child.

IV. If a node has n children then it must have n - 1 values. All the values of a particular node are in increasing order.

(a) I, II and III are correct.

(b) II, III and IV are correct.

(c) I, II and IV are correct.

(d) All the four statement are correct.

Question 57

Which of the following statements are correct about the B-tree?

I. All the values that appear on the left most child of a node are smaller than the first value of that node. All the values that appear on the right most child of a node are greater than the last value of that node.

II. If x and y are any two ith and (i + 1)th values of a node, where x < y, then all the values appearing on the (i + 1)th sub-tree of that node are greater than x and less than y.

III. All the leaf nodes should appear on the different level.

(a) I and II are correct.

(b) I and III are correct.

(c) II and III are correct.

(d) All the three statements are correct.

Question 58

Which of the following option is correct for the statements given below?

I. To insert an element to the heap, the node is inserted after the last element in the array and is compared with its parent that is present at (i/2)th position.

II. If the value present at any node is greater than all its children then such a tree is called as the max-heap or descending heap.

III. In case of a min-heap or ascending heap the value present in any node is smaller than all its children.

IV. Heap can be constructed from an array.

(a) Only I and IV are correct.

(b) Only II and III are correct.

(c) I, II and III are correct.

(d) All the four statements are correct.

Question 59

What will be the output for the program given below?

```
# include <stdio.h>
# include <conio.h>

void restoreup ( int, int * ) ;
void restoredown ( int, int *, int ) ;
void makeheap ( int *, int ) ;
void add ( int, int *, int * ) ;

int main( )
{
```

```
    int arr [20] = { 1000, 7, 10, 25, 17, 23, 27, 16, 19, 37, 42, 4, 33, 1, 5, 11 } ;
    int i, n = 15 ;
    makeheap ( arr, n ) ;
    add ( i, arr, &n ) ;
    printf ( "\n\nElement added %d.\n", i ) ;
    printf ( "\nHeap after addition of an element:\n" ) ;
    for ( i = 1 ; i <= n ; i++ )
        printf ( "%d\t", arr [i] ) ;
    return 0 ;
}
void restoreup ( int i, int *arr )
{
    int val ;
    val = arr [i] ;
    while ( arr [i / 2] <= val )
    {
        arr [i] = arr [i / 2] ;
        i = i / 2 ;
    }
    arr [i] = val ;
}
void restoredown ( int pos, int *arr, int n )
{
    int i, val ;
    val = arr [pos] ;
    while ( pos <= n / 2 )
    {
        i = 2 * pos ;
        if ( ( i < n ) && ( arr [i] < arr [i + 1] ) )
            i++ ;
        if ( val >= arr [i] )
            break ;
        arr [pos] = arr [i] ;
        pos = i ;
    }
```

```
        arr [pos] = val ;
}
void makeheap ( int *arr, int n )
{
        int i ;
        for ( i = n / 2 ; i >= 1 ; i-- )
                restoredown ( i, arr, n ) ;
}
void add ( int val, int *arr, int *n )
{
        ( *n ) ++ ;
        arr [*n] = val ;
        restoreup ( *n, arr ) ;
}
```

(a) Element added 944.
Heap after addition of an element :
944 42 33 37 23 27 16 19 17 10
4 25 1 5 11 7

(b) Element added 922
Heap after addition of an element :
922 42 33 37 23 27 16 19 17 10
4 25 1 5 11 7

(c) Element added 936.
Heap after addition of an element :
936 42 33 37 23 27 16 19 17 10
4 11 7 25 1 5

(d) Element added 936.
Heap after addition of an element :
936 42 33 37 23 27 16 19 17 10
4 25 1 5 11 7

Question 60

What would be the output fot the program given below?

```
# include <stdio.h>
# include <conio.h>

void restoreup ( int, int * ) ;
void restoredown ( int, int *, int ) ;
void makeheap ( int *, int ) ;
void add ( int, int *, int * ) ;
int replace ( int, int *, int ) ;

int main( )
{
    int arr [20] = { 1000, 7, 10, 25, 17, 23, 27, 16, 19, 37, 42, 4, 33, 1, 5, 11 } ;
    int i, n = 15 ;
    makeheap ( arr, n ) ;
    add ( i, arr, &n ) ;
    i = replace ( 2, arr, n ) ;
    printf ( "\n\nElement replaced %d.\n", i ) ;
    printf ( "\nHeap after replacement of an element:\n" ) ;
    for ( i = 1 ; i <= n ; i++ )
        printf ( "%d\t", arr [i] ) ;
    return 0 ;
}
void restoreup ( int i, int *arr )
{
    int val ;
    val = arr [i] ;
    while ( arr [i / 2] <= val )
    {
        arr [i] = arr [i / 2] ;
        i = i / 2 ;
    }
```

```
        arr [i] = val ;
}
void restoredown ( int pos, int *arr, int n )
{
        int i, val ;
        val = arr [pos] ;
        while ( pos <= n / 2 )
        {
                i = 2 * pos ;
                if ( ( i < n ) && ( arr [i] < arr [i + 1] ) )
                        i++ ;
                if ( val >= arr [i] )
                        break ;
                arr [pos] = arr [i] ;
                pos = i ;
        }
        arr [pos] = val ;
}
void makeheap ( int *arr, int n )
{
        int i ;
        for ( i = n / 2 ; i >= 1 ; i-- )
                restoredown ( i, arr, n ) ;
}
void add ( int val, int *arr, int *n )
{
        ( *n ) ++ ;
        arr [*n] = val ;
        restoreup ( *n, arr ) ;
}
int replace ( int i, int *arr, int n )
{
        int r = arr [1] ;
        arr [1] = i ;
        for ( i = n / 2 ; i >= 1 ; i-- )
```

```
        restoredown ( i, arr, n ) ;
    return r ;
}
```

(a) Element replaced 936.
Heap after replacement of an element :
42 37 33 19 23 27 16 7 17 10
4 25 1 5 11 2

(b) Element replaced 922.
Heap after replacement of an element :
42 37 23 27 33 19 16 7 17 10
4 25 1 5 11 2

(c) Element replaced 942.
Heap after replacement of an element :
42 37 33 19 23 27 16 7 17 10
4 25 1 5 11 2

(d) Element replaced 944.
Heap after replacement of an element :
42 37 33 19 23 7 17 10 27 16
4 25 1 5 11 2

Answers

Q. 1 – C	Q. 2 – D	Q. 3 – A
Q. 4 – B	Q. 5 – B	Q. 6 – A
Q. 7 – B	Q. 8 – C	Q. 9 – D
Q. 10 – B	Q. 11 – A	Q. 12 – A
Q. 13 – D	Q. 14 – B	Q. 15 – A
Q. 16 – D	Q. 17 – C	Q. 18 – D
Q. 19 – A	Q. 20 – B	Q. 21 – D
Q. 22 – B	Q. 23 – C	Q. 24 – D
Q. 25 – D	Q. 26 – D	Q. 27 – C
Q. 28 – A	Q. 29 – A	Q. 30 – B
Q. 31 – C	Q. 32 – D	Q. 33 – B
Q. 34 – C	Q. 35 – A	Q. 36 – D
Q. 37 – C	Q. 38 – A	Q. 39 – C
Q. 40 – D	Q. 41 – A	Q. 42 – B
Q. 43 – C	Q. 44 – A	Q. 45 – A
Q. 46 – B	Q. 47 – C	Q. 48 – A

Q. 49 – D	Q. 50 – B	Q. 51 – B
Q. 52 – B	Q. 53 – C	Q. 54 – C
Q. 55 – D	Q. 56 – D	Q. 57 – A
Q. 58 – D	Q. 59 – D	Q. 60 – C

8

Graphs

Question 1

The directed graph is also called as :

(a) D-graph

(b) De-graph

(c) Connected graph

(d) Digraph

Question 2

In which of the following fields can graphs be used?

(a) Analysis of electrical circuits

(b) Finding shortest routes

(c) Statistical analysis

(d) All of the above

Question 3

Which of the following algorithm is used to visit all the vertices from a given vertex in an undirected graph?

(a) Depth First Search

(b) Breadth Second Search

(c) Breadth First Search

(d) Both (a) and (c)

Question 4

The pairs of vertices in the graph are called as :

(a) Nodes

(b) Edges

(c) Path

(d) Child

Question 5

Edges of a directed graph are drawn with an arrow from the ________.

(a) Head to the tail

(b) Tail to the head

(c) Top to the bottom

(d) Bottom to the top

Question 6

In which of the following path all the vertices except first and last are distinct?

(a) Cyclic path

(b) Connected path

(c) Strongly connected path

(d) Simple path

Question 7

Which of the following are the most commonly used matrix representations for graphs?

(a) Diagonal matrix

(b) Adjacency matrix

(c) Binary matrix

(d) Triangular matrix

Question 8

Which of the following is a 2-dimensional array of size n X n where n is the number of vertices in the graph?

(a) Adjacency matrix

(b) Adjacency list

(c) D-graph

(d) Undirected graph

Question 9

For which of the following the adjacency matrix is symmetric?

(a) Undirected graph

(b) De-graph

(c) Digraph

(d) Tree

Question 10

The space needed to represent a graph using its adjacency matrix is ____ locations where N is the number of vertices in the graph.

(a) 2N

(b) N2

(c) N

(d) 2logN

Question 11

In adjacency list how many lists are used to represent one vertex in a graph?

(a) 0

(b) 1

(c) 2

(d) 3

Question 12

What will be produced by depth first traversal for an undirected graph which is not connected?

(a) 2-3 tree

(b) B-tree

(c) Spanning tree

(d) Forest

Question 13

What will be produced by depth first traversal for a connected undirected graph?

(a) 2-3 tree

(b) B-tree

(c) Spanning tree

(d) Forest

Question 14

What will be produced by depth first traversal for a connected directed graph?

(a) 2-3 tree

(b) B-tree

(c) Spanning tree

(d) Forest

Question 15

The n rows of the adjacency matrix are represented as ___ linked lists.

(a) n – 1

(b) n + 1

(c) n

(d) 2n

Question 16

In undirected graph any edge is represented by the pair

(a) < v1 , v2 >

(b) (v1 , v2)

(c) [v1 , v2]

(d) { v1 , v2 }

Question 17

In directed graph each edge is represented by the pair:

(a) < v1 , v2 >

(b) (v1 , v2)

(c) [v1 , v2]

(d) { v1 , v2 }

Question 18

The path in which first and the last vertices are same is called:

(a) Simple path

(b) Cyclic path

(c) Dashing path

(d) None of the above

Question 19

The path between two vertices is represented by

(a) Way

(b) Edge

(c) Connector

(d) All of the above

Question 20

In adjacency lists representation of an undirected graph, each edge (Vi , Vj) is represented by _____ entries.

(a) 1

(b) 2

(c) 3

(d) 4

Question 21

What is the difference between directed graph and undirected graph?

(a) In an undirected graph the order of pair of vertices is unimportant. Hence the pairs (v1, v2) and (v2, v1) represent the same edge.

As against this, in a directed graph the order of vertices representing an edge is important. This pair is represented as <v1, v2>, where v1 is the tail and v2 the head of the edge.

(b) In a directed graph the order of pair of vertices is unimportant. Hence the pairs (v1, v2) and (v2, v1) represent the same edge.

As against this, in an undirected graph the order of vertices representing an edge is important. This pair is represented as <v1, v2>, where v1 is the tail and v2 the head of the edge.

(c) The adjacency matrix for an undirected graph is symmetric. The adjacency matrix for a directed graph need not be symmetric.

(d) Both A and C.

Question 22

Which of the following edges represent the same path if a1 and a2 are the two vertices of an undirected graph?

(a) < a1 , a2 > and < a2 , a1 >

(b) < a1 , a2 > and (a2 , a1)

(c) (a1 , a2) and (a2 , a1)

(d) (a1 , a2) and < a1 , a2 >

Question 23

Select the correct alternative for the following:

I. Depth first search algorithm visits the starting vertex twice

II. Breadth first search visits each node just one time

(a) true, true

(b) true, false

(c) false, false

(d) false, true

Question 24

Graph can be represented using which of the following methods?

(a) adjacency list

(b) adjacency multilist

(c) orthogonal representation

(d) all of the above

Question 25

The spanning tree resulting from a call to depth first tree is called:

(a) depth spanning tree

(b) depth tree

(c) depth first spanning tree

(d) spanning depth tree

Question 26

The spanning tree resulting from a call to breadth first tree is called:

(a) breadth spanning tree

(b) breadth tree

(c) spanning breadth tree

(d) breadth first spanning tree

Question 27

The cost of spanning tree is :

(a) sum of costs of even edges in tree

(b) sum of costs of odd edges in tree

(c) sum of costs of the edges in tree

(d) None of the above

Question 28

Kruskal's algorithm gives

(a) largest edge in the spanning tree

(b) minimum cost spanning tree

(c) smallest edge in the spanning tree

(d) shortest path

Question 29

Which of the following algorithm gives the shortest path between two nodes?

(a) Kruskal's algorithm

(b) Dijkstra's algorithm

(c) Short-Route algorithm

(d) None of the above

Question 30

Select the correct alternative for the following :

I. A minimal spanning tree gives indication about the shortest path between two nodes.

II. In minimal spanning tree overall cost is minimized.

(a) false, false

(b) false, true

(c) true, true

(d) true, true

Question 31

While calculating the shortest path between two nodes, in the adjacency matrix the path that does not exist between two nodes is taken as :

(a) 0

(b) -1

(c) Infinity

(d) 1

Question 32

Select the correct alternative for the following :

I. To find the minimum cost of spanning using Kruskal's algorithm the edges are inserted to tree in decreasing order of their cost.

II. In Dijkstra's algorithm, to calculate the minimum cost of any edge and determine the path between two vertices, one by one each vertex is taken into consideration.

(a) true, true

(b) false, true

(c) true, false

(d) false, false

Question 33

Which of the following is a spanning tree?

(a)

```
  1
 / \
2   3
 \ /
  4
```

(b)
```
    1
   / \
    2----3
     \
      4
```

(c)
```
    1
   / \
  2   3
     /
    4
```

(d) None of the above

Question 34

The minimum cost of spanning tree is given by

(a) sum of all edges

(b) sum of cost of all even edges

(c) sum of cost of the edges that are inserted while building the spanning tree of minimum cost

(d) None of the above

Question 35

Which of the following is NOT a part of node structure of the adjacency multilist for a digraph?

(a) Next link to tail

(b) Next link to head

(c) Head

(d) Previous link to edge

Question 36

Insertion of any edge to a spanning tree form a unique cycle because

(a) for any pair of vertices there exists multiple paths between them

(b) for any pair of vertices there exists two paths between them

(c) for any pair of vertices there exists only one path between them

(d) None of the above

Question 37

Select the correct alternative for the following:

I. If v1 and v2 are two vertices of a directed graph G, then the edges <v1, v2> and <v2, v1> represent the same edge.

II. For a graph there can exist only those many spanning trees as the number of vertices.

(a) true, true

(b) false, true

(c) true, false

(d) false, false

Question 38

Select the correct alternative for the following:

I. To find minimum cost spanning tree edges are inserted in increasing order of their cost.

II. An edge being considered is included in the spanning tree only if on inclusion it forms a cycle with edges that are already present in the spanning tree.

(a) true, true

(b) false, true

(c) true, false

(d) false, false

Question 39

Which of the following paths contains all vertices in the graph?

(a) Simple Path

(b) Cyclic Path

(c) Hamilton Path

(d) Dashing Path

Question 40

Select the correct alternative for the following:

I. A directed graph is acyclic if it has no cycles.

II. A graph is said to be connected if there exists a path between any two vertices.

(a) true, true

(b) false, true

(c) true, false

(d) false, false

Question 41

What will be the minimum cost of the spanning tree given below?

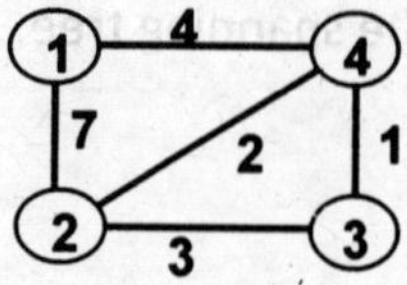

(a) 6

(b) 7

(c) 10

(d) 13

Question 42

Which of the following steps are involved in the Depth First search algorithm?

I. Visit a vertex, say v. Mark this vertex as visited.

II. Select an unvisited vertex w adjacent to v.

III. Repeat steps [I] and [II] till all adjacent vertices of w are visited.

IV. On reaching a vertex whose all adjacent vertices have been visited, go back to the last vertex visited which has an unvisited vertex adjacent to it and go back to step [I].

V. Terminate the search when no unvisited vertex can be reached from any of the visited ones.

(a) I, II and III.

(b) I, II and IV.

(c) I, II, III and IV.

(d) All the five from I to V.

Question 43

What would be the output for the program given below?

```
# include <stdio.h>
# include <conio.h>
# include <malloc.h>
# define TRUE 1
# define FALSE 0
```

```
# define MAX 8
struct node
{
    int data ;
    struct node *next ;
} ;
int visited[MAX] ;
void dfs ( int, struct node ** ) ;
struct node * getnode_write ( int ) ;
void del ( struct node * ) ;

int main( )
{
    struct node *arr[MAX] ;
    struct node *v1, *v2, *v3, *v4 ;
    int i ;

    v1 = getnode_write ( 2 ) ;
    arr[0] = v1 ;
    v1 -> next = v2 = getnode_write ( 3 ) ;
    v2 -> next = NULL ;

    v1 = getnode_write ( 1 ) ;
    arr[1] = v1 ;
    v1 -> next = v2 = getnode_write ( 4 ) ;
    v2 -> next = v3 = getnode_write ( 5 ) ;
    v3 -> next = NULL ;

    v1 = getnode_write ( 1 ) ;
    arr[2] = v1 ;
    v1 -> next = v2 = getnode_write ( 6 ) ;
    v2 -> next = v3 = getnode_write ( 7 ) ;
    v3 -> next = NULL ;

    v1 = getnode_write ( 2 ) ;
```

```
    arr[3] = v1 ;
    v1 -> next = v2 = getnode_write ( 8 ) ;
    v2 -> next = NULL ;

    v1 = getnode_write ( 2 ) ;
    arr[4] = v1 ;
    v1 -> next = v2 = getnode_write ( 8 ) ;
    v2 -> next = NULL ;

    v1 = getnode_write ( 3 ) ;
    arr[5] = v1 ;
    v1 -> next = v2 = getnode_write ( 8 ) ;
    v2 -> next = NULL ;

    v1 = getnode_write ( 3 ) ;
    arr[6] = v1 ;
    v1 -> next = v2 = getnode_write ( 8 ) ;
    v2 -> next = NULL ;

    v1 = getnode_write ( 4 ) ;
    arr[7] = v1 ;
    v1 -> next = v2 = getnode_write ( 5 ) ;
    v2 -> next = v3 = getnode_write ( 6 ) ;
    v3 -> next = v4 = getnode_write ( 7 ) ;
    v4 -> next = NULL ;

    dfs ( 1, arr ) ;
    for ( i = 0 ; i < MAX ; i++ )
        del ( arr[i] ) ;
    return 0 ;
}
void dfs ( int v, struct node **p )
{
    struct node *q ;
    visited[v - 1] = TRUE ;
```

```
        printf ( "%d\t", v ) ;
        q = * ( p + v - 1 ) ;
        while ( q != NULL )
        {
            if ( visited[q -> data - 1] == FALSE )
                dfs ( q -> data, p ) ;
            else
                q = q -> next ;
        }
}
struct node * getnode_write ( int val )
{
        struct node *newnode ;
        newnode = ( struct node * ) malloc ( sizeof ( struct node ) ) ;
        newnode -> data = val ;
        return newnode ;
}
void del ( struct node *n )
{
        struct node *temp ;
        while ( n != NULL )
        {
            temp = n -> next ;
            free ( n ) ;
            n = temp ;
        }
}
```

(a) 1 2 4 8 5 6 3 7

(b) 1 2 3 4 5 6 7 8

(c) 1 2 4 8 7 3 5 6

(d) 1 2 4 8 5 7 3 6

Question 44

What will be the output for the program given below?

```
# include <stdio.h>
# include <conio.h>
# include <malloc.h>
# define TRUE 1
# define FALSE 0
# define MAX 8

struct node
{
    int data ;
    struct node *next ;
} ;
int visited[MAX] ;
int q[8] ;
int front, rear ;

void bfs ( int, struct node ** ) ;
struct node * getnode_write ( int ) ;
void addqueue ( int ) ;
int deletequeue( ) ;
int isempty( ) ;
void del ( struct node * ) ;

int main( )
{
    struct node *arr[MAX] ;
    struct node *v1, *v2, *v3, *v4 ;
    int i ;

    v1 = getnode_write ( 2 ) ;
    arr[0] = v1 ;
```

```
v1 -> next = v2 = getnode_write ( 3 ) ;
v2 -> next = NULL ;

v1 = getnode_write ( 1 ) ;
arr[1] = v1 ;
v1 -> next = v2 = getnode_write ( 4 ) ;
v2 -> next = v3 = getnode_write ( 5 ) ;
v3 -> next = NULL ;
v1 = getnode_write ( 1 ) ;
arr[2] = v1 ;
v1 -> next = v2 = getnode_write ( 6 ) ;
v2 -> next = v3 = getnode_write ( 7 ) ;
v3 -> next = NULL ;

v1 = getnode_write ( 2 ) ;
arr[3] = v1 ;
v1 -> next = v2 = getnode_write ( 8 ) ;
v2 -> next = NULL ;

v1 = getnode_write ( 2 ) ;
arr[4] = v1 ;
v1 -> next = v2 = getnode_write ( 8 ) ;
v2 -> next = NULL ;

v1 = getnode_write ( 3 ) ;
arr[5] = v1 ;
v1 -> next = v2 = getnode_write ( 8 ) ;
v2 -> next = NULL ;

v1 = getnode_write ( 3 ) ;
arr[6] = v1 ;
v1 -> next = v2 = getnode_write ( 8 ) ;
v2 -> next = NULL ;

v1 = getnode_write ( 4 ) ;
```

```
    arr[7] = v1 ;
    v1 -> next = v2 = getnode_write ( 5 ) ;
    v2 -> next = v3 = getnode_write ( 6 ) ;
    v3 -> next = v4 = getnode_write ( 7 ) ;
    v4 -> next = NULL ;

    front = rear = -1 ;
    bfs ( 1, arr ) ;

    for ( i = 0 ; i < MAX ; i++ )
        del ( arr[i] ) ;
    return 0 ;
}
void bfs ( int v, struct node **p )
{
    struct node *u ;
    visited[v - 1] = TRUE ;
    printf ( "%d\t", v ) ;
    addqueue ( v ) ;

    while ( isempty( ) == FALSE )
    {
        v = deletequeue( ) ;
        u = * ( p + v - 1 ) ;
        while ( u != NULL )
        {
            if ( visited [u -> data - 1] == FALSE )
            {
                addqueue ( u -> data ) ;
                visited [u -> data - 1] = TRUE ;
                printf ( "%d\t", u -> data ) ;
            }
            u = u -> next ;
        }
    }
```

```
}
struct node * getnode_write ( int val )
{
      struct node *newnode ;
      newnode = ( struct node * ) malloc ( sizeof ( struct node ) ) ;
      newnode -> data = val ;
      return newnode ;
}
void addqueue ( int vertex )
{
      if ( rear == MAX - 1 )
      {
            printf ( "\nQueue Overflow." ) ;
            exit ( ) ;
      }
      rear++ ;
      q[rear] = vertex ;
      if ( front == -1 )
            front = 0 ;
}
int deletequeue( )
{
      int data ;
      if ( front == -1 )
      {
            printf ( "\nQueue Underflow." ) ;
            exit( ) ;
      }
      data = q[front] ;
      if ( front == rear )
            front = rear = -1 ;
      else
            front++ ;
      return data ;
}
```

```
int isempty( )
{
    if ( front == -1 )
        return TRUE ;
    return FALSE ;
}
void del ( struct node *n )
{
    struct node *temp ;
    while ( n != NULL )
    {
        temp = n -> next ;
        free ( n ) ;
        n = temp ;
    }
}
```

(a) 1 2 3 4 5 6 7 8

(b) Queue Underflow

(c) Queue Overflow
1 2 7 8 5 6 3 4

(d) Queue Underflow
5 6 7 8 1 2 3 4

Question 45

Which of the following operations does the following code perform?

```
# include <stdio.h>
# include <conio.h>
# include <malloc.h>
```

```
struct lledge
{
      int v1, v2 ;
      float cost ;
      struct lledge *next ;
} ;
int stree[5] ;
int count[5] ;
int mincost ;

struct lledge * kminstree ( struct lledge *, int ) ;
int getrval ( int ) ;
void combine ( int, int ) ;
void del ( struct lledge * ) ;

int main( )
{
      struct lledge *temp, *root ;
      int i ;

      root = ( struct lledge * ) malloc ( sizeof ( struct lledge ) ) ;
      root -> v1 = 4 ;
      root -> v2 = 3 ;
      root -> cost = 1 ;
      temp = root -> next = ( struct lledge * ) malloc ( sizeof ( struct lledge ) ) ;

      temp -> v1 = 4 ;
      temp -> v2 = 2 ;
      temp -> cost = 2 ;
      temp -> next = ( struct lledge * ) malloc ( sizeof ( struct lledge ) ) ;

      temp = temp -> next ;
      temp -> v1 = 3 ;
      temp -> v2 = 2 ;
      temp -> cost = 3 ;
```

```
    temp -> next = ( struct lledge * ) malloc ( sizeof ( struct lledge ) ) ;

    temp = temp -> next ;
    temp -> v1 = 4 ;
    temp -> v2 = 1 ;
    temp -> cost = 4 ;
    temp -> next = NULL ;

    root = kminstree ( root, 5 ) ;

    for ( i = 1 ; i <= 4 ; i++ )
        printf ( "\nstree[%d] -> %d", i, stree[i] ) ;
    printf ( "\n %d", mincost ) ;
    del ( root ) ;
    return 0 ;
}
struct lledge * kminstree ( struct lledge *root, int n )
{
    struct lledge *temp = NULL ;
    struct lledge *p, *q ;
    int noofedges = 0 ;
    int i, p1, p2 ;

    for ( i = 0 ; i < n ; i++ )
        stree[i] = i ;
    for ( i = 0 ; i < n ; i++ )
        count[i] = 0 ;

    while ( ( noofedges < ( n - 1 ) ) && ( root != NULL ) )
    {
        p = root ;
        root = root -> next ;
        p1 = getrval ( p -> v1 ) ;
        p2 = getrval ( p -> v2 ) ;
        if ( p1 != p2 )
```

```
        {
            combine ( p -> v1, p -> v2 ) ;
            noofedges++ ;
            mincost += p -> cost ;
            if ( temp == NULL )
            {
                temp = p ;
                q = temp ;
            }
            else
            {
                q -> next = p ;
                q = q -> next ;
            }
            q -> next = NULL ;
        }
    }
    return temp ;
}
int getrval ( int i )
{
    int j, k, temp ;
    k = i ;
    while ( stree[k] != k )
        k = stree[k] ;
    j = i ;
    while ( j != k )
    {
        temp = stree[j] ;
        stree[j] = k ;
        j = temp ;
    }
    return k ;
}
void combine ( int i, int j )
```

```
{
    if ( count[i] < count[j] )
        stree[i] = j ;
    else
    {
        stree[j] = i ;
        if ( count[i] == count[j] )
            count[j]++ ;
    }
}
void del ( struct lledge *root )
{
    struct lledge *temp ;
    while ( root != NULL )
    {
        temp = root -> next ;
        free ( root ) ;
        root = temp ;
    }
}
```

(a) The program implements the depth first search algorithm.

(b) The program implements the breadth first search algorithm.

(c) The program finds the minimum cost of the spanning tree.

(d) The program finds the shortest path between any two nodes.

Question 46

What will be the output of the program given below?

```
# include <stdio.h>
# include <conio.h>
# define INF 9999
```

```
int main( )
{
    int arr[4][4] ;
    int cost[4][4] = {
                        7, 5, 0, 0,
                        7, 0, 0, 2,
                        0, 3, 0, 0,
                        4, 0, 1, 0
                    } ;
    int i, j, k, n = 4 ;
    for ( i = 0 ; i < n ; i++ )
    {
        for ( j = 0 ; j < n ; j++ )
        {
            if ( cost[i][j] == 0 )
                arr[i][j] = INF ;
            else
                arr[i][j] = cost[i][j] ;
        }
    }

    for ( k = 0 ; k < n ; k++ )
    {
        for ( i = 0 ; i < n ; i++ )
        {
            for ( j = 0 ; j < n ; j++ )
            {
                if ( arr[i][j] > arr[i][k] + arr[k][j] )
                    arr[i][j] = arr[i][k] + arr[k][j] ;
            }
        }
    }

    printf ( "\nAdjacency matrix of lowest cost between the vertices:\n" ) ;
    for ( i = 0 ; i < n ; i++ )
```

```
    {
        for ( j = 0 ; j < n ; j++ )
            printf ( "%d\t", arr[i][j] ) ;
        printf ( "\n" ) ;
    }
    return 0 ;
}
```

(a) Adjacency matrix of lowest cost between the vertices :

```
6   6   3   2
7   5   8   7
9   3   6   5
4   4   1   6
```

(b) Adjacency matrix of lowest cost between the vertices :

```
7   5   8   7
6   6   3   2
9   3   6   5
4   4   1   6
```

(c) Adjacency matrix of lowest cost between the vertices :

```
7   5   8   7
9   3   6   5
6   6   3   2
4   4   1   6
```

(d) Adjacency matrix of lowest cost between the vertices :

```
7   5   8   7
4   4   1   6
6   6   3   2
9   3   6   5
```

Question 47

Which of the following operations is performed by the program given below?

```
# include <stdio.h>
# include <conio.h>
# include <malloc.h>
# define TRUE 1
# define FALSE 0
# define MAX 8

struct node
{
	int data ;
	struct node *next ;
} ;

int visited[MAX] ;
struct node * getnode_write ( int ) ;
int del ( struct node * ) ;
int noofvert ( struct node ** ) ;

int main( )
{
	struct node *arr[MAX] ;
	struct node *v1, *v2, *v3, *v4 ;
	int i, c ;
	int num ;

	v1 = getnode_write ( 2 ) ;
	arr[0] = v1 ;
	v1 -> next = v2 = getnode_write ( 8 ) ;
	v2 -> next = NULL ;

	v1 = getnode_write ( 1 ) ;
	arr[1] = v1 ;
	v1 -> next = v2 = getnode_write ( 3 ) ;
	v2 -> next = v3 = getnode_write ( 8 ) ;
```

```
v3 -> next = NULL ;

v1 = getnode_write ( 2 ) ;
arr[2] = v1 ;
v1 -> next = v2 = getnode_write ( 4 ) ;
v2 -> next = v3 = getnode_write ( 8 ) ;
v3 -> next = NULL ;

v1 = getnode_write ( 3 ) ;
arr[3] = v1 ;
v1 -> next = v2 = getnode_write ( 7 ) ;
v2 -> next = NULL ;

v1 = getnode_write ( 6 ) ;
arr[4] = v1 ;
v1 -> next = v2 = getnode_write ( 7 ) ;
v2 -> next = NULL ;

v1 = getnode_write ( 5 ) ;
arr[5] = v1 ;
v1 -> next = NULL ;

v1 = getnode_write ( 4 ) ;
arr[6] = v1 ;
v1 -> next = v2 = getnode_write ( 5 ) ;
v2 -> next = v3 = getnode_write ( 8 ) ;
v3 -> next = NULL ;

v1 = getnode_write ( 1 ) ;
arr[7] = v1 ;
v1 -> next = v2 = getnode_write ( 2 ) ;
v2 -> next = v3 = getnode_write ( 3 ) ;
v3 -> next = v4 = getnode_write ( 7 ) ;
v4 -> next = NULL ;
```

```
    c = noofvert ( arr ) ;
    printf ( "\n %d ", c ) ;
    return 0 ;
}
struct node * getnode_write ( int val )
{
    struct node *newnode ;
    newnode = ( struct node * ) malloc ( sizeof ( struct node ) ) ;
    newnode -> data = val ;
    return newnode ;
}
int noofvert ( struct node **p )
{
    struct node *q ;
    int i, c ;

    for ( i = 0 ; i < MAX ; i++ )
    {
        q = * ( p + i ) ;

        while ( q != NULL )
            q = q -> next ;

        c++ ;
    }
    return c ;
}
int del ( struct node *n )
{
    struct node *temp ;
    while ( n != NULL )
    {
        temp = n -> next ;
        free ( n ) ;
        n = temp ;
```

```
    }
}
```

(a) The program is to find the number of adjacent vertices.

(b) The program is to find the shortest path.

(c) The program is to find the minimum cost of spanning tree.

(d) The program is to find the number of vertices in a graph.

Question 48

What will be the output for the program given below if the number entered is 2?

```
# include <stdio.h>
# include <conio.h>
# include <malloc.h>
# define TRUE 1
# define FALSE 0
# define MAX 8

struct node
{
    int data ;
    struct node *next ;
} ;

int visited[MAX] ;

struct node * getnode_write ( int ) ;
void vertices ( int, struct node ** ) ;

int main( )
{
    struct node *arr[MAX] ;
```

```
struct node *v1, *v2, *v3, *v4 ;
int i, c ;
int num ;

v1 = getnode_write ( 2 ) ;
arr[0] = v1 ;
v1 -> next = v2 = getnode_write ( 8 ) ;
v2 -> next = NULL ;

v1 = getnode_write ( 1 ) ;
arr[1] = v1 ;
v1 -> next = v2 = getnode_write ( 3 ) ;
v2 -> next = v3 = getnode_write ( 8 ) ;
v3 -> next = NULL ;

v1 = getnode_write ( 2 ) ;
arr[2] = v1 ;
v1 -> next = v2 = getnode_write ( 4 ) ;
v2 -> next = v3 = getnode_write ( 8 ) ;
v3 -> next = NULL ;

v1 = getnode_write ( 3 ) ;
arr[3] = v1 ;
v1 -> next = v2 = getnode_write ( 7 ) ;
v2 -> next = NULL ;

v1 = getnode_write ( 6 ) ;
arr[4] = v1 ;
v1 -> next = v2 = getnode_write ( 7 ) ;
v2 -> next = NULL ;

v1 = getnode_write ( 5 ) ;
arr[5] = v1 ;
v1 -> next = NULL ;
```

```
    v1 = getnode_write ( 4 ) ;
    arr[6] = v1 ;
    v1 -> next = v2 = getnode_write ( 5 ) ;
    v2 -> next = v3 = getnode_write ( 8 ) ;
    v3 -> next = NULL ;

    v1 = getnode_write ( 1 ) ;
    arr[7] = v1 ;
    v1 -> next = v2 = getnode_write ( 2 ) ;
    v2 -> next = v3 = getnode_write ( 3 ) ;
    v3 -> next = v4 = getnode_write ( 7 ) ;
    v4 -> next = NULL ;

    printf ( "\nEnter the verices number to find its adjacent vertex :" ) ;
    scanf ( "%d", &num ) ;

    vertices ( num, arr ) ;
    return 0 ;
}
struct node * getnode_write ( int val )
{
    struct node *newnode ;
    newnode = ( struct node * ) malloc ( sizeof ( struct node ) ) ;
    newnode -> data = val ;
    return newnode ;
}
void vertices ( int num, struct node **p )
{
    struct node *q ;
    int i ;
    for ( i = 0 ; i < MAX ; i++ )
    {
        q = * ( p + i ) ;
        if ( i+1 == num )
        {
```

```
            while ( q != NULL )
            {
                printf ( " %d ", q -> data ) ;
                q = q -> next ;
            }
        }
    }
}
```

(a) 1 3 8

(b) 2 8

(c) 2 4 8

(d) 3 7

Question 49

What will be the output of the program given below?

```
# include <stdio.h>
# include <conio.h>
# define INF 9999

int main( )
{
    int arr[4][4] ;
    int cost[4][4] = {
                        5, 1, 0, 0,
                        3, 0, 0, 4,
                        0, 2, 0, 0,
                        2, 0, 3, 1
                    } ;
    int i, j, k, n = 4 ;
```

```
    for ( i = 0 ; i < n ; i++ )
    {
        for ( j = 0 ; j < n ; j++ )
        {
            if ( cost[i][j] == 0 )
                arr[i][j] = INF ;
            else
                arr[i][j] = cost[i][j] ;
        }
    }

    for ( k = 0 ; k < n ; k++ )
    {
        for ( i = 0 ; i < n ; i++ )
        {
            for ( j = 0 ; j < n ; j++ )
            {
                if ( arr[i][j] > arr[i][k] + arr[k][j] )
                    arr[i][j] = arr[i][k] + arr[k][j] ;
            }
        }
    }

    printf ( "\nAdjacency matrix of lowest cost between the vertices:\n" ) ;
    for ( i = 0 ; i < n ; i++ )
    {
        for ( j = 0; j < n ; j++ )
            printf ( "%d\t", arr[i][j] ) ;
        printf ( "\n" ) ;
    }
}
```

(a) Adjacency matrix of lowest cost between the vertices :

```
4   1   9   5
3   4   7   4
```

5 8 9 6
2 3 3 1

(b) Adjacency matrix of lowest cost between the vertices :

4 1 6 5
3 4 7 4
5 2 9 6
2 3 2 1

(c) Adjacency matrix of lowest cost between the vertices :

4 1 6 5
3 1 7 4
5 2 9 6
2 3 4 1

(d) Adjacency matrix of lowest cost between the vertices :

4 1 8 5
3 4 7 4
5 2 9 6
2 3 3 1

Question 50

What will be the output of the following program if the input entered is 7?

```
# include <stdio.h>
# include <conio.h>
# include <malloc.h>
# define TRUE 1
# define FALSE 0
# define MAX 8

struct node
{
    int data ;
```

```
    struct node *next ;
} ;

int visited[MAX] ;

struct node * getnode_write ( int ) ;
void vertices ( int, struct node ** ) ;

int main( )
{
    struct node *arr[MAX] ;
    struct node *v1, *v2, *v3, *v4 ;
    int i, c ;
    int num ;

    v1 = getnode_write ( 2 ) ;
    arr[0] = v1 ;
    v1 -> next = v2 = getnode_write ( 8 ) ;
    v2 -> next = NULL ;

    v1 = getnode_write ( 1 ) ;
    arr[1] = v1 ;
    v1 -> next = v2 = getnode_write ( 3 ) ;
    v2 -> next = v3 = getnode_write ( 8 ) ;
    v3 -> next = NULL ;

    v1 = getnode_write ( 2 ) ;
    arr[2] = v1 ;
    v1 -> next = v2 = getnode_write ( 4 ) ;
    v2 -> next = v3 = getnode_write ( 8 ) ;
    v3 -> next = NULL ;

    v1 = getnode_write ( 3 ) ;
    arr[3] = v1 ;
    v1 -> next = v2 = getnode_write ( 7 ) ;
```

```
    v2 -> next = NULL ;

    v1 = getnode_write ( 6 ) ;
    arr[4] = v1 ;
    v1 -> next = v2 = getnode_write ( 7 ) ;
    v2 -> next = NULL ;

    v1 = getnode_write ( 5 ) ;
    arr[5] = v1 ;
    v1 -> next = NULL ;

    v1 = getnode_write ( 4 ) ;
    arr[6] = v1 ;
    v1 -> next = v2 = getnode_write ( 5 ) ;
    v2 -> next = v3 = getnode_write ( 8 ) ;
    v3 -> next = NULL ;

    v1 = getnode_write ( 1 ) ;
    arr[7] = v1 ;
    v1 -> next = v2 = getnode_write ( 2 ) ;
    v2 -> next = v3 = getnode_write ( 3 ) ;
    v3 -> next = v4 = getnode_write ( 7 ) ;
    v4 -> next = NULL ;

    printf ( "\nEnter the vertices number to find its adjacent vertex :" ) ;
    scanf ( "%d", &num ) ;

    vertices ( num, arr ) ;
    return 0 ;
}

struct node * getnode_write ( int val )
{
    struct node *newnode ;
    newnode = ( struct node * ) malloc ( sizeof ( struct node ) ) ;
```

```
    newnode -> data = val ;
    return newnode ;
}

void vertices ( int num, struct node **p )
{
    struct node *q ;
    int i ;

    for ( i = 0 ; i < MAX ; i++ )
    {
        q = * ( p + i ) ;
        if ( i + 1 == num )
        {
            while ( q != NULL )
            {
                printf ( " %d ", q -> data ) ;
                q = q -> next ;
            }
        }
    }
}
```

(a) 1 2 3 7

(b) 4 5 8

(c) 2 4 8

(d) 2 8

Question 51

What will be the output of the program given below?

```
# include <stdio.h>
```

```
# include <conio.h>
# define INF 9999

int main( )
{
      int arr[4][4] ;
      int cost[4][4] = {
                              0, 1, 0, 0,
                              2, 0, 0, 3,
                              0, 3, 0, 5,
                              0, 0, 3, 1
                        } ;
      int i, j, k, n = 4 ;

      for ( i = 0 ; i < n ; i++ )
      {
            for ( j = 0 ; j < n ; j++ )
            {
                  if ( cost[i][j] == 0 )
                        arr[i][j] = INF ;
                  else
                        arr[i][j] = cost[i][j] ;
            }
      }

      for ( k = 0 ; k < n ; k++ )
      {
            for ( i = 0 ; i < n ; i++ )
            {
                  for ( j = 0 ; j < n ; j++ )
                  {
                        if ( arr[i][j] > arr[i][k] + arr[k][j] )
                              arr[i][j] = arr[i][k] + arr[k][j] ;
                  }
            }
```

```
    }

    printf ( "\nAdjacency matrix of lowest cost between the vertices:\n" ) ;
    for ( i = 0 ; i < n ; i++ )
    {
        for ( j = 0; j < n ; j++ )
            printf ( "%d\t", arr[i][j] ) ;
        printf ( "\n" ) ;
    }
    return 0 ;
}
```

(a) Adjacency matrix of lowest cost between the vertices :

```
3   1   7   4
2   3   6   3
5   3   8   5
8   6   3   1
```

(b) Adjacency matrix of lowest cost between the vertices :

```
3   1   6   4
2   3   6   3
4   3   8   5
8   6   7   1
```

(c) Adjacency matrix of lowest cost between the vertices :

```
3   1   5   4
2   3   5   3
5   3   8   5
8   9   3   1
```

(d) Adjacency matrix of lowest cost between the vertices :

```
3   2   7   4
2   3   6   3
5   3   9   5
8   6   3   4
```

Question 52

What will be the output of the program given below if the input entered is 8?

```
# include <stdio.h>
# include <conio.h>
# include <malloc.h>
# define TRUE 1
# define FALSE 0
# define MAX 8

struct node
{
    int data ;
    struct node *next ;
} ;
int visited[MAX] ;
struct node * getnode_write ( int ) ;
void vertices ( int, struct node ** ) ;
int noofvert ( struct node ** ) ;

int main( )
{
    struct node *arr[MAX] ;
    struct node *v1, *v2, *v3, *v4 ;
    int i, c ;
    int num ;

    v1 = getnode_write ( 2 ) ;
    arr[0] = v1 ;
    v1 -> next = v2 = getnode_write ( 8 ) ;
    v2 -> next = NULL ;

    v1 = getnode_write ( 1 ) ;
    arr[1] = v1 ;
```

```
v1 -> next = v2 = getnode_write ( 3 ) ;
v2 -> next = v3 = getnode_write ( 8 ) ;
v3 -> next = NULL ;

v1 = getnode_write ( 2 ) ;
arr[2] = v1 ;
v1 -> next = v2 = getnode_write ( 4 ) ;
v2 -> next = v3 = getnode_write ( 8 ) ;
v3 -> next = NULL ;

v1 = getnode_write ( 3 ) ;
arr[3] = v1 ;
v1 -> next = v2 = getnode_write ( 7 ) ;
v2 -> next = NULL ;

v1 = getnode_write ( 6 ) ;
arr[4] = v1 ;
v1 -> next = v2 = getnode_write ( 7 ) ;
v2 -> next = NULL ;

v1 = getnode_write ( 5 ) ;
arr[5] = v1 ;
v1 -> next = NULL ;

v1 = getnode_write ( 4 ) ;
arr[6] = v1 ;
v1 -> next = v2 = getnode_write ( 5 ) ;
v2 -> next = v3 = getnode_write ( 8 ) ;
v3 -> next = NULL ;

v1 = getnode_write ( 1 ) ;
arr[7] = v1 ;
v1 -> next = v2 = getnode_write ( 2 ) ;
v2 -> next = v3 = getnode_write ( 3 ) ;
v3 -> next = v4 = getnode_write ( 7 ) ;
```

```
    v4 -> next = NULL ;

    c = noofvert ( arr ) ;
    printf ( "\n No of vertices in the program = %d ", c ) ;
    printf ( "\nEnter the verices number to find its adjacent vertex :" ) ;
    scanf ( "%d", &num ) ;
    vertices ( num, arr ) ;
    return 0 ;
}

struct node * getnode_write ( int val )
{
    struct node *newnode ;
    newnode = ( struct node * ) malloc ( sizeof ( struct node ) ) ;
    newnode -> data = val ;
    return newnode ;
}

int noofvert ( struct node **p )
{
    struct node *q ;
    int i, c ;

    for ( i = 0 ; i < MAX ; i++ )
    {
        q = * ( p + i ) ;

        while ( q != NULL )
            q = q -> next ;
        c++ ;
    }
    return c ;
}

void vertices ( int num, struct node **p )
```

```
{
    struct node *q ;
    int i ;

    for ( i = 0 ; i < MAX ; i++ )
    {
        q = * ( p + i ) ;
        if ( i + 1 == num )
        {
            while ( q != NULL )
            {
                printf ( " %d ", q -> data ) ;
                q = q -> next ;
            }
        }
    }
}
```

(a) No of vertices in the program = 8
1 2 3 7

(b) No of vertices in the program = 8
5

(c) No of vertices in the program = 8
6 7

(d) No of vertices in the program = 8
4 5 8

Question 53

What will be the output of the program given below?

```
# include <stdio.h>
```

```
# include <conio.h>
# include <malloc.h>

struct lledge
{
	int v1, v2 ;
	float cost ;
	struct lledge *next ;
} ;

int stree[5] ;
int count[5] ;
int mincost ;
struct lledge * kminstree ( struct lledge *, int ) ;
int getrval ( int ) ;
void combine ( int, int ) ;
void del ( struct lledge * ) ;

int main( )
{
	struct lledge *temp, *root ;
	int i ;

	root = ( struct lledge * ) malloc ( sizeof ( struct lledge ) ) ;
	root -> v1 = 4 ;
	root -> v2 = 3 ;
	root -> cost = 1 ;
	temp = root -> next = ( struct lledge * ) malloc ( sizeof ( struct lledge ) ) ;

	temp -> v1 = 4 ;
	temp -> v2 = 2 ;
	temp -> cost = 2 ;
	temp -> next = ( struct lledge * ) malloc ( sizeof ( struct lledge ) ) ;

	temp = temp -> next ;
```

```
    temp -> v1 = 3 ;
    temp -> v2 = 2 ;
    temp -> cost = 3 ;
    temp -> next = ( struct lledge * ) malloc ( sizeof ( struct lledge ) ) ;

    temp = temp -> next ;
    temp -> v1 = 4 ;
    temp -> v2 = 1 ;
    temp -> cost = 4 ;
    temp -> next = NULL ;

    root = kminstree ( root, 5 ) ;

    for ( i = 1 ; i <= 4 ; i++ )
        printf ( "\nstree[%d] -> %d", i, stree[i] ) ;
    printf ( "\n %d", mincost ) ;
    del ( root ) ;
    return 0 ;
}

struct lledge * kminstree ( struct lledge *root, int n )
{
    struct lledge *temp = NULL ;
    struct lledge *p, *q ;
    int noofedges = 0 ;
    int i, p1, p2 ;

    for ( i = 0 ; i < n ; i++ )
        stree[i] = i ;
    for ( i = 0 ; i < n ; i++ )
        count[i] = 0 ;

    while ( ( noofedges < ( n - 1 ) ) && ( root != NULL ) )
    {
        p = root ;
```

```
            root = root -> next ;
            p1 = getrval ( p -> v1 ) ;
            p2 = getrval ( p -> v2 ) ;
            if ( p1 != p2 )
            {
                combine ( p -> v1, p -> v2 ) ;
                noofedges++ ;
                mincost += p -> cost ;
                if ( temp == NULL )
                {
                    temp = p ;
                    q = temp ;
                }
                else
                {
                    q -> next = p ;
                    q = q -> next ;
                }
                q -> next = NULL ;
            }
        }
        return temp ;
}

int getrval ( int i )
{
        int j, k, temp ;
        k = i ;
        while ( stree[k] != k )
            k = stree[k] ;
        j = i ;
        while ( j != k )
        {
            temp = stree[j] ;
            stree[j] = k ;
```

```
        j = temp ;
    }
    return k ;
}

void combine ( int i, int j )
{
    if ( count[i] < count[j] )
        stree[i] = j ;
    else
    {
        stree[j] = i ;
        if ( count[i] == count[j] )
            count[j]++ ;
    }
}

void del ( struct lledge *root )
{
    struct lledge *temp ;
    while ( root != NULL )
    {
        temp = root -> next ;
        free ( root ) ;
        root = temp ;
    }
}
```

(a) stree[1] -> 1
stree[2] -> 1
stree[3] -> 1
stree[4] -> 1
11

(b) stree[1] -> 2

stree[2] -> 2
stree[3] -> 2
stree[4] -> 2
13

(c) stree[1] -> 3
stree[2] -> 3
stree[3] -> 3
stree[4] -> 3
10

(d) stree[1] -> 4
stree[2] -> 4
stree[3] -> 4
stree[4] -> 4
7

Question 54

What will be the output of the program given below?

```
# include <stdio.h>
# include <conio.h>
# define INF 9999

int main( )
{
    int arr[4][4] ;
    int cost[4][4] = {
                        7, 0, 0, 6,
                        5, 0, 4, 0,
                        0, 3, 2, 0,
                        0, 1, 0, 2
                };
    int i, j, k, n = 4 ;
```

```
    for ( i = 0 ; i < n ; i++ )
    {
        for ( j = 0 ; j < n ; j++ )
        {
            if ( cost[i][j] == 0 )
                arr[i][j] = INF ;
            else
                arr[i][j] = cost[i][j] ;
        }
    }

    for ( k = 0 ; k < n ; k++ )
    {
        for ( i = 0 ; i < n ; i++ )
        {
            for ( j = 0 ; j < n ; j++ )
            {
                if ( arr[i][j] > arr[i][k] + arr[k][j] )
                    arr[i][j] = arr[i][k] + arr[k][j] ;
            }
        }
    }

    printf ( "\nAdjacency matrix of lowest cost between the vertices:\n" ) ;
    for ( i = 0 ; i < n ; i++ )
    {
        for ( j = 0; j < n ; j++ )
            printf ( "%d\t", arr[i][j] ) ;
        printf ( "\n" ) ;
    }
    return 0 ;
}
```

(a) Adjacency matrix of lowest cost between the vertices :

```
            printf ( "\n" ) ;
        }
        return 0 ;
}
```

(a) Adjacency matrix of lowest cost between the vertices :

5	3	9	6
2	5	6	9
6	9	3	5
5	4	3	7

(b) Adjacency matrix of lowest cost between the vertices :

5	3	9	6
2	5	7	3
6	4	8	5
1	4	3	7

(c) Adjacency matrix of lowest cost between the vertices :

5	3	9	6
2	5	6	3
6	9	8	5
1	4	3	7

(d) Adjacency matrix of lowest cost between the vertices :

5	3	9	6
2	7	6	3
6	9	8	5
1	4	9	7

Question 56

Consider the following undirected graph.

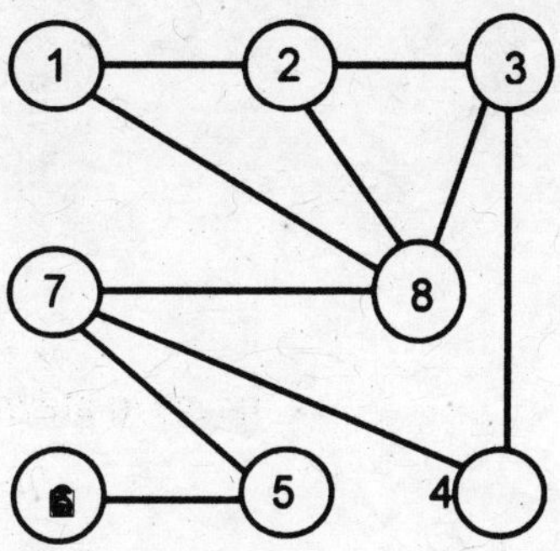

If the depth first search is initiated from vertex 1, then the vertices are visited in the order :

(a) 1, 2, 3, 4, 5, 7, 6, 8

(b) 2, 1, 4, 3, 8, 5, 6, 7

(c) 1, 8, 2, 3, 5, 6, 7, 4

(d) 1, 2, 3, 4, 7, 5, 6, 8

Question 57

What will be the output of the program given below?

```
# include <stdio.h>
# include <conio.h>
# define INF 9999

int main( )
{
      int arr[4][4] ;
      int cost[4][4] = {
                        0, 1, 0, 2,
                        3, 0, 0, 4,
                        5, 0, 0, 6,
```

```
                        7, 0, 4, 0
                    } ;
    int i, j, k, n = 4 ;

    for ( i = 0 ; i < n ; i++ )
    {
        for ( j = 0 ; j < n ; j++ )
        {
            if ( cost[i][j] == 0 )
                arr[i][j] = INF ;
            else
                arr[i][j] = cost[i][j] ;
        }
    }

    for ( k = 0 ; k < n ; k++ )
    {
        for ( i = 0 ; i < n ; i++ )
        {
            for ( j = 0 ; j < n ; j++ )
            {
                if ( arr[i][j] > arr[i][k] + arr[k][j] )
                    arr[i][j] = arr[i][k] + arr[k][j] ;
            }
        }
    }

    printf ( "\nAdjacency matrix of lowest cost between the vertices:\n" ) ;
    for ( i = 0 ; i < n ; i++ )
    {
        for ( j = 0; j < n ; j++ )
            printf ( "%d\t", arr[i][j] ) ;
        printf ( "\n" ) ;
    }
    return 0 ;
```

}

(a) Adjacency matrix of lowest cost between the vertices :

4	9	6	2
3	4	8	4
5	9	10	6
7	8	4	9

(b) Adjacency matrix of lowest cost between the vertices :

4	1	6	2
3	4	9	4
5	9	10	6
7	8	4	9

(c) Adjacency matrix of lowest cost between the vertices :

4	1	6	2
3	4	8	4
5	6	10	6
7	8	4	9

(d) Adjacency matrix of lowest cost between the vertices :

4	1	6	2
3	7	8	4
5	6	10	7
7	8	4	9

Question 58

Select Correct alternative from the following:

I. The complexity of Prim's algorithm is O (n2) for a graph having "n" vertices.

II. Prim's algorithm starts with a vertex and goes on adding edges to an already formed partial minimal spanning tree. The edge to be added is a minimum cost edge which has exactly one end belonging to the already formed minimal spanning tree.

(a) Only I is correct.

(b) Only II is correct.

(c) Neither I nor II are correct.

(d) Both I and II are correct.

Question 59

What will be the output of the program given below?

```
# include <stdio.h>
# include <conio.h>
# define INF 9999

int main( )
{
    int arr[4][4] ;
    int cost[4][4] = {
                        7, 0, 0, 6,
                        5, 0, 0, 0,
                        0, 2, 3, 0,
                        0, 1, 0, 2
                    } ;
    int i, j, k, n = 4 ;

    for ( i = 0 ; i < n ; i++ )
    {
        for ( j = 0 ; j < n ; j++ )
        {
            if ( cost[i][j] == 0 )
                arr[i][j] = INF ;
            else
                arr[i][j] = cost[i][j] ;
        }
    }
```

```
    for ( k = 0 ; k < n ; k++ )
    {
        for ( i = 0 ; i < n ; i++ )
        {
            for ( j = 0 ; j < n ; j++ )
            {
                if ( arr[i][j] > arr[i][k] + arr[k][j] )
                    arr[i][j] = arr[i][k] + arr[k][j] ;
            }
        }
    }

    printf ( "\nAdjacency matrix of lowest cost between the vertices:\n" ) ;
    for ( i = 0 ; i < n ; i++ )
    {
        for ( j = 0; j < n ; j++ )
            printf ( "%d\t", arr[i][j] ) ;
        printf ( "\n" ) ;
    }
    return 0 ;
}
```

(a) Adjacency matrix of lowest cost between the vertices :

```
7   7   9999  6
5   12  9999  11
7   2   4     13
6   1   9999  2
```

(b) Adjacency matrix of lowest cost between the vertices :

```
7   7   9999  6
5   12  9999  11
7   2   7     13
6   1   7     2
```

(c) Adjacency matrix of lowest cost between the vertices :

7	7	9999	6
5	12	9999	11
7	2	3	13
6	1	9999	2

(d) Adjacency matrix of lowest cost between the vertices :

7	7	9999	6
5	12	9999	11
7	2	3	13
6	9	9999	2

Question 60

Consider the following undirected graph:

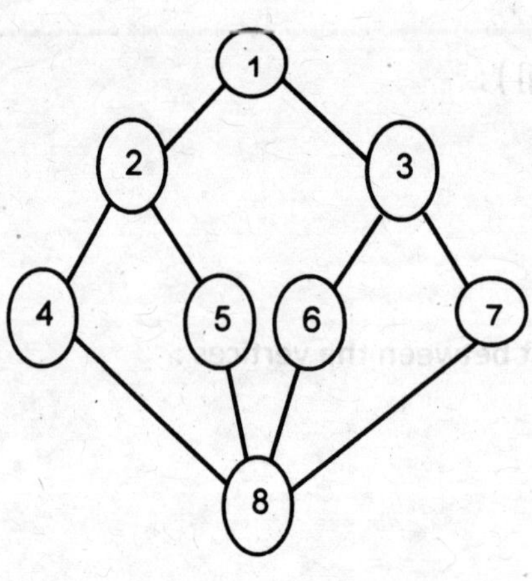

If the breadth first search is initiated from vertex 1, then the vertices are visited in the order:

(a) 1, 2, 3, 4, 5, 7, 6, 8

(b) 2, 1, 4, 3, 8, 5, 6, 7

(c) 1, 8, 2, 3, 5, 6, 7, 4

(d) 1, 2, 3, 4, 7, 5, 6, 8

Answers

Q. 1 – D	Q. 2 – D	Q. 3 – D
Q. 4 – B	Q. 5 – B	Q. 6 – D
Q. 7 – B	Q. 8 – A	Q. 9 – A
Q. 10 – B	Q. 11 – B	Q. 12 – D
Q. 13 – C	Q. 14 – D	Q. 15 – C
Q. 16 – B	Q. 17 – A	Q. 18 – B
Q. 19 – B	Q. 20 – B	Q. 21 – D
Q. 22 – C	Q. 23 – D	Q. 24 – D
Q. 25 – C	Q. 26 – D	Q. 27 – C
Q. 28 – B	Q. 29 – B	Q. 30 – B
Q. 31 – C	Q. 32 – B	Q. 33 – C
Q. 34 – C	Q. 35 – D	Q. 36 – C
Q. 37 – D	Q. 38 – C	Q. 39 – C
Q. 40 – A	Q. 41 – B	Q. 42 – D
Q. 43 – A	Q. 44 – A	Q. 45 – C
Q. 46 – B	Q. 47 – D	Q. 48 – A

Q. 49 – D	Q. 50 – B	Q. 51 – A
Q. 52 – A	Q. 53 – D	Q. 54 – A
Q. 55 – C	Q. 56 – D	Q. 57 – C
Q. 58 – D	Q. 59 – C	Q. 60 – A

9

Searching Algorithms

Question 1

What do you mean by searching an element in an array?

(a) Storing an element in the array.

(b) Finding an element in the array and replacing it with another element.

(c) Finding an element and its location in the array.

(d) Finding the position of the element after sorting the array.

Question 2

Which of the following is(are) the type(s) of Searching methods?

(a) Linear Search

(b) Tree Search

(c) Binary Search

(d) Both A and C

Question 3

Which of the following statement is correct about the linear search?

(a) Elements are searched in random order.

(b) Elements are searched in sequential order from the end.

(c) Elements are searched in sequential order from the beginning.

(d) Elements are searched in alternate fashion.

Question 4

Which of the following statement is correct about the binary search?

(a) Elements must be in sorted order.

(b) Elements should be in random order.

(c) Last element must be zero.

(d) Elements must be in binary form.

Question 5

Which of the following is the order of complexity for a linear search?

(a) O (n)

(b) O (2n)

(c) O (2n – 1)

(d) O (n2)

Question 6

Which of the following is the fastest searching method?

(a) Binary Search

(b) Sequential Search

(c) Random Search

(d) Linear Search

Question 7

Which of the following work only on sorted elements?

(a) Linear Search

(b) Tree Search

(c) Binary Search

(d) Sequential Search

Question 8

Which of the following makes the binary search efficient?

(a) After division of element searching the required element sequentially.

(b) Division of elements into two halves and checking for the required element.

(c) Reduces the number of elements to be searched from n to (n / 2).

(d) Both B and C.

Question 9

How many comparisons are required to find 28 in the following list of elements using linear search?

1, 23, 3, 6, 7, 34, 67, 900, 22, 12, 20, 1909, 28, 1, 3, 45, 67

(a) 12

(b) 13

(c) 11

(d) 14

Question 10

How many comparisons are required to find 8 in the following list of elements using binary search?

11, 3, 53, 16, 10, 4, 167, 9, 8, 12, 20, 1909, 28, 1, 3, 45, 67

(a) 2

(b) 3

(c) 1

(d) 4

Question 11

What is the number of comparisons in worst case scenario for linear search?

(a) (n – 1)

(b) N

(c) (n + 1)

(d) (n / 2)

Question 12

What is the number of comparisons in average case scenario for linear search?

(a) (n + 1)

(b) N

(c) (n – 1)

(d) (n / 2)

Question 13

How strings are compared while searching the string using any searching algorithm?

(a) Addresses of the strings are compared.

(b) Strings are compared character by character starting from the beginning to end.

(c) Strings are compared character by character starting from the end to beginning.

(d) Only the first character of the strings is compared.

Question 14

What is the best case scenario for the linear search algorithm?

(a) When the element to be searched is present at the end of the list.

(b) When the element to be searched is present at the first position.

(c) When the element to be searched is present in the middle.

(d) When the element to be searched is not present in the list.

Question 15

What is the best case scenario for the binary search algorithm?

(a) When the element to be searched is present at the end of the list.

(b) When the element to be searched is present at the first position of the list.

(c) When the element to be searched is present in the middle of the list.

(d) When the element to be searched is not present in the list.

Question 16

What is the worst case for the linear search algorithm?

(a) When the element to be searched is present in the middle of the list.

(b) When the element to be searched is present at the first position.

(c) When the element to be searched is present at the last position of the list.

(d) When the element to be searched is present just before last element in the list.

Question 17

What will be the output of the following program?

```
# include <stdio.h>
int main( )
{
    int array[ ] = { 1, 4, 3, 5, 6, 6, 4, 7, 8, 4, 3, 4 } ;
    int i ;
    for ( i = 0 ; i < 12 ; i++ )
    {
        if ( array[ i ] == 4 )
```

```
        {
            printf ( "%d", i ) ;
            break ;
        }
    }
    return 0 ;
}
```

(a) 6

(b) 9

(c) 1

(d) 11

Question 18

Which of the following statements is correct about the program given below?

```
# include <stdio.h>
int main( )
{
    int a[ ] = { 12, 8, 3, 4, 8, 9, 45, 7, 8, 6, 534, 8 } ;
    int i, k = 0 ;
    for ( i = 0 ; i < 12 ; i++ )
        if ( a[ i ] - 8 != 0 )
            ++k ;
    printf ( "%d ", k ) ;
    return 0 ;
```

a) The program counts all the occurrences of number 8.

b) The program subtracts 8 from all the elements of the array.

c) The program counts those numbers which are the multiples of 8.

(d) The program searches for the element 8, skips it if its is found and counts all other numbers.

Question 19

How the elements should be kept in an array for searching using the binary search?

(a) Elements must be in random order.

(b) Elements must be in ascending order only.

(c) Elements must be in descending order only.

(d) Elements must be in ascending or descending order.

Question 20

Which of the following is correct?

(a) When the elements are in ascending order the binary search works much faster.

(b) When the elements are in descending order the binary search works much faster.

(c) Binary search is useful when there are large numbers of elements.

(d) Binary search also works on unsorted elements.

Question 21

Which of the following statements is correct about the program given below?

```
# include <stdio.h>
int main( )
{
    FILE *fp ;
    int num, p = 0, flag = 0 ;
    fp = fopen ( "Numbers.dat", "rb" ) ;
    while ( ( num = getw ( fp ) ) != EOF )
    {
```

```
            ++p ;
            if ( num == 100 / 2 - 5 )
            {
                flag = 1 ;
                break ;
            }
        }
        if ( flag == 1 )
            printf ( "%d ", p ) ;
        else
            printf ( "0" ) ;
        return 0 ;
}
```

(a) The program counts the number of occurrences of 45 in the file Numbers.dat.

(b) The program finds the first occurrence of 45 in the file Numbers.dat. If not present in the file prints 0.

(c) The program finds the last occurrence of 45 in the file Numbers.dat.

(d) The program prints all the occurrences of 45 in the file Numbers.dat along with 0.

Question 22

What is the purpose of recursion in the following program?

```
# include <stdio.h>
# include <malloc.h>
struct LinkList
{
    int data ;
    struct LinkList *Link ;
} *start = NULL ;
void insert ( int ) ;
void display ( struct LinkList* ) ;
```

```
int main( )
{
    struct LinkList *temp ;
    insert ( 3 ) ;
    insert ( 7 ) ;
    insert ( 5 ) ;
    insert ( 7 ) ;
    insert ( 9 ) ;
    insert ( 1 ) ;
    insert ( 7 ) ;
    display ( start ) ;
    return 0 ;
}
void insert ( int n )
{
    struct LinkList *temp ;
    temp = ( struct LinkList* ) malloc ( sizeof ( struct LinkList ) ) ;
    temp -> data = n ;
    temp -> Link = NULL ;
    if ( !start )
        start = temp ;
    else
    {
        struct LinkList *t = start ;
        while ( t -> Link != NULL )
            t = t -> Link ;
        t -> Link = temp ;
    }
}
void display ( struct LinkList *ptr )
{
    static int i ;
    if ( ( ptr != NULL ) && !( ptr -> data - 7 ) )
        printf ( "%d", i ) ;
    else if ( ptr != NULL )
```

```
    {
        ++i ;
        display ( ptr -> Link ) ;
    }
}
```

(a) The recursion prints the first occurrence of element 7 from the linked list.

(b) The recursion prints the last occurrence of element 7 from the linked list.

(c) The recursion searches for the element greater than 7 from the linked list and prints the difference between them.

(d) The recursion prints all the numbers from the linked list each subtracted by 7.

Question 23

Which of the following statements are correct about the program given below?

```
# include <stdio.h>
int main( )
{
    int a[ ] = { 1, 5, 8, 3, 2, 8, 4, 1, 2, 4, 8, 7, 4 } ;
    int i = 0, j = 12, k ;
    while ( i <= j )
    {
        k = ( i + j ) / 2 ;
        if ( a[ k ] == 8 )
        {
            printf ( "%d", k ) ;
            k = 0 ;
            break ;
        }
        else if ( 8 > a[ k ] )
            i = k + 1 ;
        else
            j = k - 1 ;
```

```
    }
    if ( k )
        printf ( "Element not found" ) ;
    return 0 ;
}
```

(a) The program implements binary search and prints the output 2.

(b) The program implements binary search and prints the output 5.

(c) The program implements binary search and prints the output 10.

(d) The program prints the message Element not found.

Question 24

What will be the output of the following program?

```
# include <stdio.h>
struct Sample
{
    int Age ;
    char Name[ 25 ] ;
    float salary ;
} E[ ] = {
        { 12, "Aanand", 12000.0f },
        { 15, "Ajay", 13000.0f },
        { 17, "Bihul", 14000.0f },
        { 20, "Sharda", 15000.0f },
        { 22, "Tanisha", 15500.0f },
        { 23, "Taniya", 17000.50f },
        { 25, "Yogini", 17600.0f }
    } ;
int Take ( int ) ;
int main( )
{
```

```
    int a = 17 ;
    printf ( "%d ", Take ( a ) ) ;
    return 0 ;
}
int Take ( int y )
{
    int a = 0, b = 7, c ;
    while ( b - a >= 0 )
    {
        c = ( a + b ) ;
        if ( y == E[ c / 2 ].Age )
            return ( c / 2 ) ;
        else if ( y > E[ c / 2 ].Age )
            a = c / 2 + 1 ;
        else
            b = c / 2 - 1 ;
    }
    return ( 0 ) ;
}
```

(a) 0

(b) 2

(c) 4

(d) -1

Question 25

Which of the following function must be used so that binary search can be applied to array Etc in the program given below?

```
# include <stdio.h>
struct Count
{
```

```
    int a ;
} Etc[ ] = { 12, 2, 45, 67, 34, 1, 23, 45, 57, 78, 565, 323, 34 } ;
void MakeChange ( int ) ;
int main( )
{
    int a, b = sizeof ( Etc ) / sizeof ( struct Count ) ;
    MakeChange ( b ) ;
    /*   Apply Binary Search  */
    . . . .
    return 0 ;
}
```

(a)
```
void MakeChange ( int x )
{
    int a, c ;
    struct Count n ;
    for ( a = 0 ; a < x ; a++ )
        for ( c = 0 ; c < x - 1 - a ; c++ )
        {
            if ( Etc[ c ].a == Etc[ c + 1 ].a )
            {
                n = Etc[ c ] ;
                Etc[ c ] = Etc[ c + 1 ] ;
                Etc[ c + 1 ] = n ;
            }
        }
}
```

(b)
```
void MakeChange ( int x )
{
    int a, c ;
    struct Count n ;
    for ( a = 0 ; a < x ; a++ )
        for ( c = 0 ; c < x - 1 - a ; c++ )
        {
```

```
                if ( Etc[ c ].a != Etc[ c + 1 ].a )
                {
                        n = Etc[ c ] ;
                        Etc[ c ] = Etc[ c + 1 ] ;
                        Etc[ c + 1 ] = n ;
                }
        }
}
```

(c) void MakeChange (int x)

```
{
        int a, c ;
        struct Count n ;
        for ( a = 0 ; a < x ; a++ )
                for ( c = 0 ; c < x - 1 - a ; c++ )
                {
                        if ( Etc[ c ].a > Etc[ c + 1 ].a )
                        {
                                n = Etc[ c ] ;
                                Etc[ c ] = Etc[ c + 1 ] ;
                                Etc[ c + 1 ] = n ;
                        }
                }
}
```

(d) void MakeChange (int x)

```
{
        int a, c ;
        struct Count n ;
        for ( a = 0 ; a < x ; a++ )
                for ( c = 0 ; c < x - 1 - a ; c++ )
                {
                        if ( ! ( Etc[ c ].a != Etc[ c + 1 ].a ) )
                        {
                                n = Etc[ c ] ;
```

```
                    Etc[ c ] = Etc[ c + 1 ] ;
                    Etc[ c + 1 ] = n ;
                }
            }
    }
```

Question 26

What is the job of Mak( ) in the following program?

```
# include <stdio.h>
struct Count
{
    int a ;
} Etc[ ] = { 12,2,45,67,34,1,23,45,57,78,565,323,34 } ;
int Mak ( int ) ;
int main( )
{
    int b = sizeof ( Etc ) / sizeof ( struct Count ) ;
    printf ( "%d", Mak ( b ) ) ;
    return 0 ;
}
int Mak ( int x )
{
    int a, c ;
    struct Count n ;
    for ( a = 0 ; a < x ; a++ )
        for ( c = 0 ; c < x - 1 - a ; c++ )
        {
            if ( Etc[ c ].a > Etc[ c + 1 ].a )
            {
                n = Etc[ c ] ;
                Etc[ c ] = Etc[ c + 1 ] ;
                Etc[ c + 1 ] = n ;
            }
```

```
        }
    for ( a = 0 ; a < x ; a++ )
        if ( Etc[ a ].a == 78 )
            return ( a ) ;
    return( -1 ) ;
}
```

(a) Mak( ) is sorting the array Etc in ascending order.

(b) Mak( ) is sorting the array Etc in ascending order and finding the element 78 using binary search.

(c) Mak( ) is sorting the array Etc in descending order and finding the element 78 using linear search.

(d) Mak( ) is sorting the array Etc in ascending order and finding the element 78 using linear search.

Question 27

Which of the following statements are correct about the program given below?

```
# include <stdio.h>
struct d
{
    int day ;
    int month ;
    int year ;
} date[ ] = {
            { 12, 4, 2004 },
            { 21, 1, 2004 },
            { 10, 7, 2002 },
            { 25, 9, 1994 },
            { 12, 12, 2006 },
            { 3, 8, 2002 }
        } ;
```

```
int See ( int, int ) ;
int main( )
{
    printf ( "%d", See ( 12, 2 ) ) ;
    return 0 ;
}
int See ( int x, int y )
{
    int i ;
    for ( i = 0 ; i < 6 ; i++ )
    {
        if ( date[ i ].day == x && !( date[ i ].month - y ) )
            return ( i ) ;
    }
    return ( -1 ) ;
}
```

(a) The program searches for the record with matching date.

(b) The program searches for the record with matching date and month.

(c) The program searches for the record with matching month.

(d) The program searches for the record that won't match the given date and month.

Question 28

What will be the output of the following program?

```
# include <stdio.h>
int main( )
{
    int array[ ] = { 1, 4, 3, 5, 7, 3, 11, 7, 8, 4, 13, 3 } ;
    int i ;
    for ( i = 0 ; i < 12 ; i++ )
    {
```

```
        if ( array[ i ] % 2 != 0 && array[ i ] % 3 == 0 ) ;
        else
            array[ i ] %= array [ i ] ;
    }
    for ( i = 0 ; i < 12 ; i++ )
    {
        if ( array[ i ] == 3 )
        {
            printf ( "%d", i ) ;
            break ;
        }
    }
    return 0 ;
}
```

(a) 5

(b) 11

(c) 1

(d) 2

Question 29

Which of the following statements are correct about the program given below?

```
# include <stdio.h>
int main( )
{
    int i ;
    int arr[ ] = { 23, 45, 4, 2, 7, 89,8 } ;
    for ( i = 7 ; i >= 1 ; i-- )
    {
        if ( arr[ 7 - i ] == 23 )
        {
```

```
            printf ( "%d", 7 - i ) ;
            break ;
        }
    }
    return 0 ;
}
```

(a) The program searches the element 23 from the beginning of the array.

(b) The program searches the element 23 from the end of array.

(c) The program searches the element 23 alternately in the array.

(d) The program searches the element 23 randomly in the array.

Question 30

Which of the following statements are correct about the program given below?

```
# include <stdio.h>
int main( )
{
    FILE *fp ;
    int num ;
    fp = fopen ( "Numbers.dat", "wb+" ) ;
    if ( fp == NULL )
        printf ( "Error : Can not open the file" ) ;
    else
    {
        int s = sizeof ( int ) ;

        while ( ( scanf ( "%d", &num ) ) != EOF )
            putw ( num, fp ) ;
        rewind ( fp ) ;

        while ( ( num =  getw ( fp ) ) != EOF )
```

```
            if ( num == 58 )
            {
                fseek ( fp, -s, SEEK_CUR ) ;
                putw ( 500, fp ) ;
                break ;
            }

        rewind ( fp ) ;
        while ( ( num = getw ( fp ) ) != EOF )
            printf ( "%d ", num ) ;
        fclose ( fp ) ;
    }
    return 0 ;
}
```

(a) The program searches the position of number 58 in the file.

(b) The program searches all the occurrences of number 58 and replaces them with 500.

(c) The program searches the first occurrence of number 58 and adds the number 500 just before it.

(d) The program searches the first occurrence of number 58 and replaces that with 500.

Question 31

What will be the output of the following program?

```
# include <stdio.h>
int fun1 ( char*, char* ) ;
int main( )
{
    char str1[ ] = "OneSomethingisforSomeonetwoone" ;
    char str2[ ] = "one" ;
    printf ( "%d", fun1 ( str1, str2 ) ) ;
    return 0 ;
```

```
}
int fun1 ( char *s, char *t )
{
    int count = 0, i ;
    while ( *s )
    {
        i = 0 ;
        while ( *( t + i ) )
        {
            if ( *( s + i ) ==*( t + i ) )
                i++ ;
            else
                break ;
        }
        if ( *( t + i ) == 0 )
            return ( count ) ;
        ++count ;
        s++ ;
    }
    return ( -1 ) ;
}
```

(a) 0

(b) 27

(c) 4

(d) 21

Question 32

Which of the following statements are correct about the program given below?

```
# include <stdio.h>
int main( )
```

```
{
    int a[ ] = { 12, 8, 3, 4, 8, 9, 45, 7, 8, 6, 534, 8 } ;
    int i, k = 0 ;
    for ( i = sizeof ( a ) / sizeof ( int ) – 1 ; i >= !a[ 0 ] ; --i )
        if ( *( a + i ) == 8 )
            k = i ;
    printf ( "%d ", k ) ;
    return 0 ;
}
```

(a) The program finds the last occurrence of 8 from the beginning of the array.

(b) The program finds the number of occurrences of 8 in the array.

(c) The program finds the first occurrence of 8 in the array by searching it in reverse direction.

(d) The program goes into an infinite loop.

Question 33

What will be the output of the following program?

```
# include <stdio.h>
int main( )
{
    int array[ ] = { 17, 45, 7, 89, 3, 90, 12, 7, 7, 8, 6, 7 } ;
    int i, k ;
    for ( i = EOF, k = sizeof ( array ) / sizeof ( int ) ; k >= !9 ; k -= 1 )
        if ( *( array + k ) == *( array + 3 + EOF ) )
            i = k ;
    printf ( "%d", i ) ;
    return 0 ;
}
```

(a) -1

(b) 2

(c) 7

(d) 8

Question 34

What will be the output of the following program?

```
# include <stdio.h>
# include <string.h>
struct Rec
{
    char name[ 20 ] ;
    int pid ;
    float salary ;
} ;
int main( )
{
    struct Rec t[ ] = {
                        { "Amit", 12, 12000.0f },
                        { "Varsha", 10, 13000.0f },
                        { "Sanjay", 13, 8900.0f },
                        { "Sanjay", 14, 11000.0f },
                        { "Ramesh", 12, 7000.0f },
                        { "Sanjay", 15, 9000.0f }
                      } ;
    int i, f = 14 ;
    for ( i = 0 ; i < sizeof ( t ) / sizeof ( struct Rec ) ; i++ )
    {
        if ( !( strcmp ( t[ i ].name, "Sanjay" ) ) )
            if ( !( t[ i ].pid - f ) )
                printf ( "%d", i ) ;
```

```
    }
    return 0 ;
}
```

(a) 6

(b) 2

(c) 3

(d) 5

Question 35

Which of the following statements are correct about the program given below?

```
# include <stdio.h>
int Change ( void ) ;
int array[ ] = { 3, 56, 78, 54, 34 } ;
int main( )
{
    printf ( "%d ", Change( ) ) ;
    return 0 ;
}
int Change ( void )
{
    int i ;
    for ( i = 5 ; i >= 1 ; --i )
    {
        if ( array[ i - 1 ] == 3 )
            return ( -- i ) ;
        else
            array[ i - 1 ] = 0 ;
    }
    return ( -1 ) ;
}
```

(a) The program implements the stack and reverses the array elements.

(b) The program searches the element 3 from the beginning and makes all non-matching numbers zero.

(c) The program implements the stack and pops all the elements till element 3 is not found.

(d) The program prints the garbage.

Question 36

Which of the following statements are correct about the program given below?

```
# include <stdio.h>
# include <string.h>
struct temp
{
        char str[ 20 ] ;
} sample ;
int main( )
{
    FILE *fp ;
    int i, n = 0 ;
    char str[ ] = "Hello" ;

    fp = fopen ( "text.txt", "rb+" ) ;

    while ( ( fread ( &sample, sizeof ( sample ), 1, fp ) ) )
    {
        for ( i = 0 ; sample.str[ i ] && str[ i ] ; i++ )
            if ( sample.str[ i ] != str[ i ] )
                break ;
        if ( !sample.str[ i ] && !str[ i ] )
            ++n ;
```

```
    }

    printf ( "%d", n ) ;
    fclose ( fp ) ;
    return 0 ;
}
```

(a) The program searches and counts the number of strings in the file.

(b) The program searches and counts the occurrences of string "Hello" in the file.

(c) The program searches and counts the string containing "Hello" from the file.

(d) The program searches and counts the strings other than the "Hello" from the file.

Question 37

What will be the output of the following program?

```
# include <stdio.h>
int main( )
{
    char array1[ ] = "misandunderstanding" ;
    char array2[ ] = "misunderstanding" ;
    int i, j ;

    for ( i = j = 0 ; array1[ i ] ; )
    {
        if ( array1[ i ] != array2[ j ] )
            printf ( "%c", array1[ i++ ] ) ;
        else
        {
            ++i ;
            j++ ;
        }
    }
```

```
    return 0 ;
}
```

(a) and

(b) mis

(c) understanding

(d) andunderstanding

Question 38

What will be the output of the following program?

```
# include <stdio.h>
# include <string.h>
int main( )
{
    char *array1 = "misandmisusemissitsomis" ;
    char *p = array1+ strlen ( array1 ) - 3 ;
    int i, j, k, count = 0 ;

    for ( i = 0 ; i <= 20 ; ++i )
    {
        for ( j = 0 , k = i ; *( p + j ) ; j++ )
        {
            if ( *( array1 + k ) != *( p + j ) )
                break ;
            else
                k++ ;
        }
        if ( !*( p + j ) )
            count++ ;
    }
    printf ( "%d", count ) ;
```

```
    return 0 ;
}
```

(a) 2

(b) 4

(c) 3

(d) 5

Question 39

Which of the following statements are correct about the program given below?

```
# include <stdio.h>
# include <malloc.h>
struct LList
{
    int *data ;
    struct LList *Link ;
} *start = NULL ;
void hold ( int* ) ;
int a[ ] = { 12, 3, 4, 7, 8, 9, 4, 2, 1 } ;
int main( )
{
    int I ;
    for ( i = 0 ; i <sizeof ( a ) / sizeof ( int ) ; i++ )
        hold ( &a[ i ] ) ;
    for ( i = 0 ; i <sizeof ( a ) / sizeof ( int ) ; i++ )
        printf ( "%d ", a[ i ] ) ;
    return 0 ;
}
void hold ( int *a )
{
    struct LList *temp = ( struct LList* ) malloc ( sizeof ( struct LList ) ) ;
```

```
    temp -> data = a ;
    if ( *( temp -> data ) & 1 == 1 )
        *( temp -> data ) -= *( temp -> data ) ;
    temp -> Link = NULL ;
    if ( !start )
        start = temp ;
    else
    {
        struct LList *t = start ;
        while ( t -> Link != NULL )
            t = t -> Link ;
        t -> Link = temp ;
    }
}
```

(a) The program searches for all the odd numbers in the array and makes them zero via the linked list.

(b) The program searches for all the even numbers in the array and makes them zero via the linked list.

(c) The program makes all the elements in the array zero via the linked list.

(d) The program searches and makes all the non-zero elements in the array zero via the linked list.

Question 40

What is the purpose of Show( ) in the following program?

```
# include <stdio.h>
# include <malloc.h>
struct LList
{
    int data ;
    struct LList *Link ;
```

```
} *start = NULL ;
void Show ( struct LList* ) ;
int main( )
{
      /* insert the elements 10, 7, 5, 10, 23, 10, 10 in the linked list. */
      Show ( start ) ;
      return 0 ;
}
void Show ( struct LList *ptr )
{
      static int loc ;
      if ( ptr -> Link != NULL )
      {
            if ( !( ptr -> data - 10 ) )
                  printf ( "%d  ", loc ) ;
            loc++ ;
            Show ( ptr -> Link ) ;
      }
      else
      {
            if ( !( ptr -> data - 10 ) )
                  printf ( "%i  ", loc ) ;
            loc++ ;
      }
}
```

(a) It searches for the first occurrence of number 10 in the linked list.

(b) It searches for the last occurrence of number 10 in the linked list.

(c) It searches for the all the occurrences of number 10 in the linked list and prints them.

(d) It counts the number of locations of 10 and prints the number of locations found.

Question 41

In linear search the time taken in average and worst case is proportional to__________.

(a) n

(b) 2n

(c) n2

(d) (n + 2)

Question 42

What will be the output of the following program?

```
# include <stdio.h>
int find ( int*, int ) ;
int main( )
{
    int a[ ] = { 1, 13, 4, 5, 6, 8, 43, 3, 34, 45, 3, 56, 7, 10, 5, 3 } ;
    printf ( "%d\n", find ( a, 3 ) ) ;
    return 0 ;
}
int find ( int *a, int num )
{
    int i ;
    for ( i = 0 ; i < 16 ; i++ )
    {
        if ( a[ i ] == num )
            return ( a[ i ] += i ) ;
    }
    return ( 0 ) ;
}
```

(a) 0

(b) 10

(c) 13

(d) 19

Question 43

What will be the output of the following program?

```
# include <stdio.h>
int Check ( int ) ;
int a[ ] = { 1, 13, 4, 3, 6, 8, 43, 3, 34, 45, 3, 56, 7, 10, 5, 3 } ;
int main( )
{
    int i ;
    for ( i = 0 ; i < 16 ; i++ )
    {
        if ( a[ I ] == 3 )
        {
            a[ i ] += a[ i + 1 ] ;
            a[ i + 1 ] = a[ i ] - a[ i + 1 ] ;
            a[ i ] -= a[ i + 1 ] ;
            break ;
        }
    }
    printf ( "%d", Check ( 3 ) ) ;
    return 0 ;
}
int Check ( int num )
{
    int i ;
    for ( i = 0 ; i < 16 ; i++ )
        if ( a[ i ] == num )
            return ( i ) ;
    return ( 0 ) ;
```

```
}
```

(a) 0

(b) 8

(c) 4

(d) 11

Question 44

Which of the following statements are correct about the program given below?

```
# include <stdio.h>
# include <malloc.h>
struct LinkList
{
    int data ;
    struct LinkList *Link ;
} *start = NULL ;
void insert ( void ) ;
int sample ( int ) ;
int main( )
{
    insert ( ) ;
    printf ( "%d", sample ( 6 ) ) ;
    return 0 ;
}
void insert ( void )
{
    int i = 1 ;
    struct LinkList *temp ;
    for ( i = 10 ; i >= 1 ; i-- )
    {
        temp = ( struct LinkList* ) malloc ( sizeof ( struct LinkList ) ) ;
```

```
        temp -> data = i ;
        temp -> Link = NULL ;
        if ( !start )
            start = temp ;
        else
        {
            struct LinkList *t = start ;
            while ( t -> Link != NULL )
                t = t -> Link ;
            t -> Link = temp ;
        }
    }
}
int sample ( int n )
{
    struct LinkList *temp ;
    for ( temp = start ; temp != NULL ; temp = temp -> Link )
    {
        if ( temp -> data - n == 0 )
        {
            if ( temp -> Link != NULL )
                return ( temp -> Link -> data ) ;
            else
                return ( 0 ) ;
        }
    }
    return ( 0 ) ;
}
```

(a) The program prints the position of element 6 from the linked list.

(b) The program prints the element just before the first appearance of 6 in the linked list.

(c) The program prints the element just before the last appearance of 6 in the linked list.

(d) The program prints the element just after the first appearance of 6 in the linked list.

Question 45

What will be the output of the following program?

```
# include <stdio.h>
# include <string.h>
struct Sample
{
      int Age ;
      char Name[ 25 ] ;
      float salary ;
} E[ ] = {
            { 12, "Aanand", 12000.0f },
            { 15, "Ajay", 13000.0f },
            { 17, "Bihul", 14000.0f },
            { 20, "Sharda", 15000.0f },
            { 22, "Tanisha", 15500.0f },
            { 23, "Taniya", 17000.50f },
            { 25, "Yogini", 17600.0f }
      } ;
int Take ( char* ) ;
int main( )
{
      int a = 0, b = sizeof ( E ) / sizeof ( struct Sample ) ;
      struct Sample one ;
      for ( --b ; a <= b ; a++, b-- )
      {
            one = E[ a ] ;
            E[ a ] = E[ b ] ;
            E[ b ] = one ;
      }
      printf ( "%d", Take ( "Taniya" ) ) ;
      return 0 ;
}
int Take ( char *ptr )
```

```
{
    int a = 0, b = 7, c ;
    while ( a <= b )
    {
        c = ( a + b ) ;
        if ( strcmp ( ptr, E[ c / 2 ].Name ) == 0 )
            return ( c / 2 ) ;
        else if ( strcmp ( ptr, E[ c / 2 ].Name ) < 0 )
            a = c / 2 + 1 ;
        else
            b = c / 2 - 1 ;
    }
    return ( 0 ) ;
}
```

(a) 5

(b) 0

(c) 4

(d) 1

Question 46

Which of the following statements are correct about the program given below?

```
# include <stdio.h>
# include <string.h>
struct Example
{
    int a ;
    char n[ 25 ] ;
    float s ;
} E[ ] = {
        { 20, "Sharad", 15700.0f },
```

```
        { 12, "Anand",  12300.0f },
        { 22, "Tania", 15500.0f },
        { 25, "Yogi",  17600.0f },
        { 17, "Bihul",  14010.0f },
        { 23, "Taniya",  17500.50f },
        { 15, "Ajay",    13040.0f },
    } ;
int Execute ( char* ) ;
int main( )
{
    int a=0, c, b = sizeof ( E ) / sizeof ( struct Example ) ;
    struct Example one ;
    for ( a = 0 ; a < b ; a++ )
        for ( c = 0 ; c < b - 1 - a ; c++ )
        {
            if ( E[ c ].s < E[ c + 1 ].s )
            {
                one = E[ c ] ;
                E[ c ] = E[ c + 1 ] ;
                E[ c + 1 ] = one ;
            }
        }
    printf ( "%d", Execute ( "Tania" ) ) ;
    return 0 ;
}
int Execute ( char *ptr )
{
    int a = 0, b = 7, c ;
    while ( a <= b )
    {
        c = ( a + b ) ;
        if ( strcmp ( ptr, E[ c / 2 ].n ) == 0 )
            return ( c / 2 ) ;
        else if ( strcmp ( ptr, E[ c / 2 ].n ) < 0 )
            a = c / 2 + 1 ;
```

```
        else
            b = c / 2 - 1 ;
    }
    return ( 0 ) ;
}
```

(a) The program sorts the array E in ascending order according to 's' member and then prints the record number of Tania.

(b) The program prints the record number of the record in which the word Tania occurs.

(c) The program sorts the array E in descending order according to 's' member and then prints the record number of the record in which the word Tania occurs.

(d) The program sorts the array E in ascending order according to 'a' member and then prints the record number of the record in which the word Tania occurs.

Question 47

What will be the output of the following program?

```
# include <stdio.h>
char* fun1 ( char*, char* ) ;
int main( )
{
    char str1[ ] = "OneSomethingisforSomeonetwoone" ;
    char str2[ ] = "one" ;
    printf ( "%s", fun1 ( str1, str2 ) ) ;
    return 0 ;
}
char* fun1 ( char *s, char *t )
{
    int count = 0, i ;
    while ( *s )
    {
        i = 0 ;
```

```
        while ( *( t + i ) )
        {
            if ( *( s + i ) ==*( t + i ) )
                i++ ;
            else
                break ;
        }
        if ( *( t + i ) == 0 )
            return ( s ) ;
        ++count ;
        s++ ;
    }
    return ( s = NULL ) ;
}
```

(a) one

(b) onetwoone

(c) OneSomethingisforSomeonetwoone

(d) (null)

Question 48

What will be the output of the following program?

```
# include <stdio.h>
struct Rec
{
    char name[ 20 ] ;
    int age ;
    float salary ;
} E[ ] = {
        { "Prashant", 25, 5000.0f },
        { "Sachin", 24, 9600.0f },
```

```
        { "Rakesh", 24, 12000.0f },
        { "Vivek", 24, 3000.0f },
        { "Sanjay", 24, 7800.90f }
    };

int main( )
{
    FILE *fp ;
    struct Rec one ;
    long size, get = sizeof ( one ) ;

    fp = fopen ( "sample", "wb+" ) ;
    fwrite ( &E, sizeof ( one ), 5, fp ) ;

    size = ftell ( fp ) / sizeof ( one ) ;
    rewind ( fp ) ;

    fseek ( fp, 0L, SEEK_END ) ;
    fseek ( fp, -get, SEEK_CUR ) ;

    while ( size && ( fread ( &one, sizeof ( one ), 1, fp ) ) )
    {
        if ( ( one.age - 24 ) ) ;
        else
        {
            printf ( "%s", one.name ) ;
            break ;
        }
        fseek ( fp, -get * 2, SEEK_CUR ) ;
        size-- ;
    }
    fclose ( fp ) ;
    return 0 ;
}
```

(a) Sanjay

(b) Sachin

(c) Vivek

(d) Rakesh

Question 49

Which of the following statements are correct about the program given below?

```
# include <stdio.h>
# include <string.h>
struct Employees
{
    char N[ 20 ] ;
    int A ;
    float S ;
} Emp[ ] = {
            { "Ramesh", 22, 12000.0f },
            { "Sahil", 24, 9600.0f },
            { "Parikshit", 25, 5000.0f },
            { "Varsha", 28, 3000.0f },
            { "Samay", 30, 7800.90f }
        } ;
int main( )
{
    FILE *fp ;
    struct Employees one ;
    fp = fopen ( "sample", "wb+" ) ;
    fwrite ( &Emp, sizeof ( one ), sizeof ( Emp ) / sizeof ( one ), fp ) ;
    rewind ( fp ) ;
    while ( fread ( &one, sizeof ( one ), 1, fp ) )
    {
        if ( !( one.A - 25 ) )
```

```
        {
            strcpy ( one.N, "Parkisha" ) ;
            fseek ( fp, 0L, SEEK_CUR ) ;
            fwrite ( &one, sizeof ( one ), 1, fp ) ;
            break ;
        }
    }
    fclose ( fp ) ;
    return 0 ;
}
```

(a) The program searches for the record of Parikshit and replaces it with name Pariksha.

(b) The program searches for the record of Parikshit and deletes it.

(c) The program searches for the record of Parikshit and updates the name in previous record with the name Pariksha.

(d) The program searches for the record of Parikshit and updates the name in very next record with the name Pariksha.

Question 50

Which of the following statements are correct about the program given below? Consider the file Numbers.dat file contains the numbers 12, 4, 66, 80, 0, 13, 16, 15, 43.

```
# include <stdio.h>
int main( )
{
    FILE *fp ;
    int num, flag = 0 ;
    fp = fopen ( "Numbers.dat", "rb" ) ;
    while ( ( num = getw ( fp ) ) != EOF )
        if ( num & 1 == 1)
        {
            flag = 1 ;
```

```
            break ;
        }
    if ( flag )
        printf ( "%d", num ) ;
    else
        printf ( "0" ) ;
    return 0 ;
}
```

(a) The program will report compilation error.

(b) The program will search for all the non-zero numbers and will print the last non-zero number.

(c) The program will search for the first odd number in the file using linear search and will print that number.

(d) The program will search for all the 1s in the file and will print the number at last.

Question 51

Which of the following statements are correct about the program given below?

```
# include <stdio.h>
# include <string.h>
void display ( char* ) ;
int main( )
{
    char *ptr[ ] = {
                    "I am the beginning of the end",
                    "You can see me twice in week",
                    "But not once in day",
                    "So mam who I am?"
                };
    int i, j, k ;
    char p[ 10 ], t[ 10 ] ;
```

```
    for ( i = 0 ; i < 4 ; i++ )
    {
        for ( k = j = 0 ; *( ptr[ i ] + j ) ; j++ )
        {
            while ( *( *( ptr + i ) + j ) != ' ' && *( *( ptr + i ) + j ) != 0 )
                p [ k++ ] = *( *( ptr + i ) + j++ ) ;
            p[ k ] = 0 ;
            k = 0 ;
            strcpy ( t, p ) ;
            if ( strcmp ( t, strrev ( p ) ) == 0 )
                display ( p ) ;
            if ( *( *( ptr + i ) + j ) == 0 )
                break ;
        }
    }
    return 0 ;
}
void display ( char *word )
{
    printf ( "%s\n", word ) ;
}
```

(a) The program prints the string containing the palindrome.

(b) The program searches for the palindrome in the string and prints if any.

(c) The program prints the portion of the string from where the palindrome starts.

(d) The program prints the portion of the string till the palindrome if any.

Question 52

What will be the output of the following program?

```
# include <stdio.h>
void See ( int* ) ;
```

```
void Observe ( void ) ;
int array[ 6 ] ;

int main( )
{
        void ( *isee )( int* ) = See ;
        ( *isee )( array ) ;
        Observe( ) ;
        return 0 ;
}
void See ( int *array )
{
        int i ;
        for ( i = 0 ; i < 6 ; i++ )
                * ( array + i ) = ( array[ i ] = 0 ) + ( i + 1 ) ;
}
void Observe ( void )
{
        static int k ;
        if ( k < 6 )
        {
                k++ ;
                Observe( ) ;
                if ( *( array + k ) == 2 )
                        printf ( "%d ", k-- ) ;
                else
                        --k ;
        }
        else
                --k ;
}
```

(a) 0

(b) 2

(c) 1

(d) 4

Question 53

What will be the output of the following program?

```
# include <stdio.h>
# include <string.h>
# include <malloc.h>
struct strings
{
    char strsts[ 20 ] ;
} ;
int main( )
{
    struct strings strrst[ ] = {
                                    { "Amit" },
                                    { "Varsha" },
                                    { "Sanjay" },
                                    { "Sanjana" },
                                    { "Ramesh" },
                                    { "Suraj" }
                            } ;
    int i ;
    for ( i = 0 ; i < sizeof ( strrst ) / sizeof ( struct strings ) ; i++ )
    {
        char *ptr  = ( char* ) malloc ( 10 ) ;
        char *cptr = ( char*) malloc ( 12 ) ;
        ptr = strstr ( strrst[ i ].strsts, "ja" ) ;
        if ( ptr != NULL )
        {
            cptr = strrev ( ptr ) ;
            if ( ( strcmp ( "ja", cptr ) ) == 0 )
```

```
            {
                printf ( "%d", i ) ;
                break ;
            }
        }
    }
    if ( i == sizeof ( strrst ) / sizeof ( struct strings ) )
        printf ( "%d", i ) ;
    return 0 ;
}
```

(a) 6

(b) 2

(c) 3

(d) 5

Question 54

Which of the following statements are correct about the program given below?

```
# include <stdio.h>
# include <string.h>
struct string
{
    char str[ 20 ] ;
} obj ;
int main( )
{
    FILE *fp ;
    fp = fopen ( "strings.txt", "rb+" ) ; /* File contains several strings */
    while ( fread ( &obj, sizeof ( obj ), 1, fp ) )
    {
        char *s = obj.str ;
```

```
        char *t = s + strlen ( obj.str ) - 1 ;
        while ( s <= t )
        {
            if ( *s == *t )
            {
                s++ ;
                t-- ;
            }
            else
                break ;
        }
        if ( s > t )
            printf ( "%s\n", obj.str ) ;
    }
    fclose ( fp ) ;
    return 0 ;
}
```

(a) The program reads the strings from the file and prints them.

(b) The program reads the strings from the file and prints only those strings which are not palindromes.

(c) The program reads the strings from the file and prints only those strings which are palindromes.

(d) The program reads the string from the file and prints them in reverse order.

Question 55

What will be the output of the following program?

```
# include <stdio.h>
# include <string.h>
char* finding ( char*, char* ) ;
int main( )
```

```
{
    char string2[ ] = "takeenotakeenomedicine" ;
    char string3[ ] = "one" ;
    printf ( "%s", finding ( string2, string3 ) ) ;
    return 0 ;
}
char* finding ( char *s, char *t )
{
    int i ;
    strrev ( s ) ;
    while ( *s )
    {
        i = 0 ;
        while ( *( t + i ) )
        {
            if ( *( s + i ) == *( t + i ) )
                i++ ;
            else
                break ;
        }
        if ( *( t + i ) == 0 )
            return ( s ) ;

        s++ ;
    }
    return ( s = NULL ) ;
}
```

(a) oneekat

(b) oneekatoneekat

(c) (null)

(d) one

Question 56

Which version of the display function must be used to print only the first location of 10 starting from the reverse direction of linked list?

```
# include <stdio.h>
# include <malloc.h>
struct LinkList
{
      int data ;
      struct LinkList *Link ;
} *start = NULL ;
void insert ( int ) ;
void display ( struct LinkList* ) ;
int main( )
{
      struct LinkList *temp ;
      insert ( 10 ) ;
      insert ( 7 ) ;
      insert ( 5 ) ;
      insert ( 10 ) ;
      insert ( 23 ) ;
      insert ( 10 ) ;
      insert ( 102 ) ;
      display ( start ) ;
      return 0 ;
}
void insert ( int n )
{
      struct LinkList *temp ;
      temp = ( struct LinkList* ) malloc ( sizeof ( struct LinkList ) ) ;
      temp -> data = n ;
      temp -> Link = NULL ;
      if ( !start )
            start = temp ;
```

```
    else
    {
        struct LinkList *t = start ;
        while ( t -> Link != NULL )
            t = t -> Link ;
        t -> Link = temp ;
    }
}
```

(a)
```
void display ( struct LinkList *ptr )
{
    static int i, j ;
    if ( ptr != NULL )
    {
        display ( ptr -> Link ) ;
        i++ ;
        if ( !( ptr -> data - 10 ) && !j )
        {
            printf ( "%i  ", i ) ;
            ++j ;
        }
    }
}
```

(b)
```
void display ( struct LinkList *ptr )
{
    static int i  ;
    if ( ptr -> Link != NULL )
    {
        display ( ptr -> Link ) ;
        i++ ;
        if ( !( ptr -> data - 10 ) )
        {
            printf ( "%i  ", i ) ;
            ++j ;
```

```
            }
        }
    }
```

(c)
```
void display ( struct LinkList *ptr )
{
    static int i, j ;
    if ( ptr -> Link != NULL )
    {
        display ( ptr -> Link -> Link ) ;
        i++ ;
        if ( !( ptr -> data - 10 ) && !j )
        {
            printf ( "%i  ", i ) ;
            ++j ;
        }
    }
}
```

(d)
```
void display ( struct LinkList *ptr )
{
    static int i, j ;
    if ( ptr -> Link != NULL )
    {
        display ( ptr -> Link ) ;
        i++ ;
        if ( !( ptr -> data - 10 ) && !j )
        {
            printf ( "%i  ", i ) ;
            ++j ;
        }
    }
}
```

Question 57

Which of the following statements are correct about the program given below?

```
# include <stdio.h>
# include <string.h>
# include <malloc.h>
struct String
{
	char name[ 20 ] ;
} take ;
struct List
{
	char data[ 20 ] ;
	struct List *Link ;
} *start = NULL ;
void insert ( struct String* ) ;
int main( )
{
	FILE *fp ;
	fp = fopen ( "Data.txt", "rb+" ) ;
	while ( fread ( &take, sizeof ( take ), 1, fp ) )
		insert ( &take ) ;
	fclose ( fp ) ;
	fp = fopen ( "Data.txt", "wb" ) ;
	while ( start != NULL )
	{
		strcpy ( take.name, start -> data ) ;
		fwrite ( &take, sizeof ( take ), 1, fp ) ;
		start = start -> Link ;
	}
	fclose ( fp ) ;
	return 0 ;
}
void insert ( struct String *ptr )
```

```
{
    struct List *temp = ( struct List* ) malloc ( sizeof ( struct List ) ) ;
    if ( strcmp ( ptr -> name, "Bye" ) ==0 )
        return ;
    else
        strcpy ( temp -> data, ptr -> name ) ;
    temp -> Link = NULL ;

    if ( start == NULL )
        start = temp ;
    else
    {
        struct List *t = start ;

        while ( t -> Link != NULL )
            t = t -> Link ;
        t -> Link = temp ;
    }
}
```

(a) The program deletes all the strings from the file.

(b) The program searches for the word "Bye" from the file and deletes all "Bye"s from the file.

(c) The program searches for the "Bye" and stores in the linked list but do not change the contents of the file.

(d) The program stores only "Bye"s in the file.

Question 58

Which of the following statements are correct about the program given below?

```
# include <stdio.h>
# include <string.h>
```

```
# include <malloc.h>
char *ptr[ ] = {
                    "impossible", "misunderstanding", "poor", "misuse", "simbian"
          } ;
void Search ( int ) ;
int main( )
{
    Search ( 0 ) ;
    return 0 ;
}
void Search ( int num )
{
    char search[ ] = { *( ptr[ 3 ] + 2 ), *( ptr[ 3 ] + 1 ), *ptr[ 3 ], 0 } ;
    static int k = 1 ;
    if ( num < 5 )
    {
        Search ( num + 1 ) ;
        {
            char *ch = ( char* ) malloc ( sizeof ( char ) * 20 ) ;
            int i, j ;

            for ( i = 0 ; *( ptr[ num ] + i ) ; i++ ) ;

            for ( j = 0, --i ; i >= 0 ; i--, j++ )
                *( ch + j ) = *( ptr[ num ] + i ) ;
            *( ch + j ) = 0 ;
            if ( strstr ( ch, search ) != NULL && k )
            {
                printf ( "%s", strstr ( ch, search ) ) ;
                k = !k ;
            }
            free ( ch ) ;
        }
    }
}
```

(a) The program searches from the beginning of the array ptr and prints all the strings containing the substring "mis".

(b) The program searches in reverse direction of the array ptr and prints only one string containing the substring "mis".

(c) The program searches in reverse direction of the array ptr and prints only one string containing the substring "sim".

(d) The program searches from the beginning of the array ptr and prints all the string containing the substring "sim".

Question 59

Which of the following statements are correct about the program given below?

```
# include <stdio.h>
# include <string.h>
# include <malloc.h>
struct String
{
    char name[ 20 ] ;
} take ;
struct List
{
    char data[ 20 ] ;
    struct List *Link ;
} *start = NULL ;
void insert ( struct String* ) ;
int main( )
{
    FILE *fp ;
    fp = fopen ( "Data.txt", "rb+" ) ;
    while ( fread ( &take, sizeof ( take ), 1, fp ) )
        insert ( &take ) ;
```

```
    rewind ( fp ) ;
    while ( start != NULL )
    {
        strcpy ( take.name, start -> data ) ;
        fwrite ( &take, sizeof ( take ), 1, fp ) ;
        start = start -> Link ;
    }
    fclose ( fp ) ;
    return 0 ;
}
void insert ( struct String *ptr )
{
    struct List *temp = ( struct List* ) malloc ( sizeof ( struct List ) ) ;
    if ( strcmp ( ptr -> name, "Hello" ) == 0 )
        strcpy ( temp -> data, "Bye" ) ;
    else
        strcpy ( temp -> data, ptr -> name ) ;
    temp -> Link = NULL ;
    if ( start == NULL )
        start = temp ;
    else
    {
        struct List *t = start ;

        while ( t -> Link != NULL )
            t = t -> Link ;
        t -> Link = temp ;
    }
}
```

(a) The program reads the strings from the file, stores in the linked list and stores them back in the file as it is.

(b) The program reads the strings from the file, stores only "Hello" in the linked list.

(c) The program reads the strings from the file and places "Bye" just after the "Hello" in the file.

(d) The program searches and replaces the each "Hello" in the file by "Bye".

Question 60

Which of the following statements are correct about the program given below?

```
# include <stdio.h>
struct Employees
{
    char N[ 20 ] ;
    int A ;
    float S ;
} Emp[ ] = {
            { "Ramesh", 22, 12000.0f },
            { "Sahil", 24, 9600.0f },
            { "Parikshit", 25, 5000.0f },
            { "Varsha", 28, 3000.0f },
            { "Samay", 30, 7800.90f }
        } ;
int main( )
{
    FILE *fp ;
    struct Employees one ;
    int a = 0, b = sizeof ( Emp ) / sizeof ( one ), c ;
    int size = sizeof ( one ), flag = 0, t = 28 ;
    fp = fopen ( "sample", "wb+" ) ;
    fwrite ( &Emp, sizeof ( one ), b, fp ) ;
    while ( a <= b )
    {
        c = ( a + b ) / 2 ;
        rewind ( fp ) ;
        fseek ( fp, size * c, SEEK_CUR ) ;
        fread ( &one, sizeof ( one ), 1, fp ) ;
```

```
        if ( !( one.A - t ) )
        {
            flag = 1 ;
            printf ( "%d", c + 1 ) ;
            break ;
        }
        else if ( one.A - t < 0 )
            a = c + 1 ;
        else
            b = c - 1 ;
    }
    if ( !flag )
        printf ( "-1" ) ;
    fclose ( fp ) ;
    return 0 ;
}
```

(a) The program will print the output -1.

(b) The program searches for the record containing the value of one.A as 28 using linear search.

(c) The program will print the output 0.

(d) The program implements the binary search algorithm to search the record containing the value of one.A as 28 and prints its location in the file.

Answers

Q. 1 – C	Q. 2 – D	Q. 3 – C
Q. 4 – A	Q. 5 – A	Q. 6 – A
Q. 7 – C	Q. 8 – B	Q. 9 – B
Q. 10 – C	Q. 11 – B	Q. 12 – D
Q. 13 – B	Q. 14 – B	Q. 15 – C
Q. 16 – C	Q. 17 – C	Q. 18 – D
Q. 19 – D	Q. 20 – C	Q. 21 – B
Q. 22 – A	Q. 23 – D	Q. 24 – B
Q. 25 – C	Q. 26 – D	Q. 27 – B
Q. 28 – D	Q. 29 – A	Q. 30 – D
Q. 31 – D	Q. 32 – C	Q. 33 – B
Q. 34 – C	Q. 35 – D	Q. 36 – B
Q. 37 – A	Q. 38 – B	Q. 39 – A
Q. 40 – C	Q. 41 – A	Q. 42 – B
Q. 43 – C	Q. 44 – D	Q. 45 – D
Q. 46 – C	Q. 47 – B	Q. 48 – A

Q. 49 – D	Q. 50 – C	Q. 51 – B
Q. 52 – C	Q. 53 – A	Q. 54 – C
Q. 55 – B	Q. 56 – D	Q. 57 – B
Q. 58 – C	Q. 59 – D	Q. 60 – D

10

Sorting Algorithms

Question 1

What do you mean by algorithm?

(a) It is a program written in C Language.

(b) It is a program written in any Language.

(c) It is a sequence of steps written in particular order to accomplish the given task.

(d) It is a sequence of steps written in random order to complete the given task.

Question 2

What is sorting?

(a) The process of mixing the set of numbers.

(b) The process of collecting the set of numbers.

(c) The process of arranging the set of numbers in particular order.

(d) The process of arranging the set of numbers in random order.

Question 3

Which of the following is not a sorting technique?

(a) Bubble Sort

(b) Radix Sort

(c) Heap Sort

(d) Stack Sort

Question 4

How many passes are required to sort the set of N numbers using Bubble Sort?

(a) N

(b) N + 1

(c) N – 1

(d) N + 2

Question 5

Which of the following is implemented to sort the set of numbers?

(a) deletion of elements

(b) swapping of elements

(c) copying elements

(d) adding new elements

Question 6

Which of the following calculates the pivot element to sort the set of numbers?

(a) Insertion sort

(b) Radix sort

(c) Heap sort

(d) Quick sort

Question 7

What is(are) the order(s) in which elements can be sorted ?

(a) Ascending order

(b) Descending order

(c) Random order

(d) Both A and B

Question 8

Which elements are compared in Bubble sort?

(a) All elements with the first element

(b) All elements with the last element

(c) Adjacent elements

(d) Alternate elements

Question 9

Which of the following sorting algorithm is more efficient as compared to others?

(a) Heap sort

(b) Merge sort

(c) Bubble sort

(d) Quick sort

Question 10

How many elements can be sorted using sorting algorithm?

(a) Odd number of elements

(b) Even number of elements

(c) Any number of elements

(d) 2048 elements only

Question 11

As the number of elements to be sorted increases, the efficiency of Bubble sort ________.

(a) increases

(b) decreases

(c) stays medium

(d) doesn't change

Question 12

Which of the following has the worst-case complexity "n2"?

(a) Bubble sort

(b) Selection sort

(c) Heap sort

(d) Both A and B

Question 13

What is Complexity of an algorithm?

(a) Complexity is the execution time and the space required by the algorithm.

(b) Complexity is the execution time required by the algorithm.

(c) Complexity is the amount space required by the algorithm.

(d) Complexity is the difference between execution time and the space required by the algorithm.

Question 14

What are the types of Complexities of an algorithm?

(a) Constraints complexity

(b) Time complexity

(c) Space complexity

(d) Both B and C

Question 15

What is compared while sorting the strings?

(a) The addresses of the strings.

(b) The length of the strings.

(c) The ASCII values of characters in the strings.

(d) The first and last character in the strings.

Question 16

Which of the following mechanisms can be used to sort a set of numbers?

(a) Switch statements

(b) Loops

(c) Recursion

(d) Both B and C

Question 17

Which of the following algorithm sorts the numbers in the way given below?

I. It divides the set of number in different sets and sorts each set separately.

II. Combines two set and sort them and so on.

(a) Radix sort

(b) Heap sort

(c) Merge sort

(d) Insertion sort

Question 18

Which of the following is correct about the efficient sorting?

(a) The program should take long time to sort the numbers.

(b) The program should contain large number to sort the numbers.

(c) The program should occupy large space in memory.

(d) The program should take minimum space as well as time for sorting.

Question 19

Which of the following compares the first element with rest of the elements and then second element and so on?

(a) Selection sort

(b) Bubble sort

(c) Insertion sort

(d) Heap sort

Question 20

What is Space complexity?

(a) Space required for the source program and its executable file.

(b) Space required for the executable program while running in memory.

(c) Space required for the header files in the source program.

(d) Space required for the source program.

Question 21

Which of the following uses recursion to sort the set of numbers?

(a) Bubble sort

(b) Selection sort

(c) Merge sort

(d) Quick sort

Question 22

What is the Best-case complexity of Merge sort?

(a) O (log n)

(b) O (n log n)

(c) O (log n2)

(d) O (log n / 2)

Question 23

In quick sort the element that splits the set into two parts is known as ______.

(a) middle element

(b) pivot element

(c) central element

(d) median element

Question 24

Which of the following has the worst as well as average-case complexity "n2"?

(a) Heap sort

(b) Merge sort

(c) Quick sort

(d) Bubble sort

Question 25

What is the Average case complexity of Merge sort?

(a) O (n2)

(b) O 2 log (n2)

(c) O (n log n)

(d) O (2n2)

Question 26

Which of the following is correct about the program given below?

```
# include <stdio.h>
int main( )
{
    int a[ ] = { 15, 42, 32, 2, 12 } ;
    int i, j, t ;
    for ( i = 0 ; i < 5 ; i++ )
    {
        for ( j = 0 ; j < 4 – i ; j++ )
        {
            if ( a[ j ] >= a[ j + 1 ] )
            {
                t = a[ j ] ;
                a[ j ] = a[ j + 1 ] ;
                a[ j + 1 ] = t ;
            }
        }
    }
    return 0 ;
}
```

(a) The program arranges all the numbers in descending order.

(b) The program arranges left half of numbers in descending order.

(c) The program arranges all the numbers in ascending order.

(d) The program arranges right half of numbers in ascending order.

Question 27

Which of the following are the categories of sorting?

(a) Internal sorting, External sorting

(b) Complete sorting, Fragment sorting

(c) Partial Sorting, External sorting

(d) Both B and C

Question 28

Which of the following is correct?

(a) Quick sort is also known as Exchange sort.

(b) Quick sort is also known as Pivot sorting.

(c) Quick sort is also known as Partition Exchange sort.

(d) Quick sort is also known as Partial Exchange sort.

Question 29

What is the average-case complexity of quick sort?

(a) O (log2n)

(b) O (log n)

(c) O (2n log n)

(d) O (n2)

Question 30

Which of the following is correct about the program given below?

```
# include <stdio.h>
int main( )
{
    int a[ ] = { 5, 4, 3, 2, 12, 5, 4, 3, 2, 1 };
    int i, j, t, *ptr = a ;

    for ( i = 0 ; i < 10 ; i++ )
    {
        for ( j = 0 ; j < ( 9 – i ) / 2 ; j++ )
        {
            if ( *( ptr + j ) <= a[ j + 1 ] )
            {
                t = *( ptr + j ) ;
                *( ptr + j ) = a[ j + 1 ] ;
                a[ j + 1 ] = t ;
            }
        }
    }
    return 0 ;
}
```

(a) The program arranges all the numbers in descending order.

(b) The program arranges left half of numbers in descending order.

(c) The program arranges all the numbers in ascending order.

(d) The program arranges right half of numbers in descending order.

Question 31

Which of the following is correct?

(a) The efficiency of the quick sort method can be improved by eliminating recursion.

(b) The efficiency of the quick sort method cannot be improved by eliminating recursion.

(c) The heap sort is an alternative to the quick sort in the area of efficiency.

(d) The radix sort works much faster than quick sort.

Question 32

Which type of tree is used by the binary tree sort?

(a) Simple tree

(b) Binary search tree (BST)

(c) Multiway search tree

(d) 2-3 Tree

Question 33

What is the best-case complexity of the quick sort?

(a) O (2n log n)

(b) O (2 log n)

(c) O (log2n)

(d) O (n2)

Question 34

Consider the following program :

```
# include <stdio.h>
int main( )
{
    . . .
    for ( i = 0 ; i <= ( n – 2 ) ; i++ )
    {
        for ( j = i +1 ; j <= ( n – 1 ) ; j++ )
        {
```

```
                if ( a[ i ] > a[ j ] )
                {
                    t = a[ i ] ;
                    a[ i ] = a[ j ] ;
                    a[ j ] = t ;
                }
           }
      }
      . . .
      return 0 ;
}
```

Which sorting algorithm is implemented in the above program?

(a) Bubble sort

(b) Selection sort

(c) Insertion sort

(d) Radix sort

Question 35

Consider the following program :

```
# include <stdio.h>
int main( )
{
      . . .
      for ( i = 0 ; i <= ( n – 2 ) ; i++ )
      {
           for ( j = i +1 ; j <= ( n – 1 ) ; j++ )
           {
                if ( ! ( a[ i ] <= a[ j ] ) )
                {
```

```
                t = a[ i ] ;
                a[ i ] = a[ j ] ;
                a[ j ] = t ;
            }
        }
    }
    . . .
    return 0 ;
}
```

In which order the elements of array 'a' will be sorted?

(a) Ascending order

(b) Descending order

(c) Random order

(d) The elements will not be sorted at all.

Question 36

What is the worst-case complexity of merge sort?

(a) O (2n2)

(b) O (2log 2n)

(c) O (log 2n)

(d) O (n log n)

Question 37

Which sorting technique is implemented by the following program?

```
# include <stdio.h>
int main( )
{
```

```
    int a[ ] = { 15, 42, 32, 2, 12 } ;
    int i, j, t ;
    for ( i = 0 ; i < 5 ; i++ )
    {
        for ( j = 0 ; j < 4 – i ; j++ )
        {
            if ( a[ j ] >= a[ j + 1 ] )
            {
                t = a[ j ] ;
                a[ j ] = a[ j + 1 ] ;
                a[ j + 1 ] = t ;
            }
        }
    }
    return 0 ;
}
```

(a) Selection sort

(b) Bubble sort

(c) Insertion sort

(d) Radix sort

Question 38

Which of the following has "n log n" as average complexity?

(a) Bubble sort

(b) Heap sort

(c) Insertion sort

(d) Selection sort

Question 39

When external sorting method is used?

(a) When the data to be sorted is available in arrays.

(b) When the data to be sorted is so large and that data is stored in auxiliary memory.

(c) When the data to be sorted is so small and that data is stored in main memory.

(d) When the data to be sorted is so large that some of the data is in memory and rest of it in auxiliary memory.

Question 40

Which of the following has the same average and worst-case complexities?

(a) Binary Sort Tree

(b) Quick Sort

(c) Insertion sort

(d) Both A and C

Question 41

Which of the following uses the "Divide-and-Conquer" scheme for sorting the numbers?

(a) Merge Sort

(b) Bubble sort

(c) Quick sort

(d) Both A and C

Question 42

Which of the following statement is correct about the following program?

```
# include <stdio.h>
```

```
# include <string.h>
int main( )
{
    char *pointer[ ] = { "Shyam", "Ram", "Ajay", "Ramu", "Ritesh" } ;
    char *t ;
    int i, j ;

    for ( i = 0 ; i < 5 ; i++ )
    {
        for ( j = 0 ; j < 5 - 1 - i ; j++ )
        {
            if ( strcmp ( pointer[ j ], pointer[ j + 1 ] ) > 0 )
            {
                t = pointer[ j ] ;
                pointer[ j ] = pointer[ j + 1 ] ;
                pointer[ j + 1 ] = t ;
            }
        }
    }
    for ( i = 0 ; i < 5 ; i++ )
        printf ( "%s ", pointer[ i ] ) ;
    return 0 ;
}
```

(a) The program will report the Runtime error.

(b) The program will sort the array in descending order.

(c) The program will sort the array in ascending order.

(d) The program will arrange the similar words adjacent to each other.

Question 43

Which of the following will arrange the integer array 'a' of size 'n' in descending order using insertion sort?

(a)
```
...
for ( i = 1 ; i <= ( n – 1 ) ; i++ )
{
    for ( j = 0 ; j < i ; j++ )
    {
        if ( a[ j ] > a[ i ] )
        {
            t = a[ j ] ;
            a[ j ] = a[ i ] ;
            for ( k = i ; k > j ; k-- )
                a[ k ] = a[ k – 1 ] ;
            a[ k + 1 ] = t ;
        }
    }
}
...
```

(b)
```
...
for ( i = 1 ; i <= ( n – 1 ) ; i++ )
{
    for ( j = 0 ; j < i ; j++ )
    {
        if ( a[ j ] > a[ i ] )
        {
            t = a[ j ] ;
            a[ j ] = a[ i ] ;
            a[ i ] = a[ j ] ;
        }
    }
}
...
```

(c)
```
...
for ( i = 0 ; i <= ( n – 1 ) ; i++ )
{
```

```
        for ( j = 0 ; j < ( n – 1 ) – i ; j++ )
        {
            if ( a[ j ] > a[ j + 1 ] )
            {
                t = a[ j ] ;
                a[ j ] = a[ j +1 ] ;
                a[ j + 1 ] = t ;
            }
        }
    }
    . . .
```

(d)
```
    . . .
    for ( i = 0 ; i <= ( n – 2 ) ; i++ )
    {
        for ( j = 1 ; j < i ; j++ )
        {
            if ( a[ j ] > a[ i ] )
            {
                t = a[ j ] ;
                a[ j ] = a[ i ] ;
                for ( k = i ; k > j + i ; k-- )
                    a[ k ] = a[ k – 1 ] ;
                a[ k + 1 ] = t ;
            }
        }
    }
    . . .
```

Question 44

When an ordered balanced binary tree is called a max-heap?

(a) When the value at the root of any sub-tree is more than or equal to the value of either of its children.

(b) When the value at the root of any sub-tree is less than the value of either of its children.

(c) When the value at the root of any sub-tree is less than or equal to the value of either of its children.

(d) When the value at the root of any sub-tree is more the value of either of its children.

Question 45

How should the elements be accessed to get them in ascending order using the binary search tree?

(a) pre-order traversal

(b) post-order traversal

(c) in-order traversal

(d) Elements can not be sorted using the binary search tree

Question 46

Which field of structure 'emp' will be used to sort the structure in the following program?

```
# include <stdio.h>
# include <string.h>
int fun ( struct emp*, struct emp* ) ;
int fun1 ( int*, int* ) ;
struct emp
{
    char name[ 20 ] ;
    int age ;
    float salary ;
};
int main( )
{
    struct emp e[ ] = {
```

```
                    { "Deepak", 12, 12000.0f },
                    { "Ashok", 23, 14000.f },
                    { "Zem", 13, 13000.f },
                    { "Swapnali", 23, 12800.f }
                };
    int i ;
    qsort ( e, 4, 24 + sizeof ( int ), fun ) ;
    qsort ( e, 4, 24 + sizeof ( int ), fun1 ) ;
    return 0 ;
}
int fun ( struct emp *p, struct emp *t )
{
    return ( strcmp ( p->name, t->name ) ) ;
}
int fun1 ( struct emp *p, struct emp *t )
{
    return ( p->age - t->age ) ;
}
int fun2 ( struct emp *p, struct emp *t )
{
    return ( p->salary - t->salary ) ;
}
```

(a) name

(b) age

(c) salary

(d) The records will be sorted randomly

Question 47

Which of the following algorithm has all of its three complexities equal?

(a) Quick sort

(b) Insertion sort

(c) Binary Tree sort

(d) Heap sort

Question 48

Which of the following function should be used for sorting using the merge sort algorithm?

```
# include <stdio.h>
# include <string.h>

char *arr1[ ] = { "Aarti", "Shyam", "Kiran" } ;
char *arr2[ ] = { "Shweta", "Pooja", "Aakansha" } ;
char *arr[ 6 ] = { NULL, NULL, NULL, NULL, NULL, NULL } ;
void sort ( void ) ;
int main( )
{
    int i ;
    sort( ) ;    /* Write the function definition */
    printf ( "After  Sorting : \n" ) ;
    for ( i = 0 ; i < 6 ; i++ )
        printf ( "%s\n", arr[ i ] ) ;
    return 0 ;
}
```

(a)
```
void sort ( void )
{
    int i, j, k ;
    for ( i = 0 ; i <= 1 ; i++ )
    {
        for ( j = i + 1 ; j < 2 ; j++ )
        {
            if ( strcmp ( arr2[ i ], arr2[ j ] ) < 0 || strcmp ( arr2[ i ], arr2[ j ] ) == 0 )
                ;  /* null statement */
```

```
                else
                {
                        char *ptr = arr2[ i ] ;
                        arr2[i ] = arr2[ j ] ;
                        arr2[ j ] = ptr ;
                }

                if ( strcmp ( arr1[ i ], arr1[ j ] ) > 0 )
                {
                        char *ptr = arr1[ i ] ;
                        arr1[ i ] = arr1[ j ] ;
                        arr1[ j ] = ptr ;
                }
            }
        }
    }
```

(b)
```
    void sort ( void )
    {
        int i, j, k ;
        for ( i = 0 ; i < 1 ; i++ )
        {
            for ( j = i + 1 ; j < 2 ; j++ )
            {
                if ( strcmp ( arr2[ i ], arr2[ j ] ) < 0 || strcmp ( arr2[ i ], arr2[ j ] ) == 0 )
                        ;  /* null statement */
                else
                {
                        char *ptr = arr2[ i ] ;
                        arr2[i ] = arr2[ j ] ;
                        arr2[ j ] = ptr ;
                }

                if ( strcmp ( arr1[ i ], arr1[ j ] ) > 0 )
                {
```

```
                        char *ptr = arr1[ i ] ;
                        arr1[ i ] = arr1[ j ] ;
                        arr1[ j ] = ptr ;
                    }
                }
            }

            for ( ; i < 3 || j < 3 ; )
            {
                if ( i == 3 )
                    arr[ k++ ] = arr2[ j++ ] ;
                else
                    arr[ k++ ] = arr1[ i++ ] ;
            }
        }
```

(c)
```
    void sort ( void )
    {
        int i, j, k ;
        for ( i = 0 ; i <= 1 ; i++ )
        {
            for ( j = i + 1 ; j <= 2 ; j++ )
            {
                if ( strcmp ( arr2[ i ], arr2[ j ] ) < 0 || strcmp ( arr2[ i ], arr2[ j ] ) == 0 )
                    ; /* null statement */
                else
                {
                    char *ptr = arr2[ i ] ;
                    arr2[i ] = arr2[ j ] ;
                    arr2[ j ] = ptr ;
                }
                if ( strcmp ( arr1[ i ], arr1[ j ] ) > 0 )
                {
                    char *ptr = arr1[ i ] ;
                    arr1[ i ] = arr1[ j ] ;
```

```
                arr1[ j ] = ptr ;
            }
        }
    }

    for ( i = j = k = 0 ; k < 6 ; )
    {
        if ( strcmp ( arr1[ i ], arr2[ j ] ) <= 0 )
            arr[ k++ ] = arr1[ i++ ] ;
        else
            arr[ k++ ] = arr2[ j++ ] ;

        if ( i == 3 || j == 3 )
            break ;
    }

    for ( ; i < 3 || j < 3 ; )
    {
        if ( i == 3 )
            arr[ k++ ] = arr2[ j++ ] ;
        else
            arr[ k++ ] = arr1[ i++ ] ;
    }
}
```

(d)
```
void sort ( void )
{
    int i, j, k ;
    for ( i = 0 ; i <= 1 ; i++ )
    {
        for ( j = i + 1 ; j <= 2 ; j++ )
        {
            if ( strcmp ( arr2[ i ], arr2[ j ] ) < 0 || strcmp ( arr2[ i ], arr2[ j ] ) == 0 )
                ; /* null statement */
            else
```

```
                {
                    char *ptr = arr2[ i ] ;
                    arr2[i ] = arr2[ j ] ;
                    arr2[ j ] = ptr ;
                }

                if ( strcmp ( arr1[ i ], arr1[ j ] ) > 0 )
                {
                    char *ptr = arr1[ i ] ;
                    arr1[ i ] = arr1[ j ] ;
                    arr1[ j ] = ptr ;
                }
            }
        }

        for ( i = j = k = 0 ; k < 6 ; )
        {
            if ( strcmp ( arr1[ i ], arr2[ j ] ) <= 0 )
                arr[ k++ ] = arr1[ i++ ] ;
            else
                arr[ k++ ] = arr2[ j++ ] ;

            if ( i == 3 || j == 3 )
                break ;
        }

        for ( ; j < 3 ; )
        {
            if ( i == 3 )
                arr[ k++ ] = arr2[ j++ ] ;
            else
                arr[ k++ ] = arr1[ i++ ] ;
        }
    }
```

Question 49

What is the advantage of Heap sort over the binary tree sort?

(a) Heap sort takes the additional space to create the tree.

(b) Heap sort creates the nodes as compared to that of binary tree sort.

(c) Both A and B.

(d) Heap sort doesn't create the nodes. Instead it builds a heap by adjusting the position of elements within the array itself.

Question 50

Which sorting algorithm is implemented in the following program?

```
# include <stdio.h>
# include <string.h>
int main( )
{
    char *cities[ ] = {
                        "Nagpur",
                        "Pune",
                        "Mumbai",
                        "Yavatmal",
                        "Nashik"
                    } ;
    int i, j ;
    for ( i = 0 ; i < 4 ; i++ )
        for ( j = i + 1 ; j < 5 ; j++ )
        {
            if ( strcmp ( cities[ i ], cities[ j ] ) > 0 )
            {
                char *t = cities[ i ] ;
                cities[ i ] = cities[ j ] ;
                cities[ j ] = t ;
```

```
            }
        }
    return 0 ;
}
```

(a) Bubble sort

(b) Selection sort

(c) Merge sort

(d) Insertion sort

Question 51

Which of the following sort function should be used to sort the linked list assuming that there are 5 elements in the linked list?

```
# include <stdio.h>
# include <malloc.h>

void sort ( void ) ;
void display ( void ) ;

struct Linked_List
{
    int info ;
    struct Linked_List *Link ;
} *start = NULL ;

int main( )
{
    ....
    printf ( "Before Sorting :" ) ;
    display( ) ;
    sort( ) ;    /* write function definition */
    printf ( "After  Sorting :" ) ;
```

```
    display( ) ;
    return 0 ;
}
void display ( void )
{
    struct Linked_List *t = start ;
    while ( t != NULL )
    {
        printf ( " %d", t -> info ) ;
        t = t -> Link ;
    }
}
```

(a)
```
void sort ( void )
{
    struct Linked_List *temp ;
    int m, n, t ;
    m = 0 ;
    while ( m < 4 )
    {
        n = 0 ;
        temp = start ;
        while ( n < 4 - m )
        {
            if ( temp -> info > temp -> Link -> info )
            {
                t = temp -> info ;
                temp -> info = temp -> Link -> info ;
                temp -> Link -> info = t ;
            }
            temp = temp -> Link -> Link ;
            ++n ;
        }
        ++m ;
    }
```

```
}
```

(b)
```
void sort ( void )
{
    struct Linked_List *temp = start ;
    int m, n, t ;
    m = 0 ;
    while ( m < 4 )
    {
        n = 0 ;
        while ( n < 4 - m )
        {
            if ( temp -> info > temp -> Link -> info )
            {
                t = temp -> info ;
                temp -> info = temp -> Link -> info ;
                temp -> Link -> info = t ;
            }
            temp = temp -> Link ;
            ++n ;
        }
        ++m ;
    }
}
```

(c)
```
void sort ( void )
{
    struct Linked_List *temp ;
    int m, n, t ;
    m = 0 ;
    while ( m < 4 )
    {
        n = 0 ;
        temp = start ;
        while ( n < 4 - m )
```

```
        {
            if ( temp -> info > temp -> Link -> info )
            {
                t = temp -> info ;
                temp -> info = temp -> Link -> info ;
                temp -> Link -> info = t ;
            }
            temp = temp -> Link ;
            ++n ;
        }
        ++m ;
    }
}
```

(d)
```
void sort ( void )
{
    struct Linked_List *temp ;
    int m, n, t ;
    m = 0 ;
    while ( m < 4 )
    {
        n = 0 ;
        temp = start ;
        while ( n < 4 - m )
        {
            if ( temp -> info > temp -> Link -> info )
            {
                t = temp -> info ;
                temp -> info = temp -> Link -> info ;
                temp -> Link -> info = t ;
            }
            temp -> Link = temp -> Link -> Link;
            ++n ;
        }
        ++m ;
```

```
        }
    }
```

Question 52

Which algorithm is implemented by the following program to sort the linked list? Assume that there are 5 elements in the linked list.

```
# include <stdio.h>
# include <malloc.h>
void sort ( void ) ;
void display ( void ) ;

struct LinkedList
{
    int info ;
    struct LinkedList *Link ;
} *start = NULL ;

int main( )
{
    . . . .
    printf ( "Before Sorting :" ) ;
    display( ) ;
    sort( ) ;
    printf ( "After  Sorting :" ) ;
    display( ) ;
}
void display ( void )
{
    struct LinkedList *t = start ;
    while ( t != NULL )
    {
        printf ( " %d", t -> info ) ;
        t = t -> Link ;
```

```
    }
    printf ( "\n" ) ;
}
void sort ( void )
{
    struct LinkedList *temp = start, *more ;
    int i, j, t ;
    for ( i = 0, temp = start ; i < 4 ; i++, temp = temp -> Link )
    {
        for ( j = i + 1, more = temp -> Link ; j < 5 ; j++, more = more -> Link )
        {
            if ( temp -> info > more -> info )
            {
                t = temp -> info ;
                temp -> info = more -> info ;
                more -> info = t ;
            }
        }
    }
}
```

(a) Insertion sort

(b) Selection sort

(c) Bubble sort

(d) Quick sort

Question 53

Which of the following function should be used to sort an array a using the binary tree sort? Consider insert( ) is provided to build a tree.

```
# include <stdio.h>
# include <malloc.h>
```

```
void insert ( struct Tree**, int ) ;
struct Tree
{
      struct Tree *left ;
      int info ;
      struct Tree *right ;
} *start = NULL ;

int main( )
{
      int a[ ] = { 5, 6, 2, 3, 8, 12 } ;
      int k ;
      for ( k = 0 ; k < 6 ; k++ )
            insert ( &start, a[ k ] ) ; /* Consider insert( ) unction is provided */

      /* Call the appropriate function to have sorted array */
      return 0 ;
}
```

(a)
```
void inorder ( struct Tree *E )
{
      if ( E != NULL )
      {
            inorder ( E -> left ) ;
            printf ( "%d ", E -> info ) ;
            inorder ( E -> right ) ;
      }
}
```

(b)
```
void preorder ( struct Tree *E )
{
      if ( E != NULL )
      {
            printf ( "%d ", E -> info ) ;
```

```
            preorder ( E -> left ) ;
            preorder ( E -> right ) ;
        }
    }
```

(c)
```
    void postorder ( struct Tree *E )
    {
        if ( E != NULL )
        {
            postorder ( E -> left ) ;
            postorder ( E -> right ) ;
            printf ( "%d ", E -> info ) ;
        }
    }
```

(d) Just printing the array 'a' is sufficient.

Question 54

Which of the following statement is correct about the following program?

```
# include <stdio.h>
# include <malloc.h>

struct LinkList
{
    int info ;
    struct LinkList *Link ;
} *start = NULL ;

int count ;
void add ( int ) ;
void display ( void ) ;

int main( )
{
```

```
    FILE *fp ;
    struct LinkList *temp = start, *more ;
    int i, j, t, num ;
    fp = fopen ( "Numbers.dat", "rb" ) ;
    for ( ; ( num = getw ( fp ) ) != EOF ; count++ )
        add ( num ) ;

    fclose ( fp ) ;

    for ( i = 0, temp = start ; i < count - 1 ; i++, temp = temp -> Link )
    {
        for ( j = i + 1, more = temp -> Link ; j < count ; j++, more = more -> Link )
        {
            if ( temp -> info > more -> info )
            {
                t = temp -> info ;
                temp -> info = more -> info ;
                more -> info = t ;
            }
        }
    }
    display( ) ;
    return 0 ;
}
void add ( int num )
{
    if ( start == NULL )
    {
        start = ( struct LinkList* ) malloc ( sizeof ( struct LinkList ) ) ;
        start -> info = num ;
        start -> Link = NULL ;
    }
    else
    {
        struct LinkList *temp = start ;
```

```
        struct LinkList *t = ( struct LinkList* ) malloc ( sizeof ( struct LinkList ) ) ;
        t -> info = num ;
        t -> Link = NULL ;

        while ( temp -> Link != NULL )
            temp = temp -> Link ;
        temp -> Link = t ;
    }
}
void display ( void )
{
    struct LinkList *t = start ;
    while ( t != NULL )
    {
        printf ( "%d ", t -> info ) ;
        t = t -> Link ;
    }
    printf ( "\n" ) ;
}
```

(a) The program reads the numbers from the Numbers.dat file and prints on the screen after storing them in the linked list.

(b) The program reads the numbers from the Numbers.dat file and stores back into it in reverse order after printing on the screen.

(c) The program reads the numbers from Numbers.dat file, stores them in the linked list and after sorting the linked list, numbers are displayed on the screen.

(d) The program reads the numbers from Numbers.dat file, stores them in the linked list and after sorting the linked list, numbers are stored back in the file and also displays on the screen.

Question 55

Which of the following statement is NOT correct?

(a) In binary tree sort when the tree is traversed in in-order fashion, we will get elements in ascending order.

(b) Binary tree sort uses the binary search tree (BST).

(c) Heap sort doesn't create the nodes, instead it builds the heap by adjusting the position of elements within the array itself.

(d) In binary tree sort when the tree is traversed in pre-order fashion, we will get elements in descending order.

Question 56

Which of the following statement is correct about the program given below?

```
# include <stdio.h>
# include <malloc.h>

struct LinkList
{
    int info ;
    struct LinkList *Link ;
} *start = NULL ;

int num ;
void add ( int ) ;
void sort ( void ) ;
void display ( void ) ;

int main( )
{
    add ( 2 ) ;
    add ( 24 ) ;
    add ( 13 ) ;
    add ( 4 ) ;
    add ( 51 ) ;
    printf ( "Linked List : " ) ;
```

```
    display( ) ;
    return 0 ;
}

void add ( int n )
{
    if ( start == NULL)
    {
        start = ( struct LinkList* ) malloc ( sizeof ( struct LinkList ) ) ;
        start -> info = n ;
        start -> Link = NULL ;
        ++num ;
    }
    else
    {
        void ( *ptr )( void ) = sort ;
        struct LinkList *t = start, *temp = ( struct LinkList* ) malloc ( sizeof ( struct LinkList )
) ;
        temp -> info = n ;
        temp -> Link = NULL ;

        while ( t -> Link != NULL )
            t = t -> Link ;
        t -> Link = temp ;

        ++num ;
        ( *ptr )( ) ;
    }
}

void display ( void )
{
    struct LinkList *k = start ;
    while ( k != NULL )
    {
```

```
        printf ( "%d  ", k -> info ) ;
        k = k -> Link ;
    }
    printf ( "\n" ) ;
}

void sort ( void )
{
    struct LinkList *temp ;
    int i,  j ;

    for ( i = 0, temp = start ; i < num ; i++, temp = start )
    {
        for ( j = 0 ; j < ( num – 1 ) – i ;  j++ )
        {
            if ( temp -> info > temp -> Link -> info )
            {
                int t = temp -> info ;
                temp -> info = temp -> Link -> info ;
                temp -> Link -> info = t ;
            }
            temp = temp -> Link ;
        }
    }
}
```

(a) The program will give compilation error.

(b) The program will sort the linked list after the insertion of all the elements.

(c) The program will throw runtime exception.

(d) The program will sort the linked list each time when the element is inserted in it.

Question 57

What does the following program do?

```
# include <stdio.h>
# include <malloc.h>

struct LL
{
    int info ;
    struct LL*Link ;
} *start = NULL ;

void display ( void ) ;
int main( )
{
    struct LL*t1 = start, *t2 ;
    int i, j, t ;

    for ( i = 0, t1 = start ; i < 4 ; i++, t1 = t1 -> Link )
    {
        for ( j = i + 1, t2 = t1 -> Link ; j < 5 ; j++ )
        {
            if ( ! t1 -> info < t2 -> info )
            {
                t = t1 -> info ;
                t1 -> info = t2 -> info ;
                t2 -> info = t ;
            }
            t2 = t2 -> Link ;
        }
    }
    display( ) ;
    return 0 ;
}
```

```
void display ( void )
{
      struct LL *t = start ;
      while ( t != NULL )
      {
            printf ( "%d  ", t -> info ) ;
            t = t -> Link ;
      }
      printf ( "\n" ) ;
}
```

(a) The program sorts the linked list in ascending order.

(b) The program sorts the linked list in descending order.

(c) The program sorts the half numbers in linked list in ascending order and remaining numbers in descending order.

(d) The program does not sort the linked list.

Question 58

Which of the following is correct?

(a) When the binary search tree in binary tree sort is traversed in left-right-root fashion, we will get the elements in descending order.

(b) When the binary search tree in binary tree sort is traversed in left-root-right fashion, we will get the elements in ascending order.

(c) When the binary search tree in binary tree sort is traversed in root-left-right fashion, we will get the elements in descending order.

(d) When the binary search tree in binary tree sort is traversed in root-left-right fashion, we will get the elements in ascending order.

Question 59

Which of the following function should be used to display the sorted linked list in descending order?

Assume that base address of the linked list "LinkList" is stored in pointer start.

(a)
```
void display ( struct LinkList *start )
{
    while ( start != NULL )
    {
        display ( start -> Link ) ;
        continue ;
        printf ( "%d  ", start -> info ) ;
    }
}
```

(b)
```
void display ( struct LinkList *start )
{
    if ( start != NULL )
    {
        display ( start -> Link ) ;
        printf ( "%d  ", start -> info ) ;
    }
}
```

(c)
```
void display ( void )
{
    struct LinkList *k = start ;
    while ( k != NULL )
    {
        k = k -> Link ;
        continue ;
        printf ( "%d  ", k -> info ) ;
    }
    printf ( "\n" ) ;
}
```

(d)
```
void display ( struct LinkList *start )
{
        if ( start != NULL )
                display ( start -> Link ) ;
        printf ( "%d  ", start -> info ) ;
}
```

Question 60

What does the following program do?

```
# include <stdio.h>
# include <malloc.h>

struct LinkList
{
        int info ;
        struct LinkList *Link ;
} *start = NULL ;

int count ;
void add ( int ) ;

int main( )
{
        FILE *fp ;
        struct LinkList *temp = start, *more ;
        int i, j, t, num ;

        fp = fopen ( "Numbers.dat", "rb+" ) ;
        for ( ; ( num = getw ( fp ) ) != EOF ; count++ )
                add ( num ) ;
        fseek ( fp, 0L, SEEK_SET ) ;
```

```
    for ( i = 0, temp = start ; i < count - 1 ; i++, temp = temp -> Link )
    {
        for ( j = i + 1, more = temp -> Link ; j < count ; j++, more = more -> Link )
        {
            if ( ! ( temp -> info < more -> info ) )
            {
                t = temp -> info ;
                temp -> info = more -> info ;
                more -> info = t ;
            }
        }
    }
    for ( temp = start ; temp != NULL ; temp = temp -> Link )
        putw ( temp -> info, fp ) ;
    fclose ( fp ) ;
    return 0 ;
}

void add ( int num )
{
    if ( start == NULL )
    {
        start = ( struct LinkList* ) malloc ( sizeof ( struct LinkList ) ) ;
        start -> info = num ;
        start -> Link = NULL ;
    }
    else
    {
        struct LinkList *temp = start ;
        struct LinkList *t = ( struct LinkList* ) malloc ( sizeof ( struct LinkList ) ) ;
        t -> info = num ;
        t -> Link = NULL ;
        while ( temp -> Link != NULL )
            temp = temp -> Link ;
        temp -> Link = t ;
```

```
    }
}
```

(a) The program sorts the linked list only in descending order.

(b) The program sorts the file Numbers.dat in descending order.

(c) The program sorts the file Numbers.dat in ascending order.

(d) The program sorts the linked list only in ascending order.

Answers

Q. 1 – C	Q. 2 – C	Q. 3 – D
Q. 4 – C	Q. 5 – B	Q. 6 – D
Q. 7 – D	Q. 8 – C	Q. 9 – D
Q. 10 – C	Q. 11 – B	Q. 12 – D
Q. 13 – A	Q. 14 – D	Q. 15 – C
Q. 16 – D	Q. 17 – C	Q. 18 – D
Q. 19 – A	Q. 20 – B	Q. 21 – D
Q. 22 – B	Q. 23 – B	Q. 24 – B
Q. 25 – C	Q. 26 – C	Q. 27 – A
Q. 28 – C	Q. 29 – A	Q. 30 – B
Q. 31 – A	Q. 32 – B	Q. 33 – C
Q. 34 – B	Q. 35 – A	Q. 36 – D
Q. 37 – B	Q. 38 – B	Q. 39 – D
Q. 40 – C	Q. 41 – D	Q. 42 – C
Q. 43 – A	Q. 44 – A	Q. 45 – C
Q. 46 – B	Q. 47 – D	Q. 48 – C

Q. 49 – D	Q. 50 – B	Q. 51 – C
Q. 52 – B	Q. 53 – A	Q. 54 – C
Q. 55 – D	Q. 56 – D	Q. 57 – D
Q. 58 – B	Q. 59 – B	Q. 60 – C